KRISTIN ZIEMKE & KATIE MUHTARIS

READ THE WORLD

Rethinking Literacy for Empathy and Action in a Digital Age

HEINEMANN
PORTSMOUTH, NH

Heinemann
361 Hanover Street
Portsmouth, NH 03801–3912
www.heinemann.com

Offices and agents throughout the world

The authors and publisher wish to thank those who have generously given permission to reprint borrowed material:

Six Strategic Comprehension Strategies and Thinksheets from *The Primary Comprehension Toolkit*, Second Edition, and *The Intermediate Comprehension Toolkit*, Second Edition, by Stephanie Harvey and Anne Goudvis. Copyright © 2016 by Stephanie Harvey and Anne Goudvis. Published by Heinemann, Portsmouth, NH. All rights reserved.

Library of Congress Cataloging-in-Publication Data
Names: Ziemke, Kristin, author. | Muhtaris, Katie, author.
Title: Read the world : rethinking literacy for empathy and action in a
    digital age / Kristin Ziemke, Katie Muhtaris.
Description: Portsmouth, NH : Heinemann, [2020] | Includes bibliographical
    references.
Identifiers: LCCN 2019026083 | ISBN 9780325108919
Subjects: LCSH: Language arts. | Literacy—Study and teaching. |
    Empathy—Study and teaching. | Language arts—Social aspects. | Internet
    in education. | Multicultural education.
Classification: LCC LB1576 .Z54 2020 | DDC 372.6—dc23
LC record available at https://lccn.loc.gov/2019026083

Acquisitions Editor: Tobey Antao
Production Editor: Seán Moreau
Cover and Interior Designer: Monica Ann Crigler
Typesetter: Shawn Girsberger
Manufacturing: Steve Bernier

Printed in the United States of America on acid-free paper

23 22 21 20 19 VP 1 2 3 4 5

For Meghan and Moey.

From before to beyond.

We carry you with us always.

Paul –
Thank you for
inviting me to work
with your team! I
had a blast and
love your cohort.
Let's go Read the
World!

♥ Kristin

Contents

Online Resources

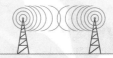

Read the World Online Resources

To access the online resources for *Read the World,* either scan this QR code or visit Hein.pub/RTW-Resources.

Hein.pub/RTW-Resources

Acknowledgments

We are forever grateful to our professional network; those educators whose conversations, workshops, posts, and tweets continually challenge and change our thinking. We are better people because of you, and we continue to learn from you every day. To Stephanie Harvey and Smokey Daniels, our professional mentors: you helped us find our voice in the service of children and teachers. Penny Kittle: you have been our writing champion. Thank you for helping us keep perspective. Sara Ahmed: your friendship and inspiration know no limits. Donalyn Miller: your wisdom at just the right time fueled our belief that we could do this. Kylene Beers: thank you for lifting us up. Lucy Calkins: thank you for honoring this work and inviting us to share with educators at the Teachers College Reading and Writing Project. To Barbara Kent: thank you for creating an environment where we could all learn and grow. Your legacy shines bright.

To the team at Heinemann: you are truly miracle workers. Your support, dedication, and creativity is boundless. Vicki Boyd: we are so honored by your wisdom and support. Thank you for your patience and for believing in us and our work. Stephen Perepeluk: your energy for this work is impacting students across the world. Roderick Spelman: thank you for thinking toward the future and valuing work that lives in a digital space. Thank you for listening and helping us craft a vision for this project.

To our Heinemann flight crew: it takes a huge team of collaborative, creative, and dedicated professionals to get all the working parts in order. Tobey: thank you for helping us launch this rocket even though sometimes we were building it as we were flying and it felt like both engines were on fire. Your thoughtfulness, thoroughness, and friendship are much appreciated. Thank you to Monica Crigler and Suzanne Heiser for the insightful and fearless design; it's what our hearts were looking for. You get us! Sean Moreau: you landed this baby right on the numbers. Jaclyn Karabinas: thank you for your early feedback during the writing and revising process. Your thoughts were so valuable. Catrina Marshall: your support with art and permissions was much needed. Thank you for your patience. Sherry Day: we would be lost without your complimentary editing skills and energy. Michael Grover and Lauren Audet: you both are our picture and podcast dream team. Brett Whitmarsh: you are innovator extraordinaire.

Also a huge thank you to: Patty Adams, Steve Bernier, Eric Chalek, Maria Czop, Sarah Fournier, Steph George, Shawn Girsberger, Jennifer Greenstein, Stacy Holly, Erik Ickes, Roberta Lew, Jane Orr, Elizabeth Silvis, and Lynette Winegarner. You are the best mission control a flight team could ask for. Thank you to Sam Brown, Mim Easton, Michelle Flynn, and Cheryl Savage who help authors continue the learning in person and online. We'd also like to acknowledge Holly Kim Price who helped to begin the conversation on this project and worked with us on our early ideas. And Lisa Fowler whose wisdom and kindness keep giving. Also, a special thank-you to our outside reviewer who helped push our thinking. Your feedback was powerful and appreciated.

To all the amazing educators teaching students to be curious, to practice compassion and to look at learning through a new lens, thank you for your energy for this work. Most importantly, to the kids living, loving, and doing the work—we hear you, we see you, and we stand with you as you continue to inspire the world around us.

— • —

From Kristin

To my parents: thank you for raising me to be a reader. I have read the world through the titles and texts you placed in my hands.

Kirk: you lift me up in more ways than I can count. Your ideas, coaching, and consistency inspire me to grow. Let's keep moving through life like a long slow fall.

To Katie: for your tenacity and enduring optimism that we would finish this book. You are the best writing partner I could ever have, and I am grateful we get to continue this work together.

This book wouldn't have been possible without the support of my Big Shoulders crew—especially Josh Hale, Rebecca Lindsay-Ryan, Eliza Bryant, and Liz Bartley—your passion for this work fuels the world. Thank you to our entire team for advocating for our kiddos 365 days of the year. Para los niños!

To my colleagues who are always up for anything— Diniah Dean, Kathleen Fox, Gretchen Geerts, Stacy Ginocchio, Staccy Kabat, Griffin Muckley, and Maggie Writt—and all their students who are willing to learn alongside us at SMOS, ASBA, De La Salle, St. Ann, and Christ the King, thank you for all you have taught me.

To the many principals who welcomed me into your schools, thank you. Special gratitude to Phyllis Cavallone, Shauntae Davis, Jennifer Farrand, Pat Murphy, Deb Oi, Kevin Powers, Clint Prohaska, Shaka Rawls, and Katie Scully.

A big shout-out to my colleagues in EPS! Lara Alford, Rena Bekris, Michele Dick, Scott Eppinger, Becky Kadrmas, Lindsay Kralj, Angie Mitchell, Erin Pinning, Tracy Schuster, Roseann Thomson, and Rose Treacy, and the students and teachers at Hearthwood, Fircrest, Fisher's Landing, and Sifton—you rock! Katie Plamondon and Eric Webb—thank you for allowing me to try new things in your classroom and share your instructional awesomeness in this book.

Chad Everett and Katharine Hsu: thank you. For everything.

Ben Kovacs, Nessy Moos, and Carolyn Skibba: let's learn together forever.

To the people who hold me up even when we are not physically together: Jeff Crews, Darren Hudgins, Nancy Mangum, Dean Phillips (NEST), Keri-Lee Beasley, Alison Cardoso, Jodi Courts, Janet Fastabend, Stacy Hansen, Shaun Jacob, Jennifer Lagarde, Tim Lauer, Audrey O'Clair, Ingvi Hrannar Ómarsson, Kimberly Querrey, Larry Reiff, Franki Sibberson, Sabrina Silverstein, and Lou Simpson, thank you. Your support means more than you know.

To my retro Burley crew—I carry you with me every single day.

Mark: this book started on a plane with you. Thank you for believing in me from day one. B.L.E.

— • —

From Katie

To my family: thank you for your support during this process. I could not do this work without you. For my girls, I hope that somehow my work will make this world a kinder place for you to be a part of. Kons: thank you for supporting me in reaching for my dreams.

To Kristin: I don't even know how we got here! I have learned so much writing and working with you. Toss and boss!

Thank you to my coach crew: Nirda Derose, Sara Dime, Kate Karasek, Joslyn Katz, Sean McGann, Amy Pelletiere, Kelly Pinta, and Lisa Riley. You are all a wicked smart group of educators. A special shout-out to Laura Meehan—my day-to-day think partner and lunch buddy—I learn so much from you every day! To Jennifer Burton: you've been so instrumental in my evolution of thought over the last few years. Thank you for your friendship and mentorship. I can't wait until the day I come to your classroom for some whisper coaching. And to our chief in charge of herding cats: Dr. Becky Gill, thank you for your support, coaching, and constant push to be better. I wouldn't have it any other way.

To the Barrington 220 School District: thank you for creating an environment for teachers and students to thrive.

To the teachers and staff at Grove Elementary and Hough Elementary: thank you for everything you do each day. You show up for kids, you do the work, and you give your best. Jim Aalfs and Katie Mathews: thank you for your support with this project.

Thank you to the teachers who opened their classrooms to pilot lessons or allow me to photograph as you and your students worked, and to those that would have if we'd only had more time. A special thanks go out to: Sandra Chang, Michele Giovanelli, Sarah Goitein, Kelly Haradon, Kathleen Holmberg, Bridgette Hurst, and Jen Magdelener for opening your rooms to piloting some of the work in this book and/or allowing me to invade your space with my camera. Bridgette: thank you for your willingness to push the line and dig into the hard stuff, and for your inspiring work on letters home to parents in Chapter 3. An extra special thank-you to Christa Gillespie and Jen Magdelener for allowing me to work with your students as I did my National Board recertification while also writing this book.

I will be forever grateful to my Burley crew and the magic we made.

Model guide collaborate

pedagogy
reflect reflect reflect
feedback paths

writing
tech
supports
It's SHARE
ALL STORY
IDENTITY THIS:

audience O O O

→ man

Henry Jenki

participator Culture

is literacy
today!
branding
△ change
responsive
relationship + community
teaching the

NOT life digital
projects
video
image
brain
#StuVoice
Print
you have
a read the world
Digital to tell.

Ss passi
interest fu
lea
and

Sharpie FLIP CHART

to brain
of reading
ailments + pharmacology

story story story
Media
Donald Graves
authentic
unfiltered polished

Words Matter
Choice wor
Student a

another SHIFT
graphic
literacy does not mean
SAT color emotion mood
ask Ss about Ts Must be
onscreen vs.
informed! - AP
- comm
- clicks,

VIS
INTEL

reness ≠
understanding their
news
access +
entry for
All

Kids do the work
Tell your stor

A Letter to Readers

Dear Reader,

When we first began the journey of this project, we were driven by the idea of stories and how the world and our students were desperately in need of the power of story. Stories connect the past to the present and individuals to one another; stories bring the human experience to life. We believe stories can save us from the hyper-inflamed, fast-paced mistruths of the internet. Stories can save us from living closed-off lives, believing that one experience—ours—is the only one that matters. Stories can inspire us toward a more caring, engaged, and contemplative citizenry. As the world around us changes, the human story endures. This book represents a chapter of our story and we invite you to be a part of it. We hope that you will see the connection between the practical lessons and suggestions in this book and the power of people to take the tools we've created and master them in a way that benefits humanity.

In 1987, Paulo Freire, author of the transformational text *Pedagogy of the Oppressed*, published a lesser-known title, *Literacy: Reading the Word and the World*. He believed that literacy and the impact of literacy went far beyond merely reading words on the page, extending to reading the world; a juxtaposition of text and context. We cannot understand or use what we read, without comprehending the people, events, social movements, and inequalities that impact us. Freire states, "We need to go beyond the rigid comprehension of literacy and begin to view it as the relationship of learners to the world" (viii). These ideas take on even more significance in a digital age. His work still inspires us, and even inspired the title for this book! Today we ground ourselves in pedagogy as we rethink literacy, adapt and adopt our practices to meet the needs of today's learner, and embrace the relationships and social connections that develop along the journey to understanding. Together, we strive to redefine what it means to read and find our humanity in doing so.

As we rethink literacy, we ask you to interact with this book in a way that balances text and tech. You will see interactive pages where we invite you to coauthor this book with us. In these interactive pages, we ask you to write with us, to be our think partner as we tackle familiar and new ideas. As you read and write, we also ask you to connect with others; share your thinking and questions with the education community on social media using the hashtag #ReadTheWorldNow, reach out to us directly, or share something you've tried with students.

Changing language is part of the process of changing the world.

—Paulo Freire, *Pedagogy of the Oppressed*, 1970 (68)

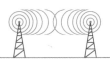

This book is about stories and we want to hear yours. You'll also find a series of links and QR codes that will take you to audio recordings of our candid conversations as we add on to ideas in the book, talk through our struggles, question that which we're still unsure of, and anticipate next steps as the tools and times continue to change.

As you read, we hope that you will find an entry point into this book—something that feels accessible and familiar. We hope that you unpack some of the Try Its within and think, "Yes! This is what I've been looking for!" We also hope that you find classroom work that you question or challenge, because it's in this dissonance that we know real growth occurs. If we aren't challenged, we aren't changed. Open your heart and your mind to this journey, allow yourself to evolve, and leave this book a different person than when you entered. We're excited to have you join us as we update our vision, understanding, and practice of what it means to "read the world."

— • —

A Note About Student Photos in This Book

As we have captured photos of the students in the schools where we work, we have been mindful to represent the varied populations of those schools. While we realize that these populations may not represent the full continuum of student diversity, we continue to work toward equitable representation in our projects while honoring families' wishes with respect to their children.

1

Laying the Groundwork
Foundational Structures for Today's Learner

When we—Kristin and Katie—were in elementary school, there weren't many options for discovering new information beyond what was presented in a textbook. Perhaps this sounds familiar? A teacher would assign you a topic related to whatever you were studying, and you would march down to the library, note cards in hand, to sift through the card catalog, a mysterious contraption made up of tiny drawers. Despite encouragement from the librarian to use multiple sources, you almost certainly stuck to the encyclopedia for the bulk of your information, peppering it with tidbits from other books. Or, if you were really lucky, a newspaper article from the microfiche machine. Students today have the collective knowledge of humanity (practically!) on a smartphone in their pocket. Not only can they access this information with their device, but they can produce, publish, and connect with the world to build and share knowledge.

Now, recalling our half-hearted attempts at research strikes us with equal parts nostalgia for the good ol' days and awe at what's possible for students in this digital age. Things sure have changed. In today's classrooms, you will still find cups with pencils sharpened to the nub and chewed erasers, stacks of colorful paper, and glue bottles with dried glue plugs that you have to peel off before using. But today's classrooms give equal real estate to smart technology with computers or tablets, interactive whiteboards, projectors, and robotics.

And still, this modern-day picture is changing—evolving as schools move toward more minimalistic and flexible classrooms and teachers wonder: Is this the new vogue of education or something here to stay?

But it's not just our rooms and our technology that are different. We are different too. Look around; the educators who surround us carry a wide span of experiences and ideas about technology. We have worked with early adopters, teachers who have taken a more conservative approach to technology, and everyone in between. Yet, in our students' worlds, there is no line between the tech world and the nontech world. To best serve the students

Technology alone is not enough. It is technology married with the liberal arts, married with the humanities that make our hearts sing. When you keep people at the center of what you do, it can have an enormous impact.

—Tim Cook, Apple CEO, 2017

The question has to do with how do we harness this technology in a way that allows a multiplicity of voices, allows a diversity of views, but doesn't lead to a Balkanisation of society and allows ways of finding common ground.

—President Barack Obama, 2017 (quoted in Meixler 2017)

Join the Conversation:
How Things Have Changed!

"That's why I'm so excited about technology, because it gives me the opportunity to learn right alongside students."

#ReadTheWorldNow

Hein.pub/RTW1.1

in our classrooms today, we educators can all be aware of each other, the strengths we bring, and the gaps that others can help us fill. We build our story together with learning from all sides and a clear focus on our students.

What Can We All Agree On?

When pedagogy and technology meet, it can feel polarizing at times. On one hand, there is the drive for innovation, the reimagining of what currently exists, and a sense of trying to keep up with new tools, strategies, or mindsets. On the other hand, there is the anchor of practices that are proven to work: structures, strategies, and scaffolds that endure time and time again. It can be easy to sort people into "tech savvy" or "not tech savvy." These kinds of judgments can quickly divide us and prevent us from the practices that will help us all grow: listening to one another, listening to our students, and considering what the purpose of education is in the first place.

We all come to this digital teaching life from a different place. With our experiences, we bring biases and memories of our own prior successes or flops in the classroom. So how can we come together? We can anchor ourselves by considering how each learning experience our students engage in promotes their own sense of agency in the process.

Promoting children's sense of agency is not a new idea—it is central to the work of visionary educators such as John Dewey and Maria Montessori. However, as technology continues to shape our daily lives, the tools and methods we use to promote agency in children must also evolve.

Realizing the Promise of Technology

Today, we find ourselves in an era in which information is ubiquitous and processed and distributed faster than ever before (Berger 2014). Ninety-eight percent of US homes with children under the age of eight have access to a mobile device (up from 52 percent in 2011). Seventy-four percent of lower-income households (below $30,000) surveyed report access to high-speed internet in 2017 (Rideout 2017, 9).

Technology, and the ability to share information quickly on a large scale, has grown our collective knowledge repository to a point where there is more and more to sift through as we access, form opinions, and build new understanding. Because there are more "bits" to sort through, we are forced to evaluate, summarize, and synthesize a larger body of work—and that body of work often contains more than the printed word. All of us—we teachers and our students—can see, hear, and feel stories from around the world in many different formats. We can view successes, failures, and struggles in live time. We can interact with those like us and those who may be different from us with just the push of a button. As we look at the young faces sitting on our rugs, we recognize that, to be truly literate in today's society, they must learn to evaluate all the information they encounter to make sense of the world.

Technology brings us an infinite number of bits of information, but human beings do not understand the world in terms of bits of information. Instead, we shape those bits of information into stories. Story links information to emotion and creates meaning (Furedi 2015). A new headline might become part of the stories we tell ourselves about what is wrong—or right—about the world. So, when technology brings us voices we've not heard before, information that challenges our views, or material from another person's perspective, it is bringing us new stories and affecting the stories that we use to make sense of our lives. As a vehicle for story, technology gives us new opportunities to learn, consider, communicate, empower, and tell.

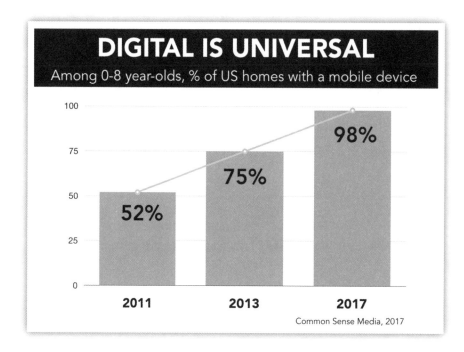

DIGITAL IS UNIVERSAL

Among 0-8 year-olds, % of US homes with a mobile device

- 2011: 52%
- 2013: 75%
- 2017: 98%

Common Sense Media, 2017

Of course, there are dark stories in the digital realm. The anonymity of technology seems to amplify the very weaknesses of human society. From a US election riddled with accusations of fake news to bots that drive online content to online bullying that threatens our children, many have proclaimed that digital interconnectedness may be the end of humanity as we know it.

Yet, if we look at the quotations at the beginning of this chapter from two of the most powerful and influential leaders of our time, we see that they share the same view of technology: it is not the tools of technology that matter but how people leverage them to affect the world. Obama and Cook share an optimism that technology can bring people together, can give everyone a voice on a global scale, and can, ultimately, enrich our lives. It's all about how we use it.

This optimism is neither new nor unfounded.

Paulo Freire, author of *Pedagogy of the Oppressed*, and Donald Macedo explained, "Reading does not consist merely of decoding the written word or language; rather, it is preceded by and intertwined with knowledge of the world" (1987, 29). Prior to ever reading print, we are surrounded by a multitude of stimuli that help us comprehend the world. Freire and Macedo saw that reading, alone, was not enough: it is art, music, architecture, and modes of communication that influence one's perspective and comprehension of life. Their words are as true today as when they wrote them, but now we have much more to "read"—digital videos, texts, infographics, images, art, audio, virtual reality, social media, and more. Freire reminded us that it is our own experience, input, and actions that give meaning to the stories we encounter.

WRITE WITH US

⏻ **How did you use technology when you were growing up?**

⏻ **How is technology—and how you use it—different now?**

⏻ **Find a colleague and ask them the questions above. Share your responses, as well, and discuss with them how your experiences are different and how they are the same. Jot down your new learning here.**

⏻ **What, from your early experiences with technology, might seem strange or puzzling to your students today? What, from their current experiences with technology, feels puzzling or strange to you?**

⏻ **Share your ideas. #ReadTheWorldNow**

There's also ample evidence that technology can be a force for good in our lives. Each day, the majority of people can head out into the world knowing what the weather will be, how to call for help immediately if they need it, what current events may affect them, how to get to the places they need to go, and how to stay in contact with everyone they need to reach. And that's not even considering how people use technology for deeper research: advances in the sciences, technology, and society as a whole rely on a free flow of information. Human history teaches us that knowledge and power are interrelated. Now, anyone with access to the internet has access to the collected knowledge and stories of the world. To anyone born just a few generations ago, this might seem like wizardry or science fiction.

This book aims to teach our students how to thrive in the society in which we currently live: a society that is flooded with technology, but that often forgets that it is our humanity—the stories that technology transmits—that makes technology meaningful. This book marries technology, proven teaching strategies, and student-centered pedagogy as a means for amplifying the thinking work our students do. In Chapter 2 you'll find ideas to use with students on how to access, engage with, and understand stories in varied digital media. Chapter 3 builds on this new look at consumption by coaching students (and teachers) to use new tools to think critically and compassionately about the world. Chapter 4 invites students and teachers to use the skills they've learned to exercise their own agency and take meaningful action upon issues to benefit their own lives and the lives of others.

Practices with More Impact	Practices with Less Impact
▶ Real-world work that connects to kids' lives as learners and helps them see the greater purpose in their learning	▶ Busywork that lacks relevant connections to students' lives and purposes for learning
▶ Time for kids to practice, internalize, transfer, and approximate independence and understanding	▶ Teacher talk; domination of the classroom by teachers' voices; and assign-and-assess-style teaching
▶ Choice, personalization, and differentiation	▶ One-size-fits-all curriculum and resources
▶ Real-world work connected to an authentic audience	▶ Assignments for the teachers' eyes only
▶ Innovation, creativity, and risk taking (teachers and students) with reflection	▶ Doing things the same way we've always done them and innovation without reflection on impact
▶ Instruction connected to skills our students need now and for the future; visual literacy and critical thinking around digital resources; and collaboration in face-to-face and digital environments	▶ Instruction from boxed curriculums without considering what our students need; focus on skills that no longer serve our students; and use of only text-based learning with passive viewing and reading and no visual or audio components
▶ Learning from multiple sources (print and digital) and through different lenses and perspectives	▶ Learning from one source, one perspective, or through an oversimplified resource
▶ Diverse and multifaceted resources that every student can access and practice with and that every student can see themselves in	▶ Resources that feature only one type of person, character, or perspective; resources that our students don't see themselves in; and resources our students can't access—textbooks at one reading level
▶ Work that is connected to overarching ideas and questions that will help students make sense of the world	▶ Work in isolation and a series of unconnected learning experiences that focus on memorizing content or isolated skill practice
▶ Access, equity, and agency	▶ Students as passive participants in the school day

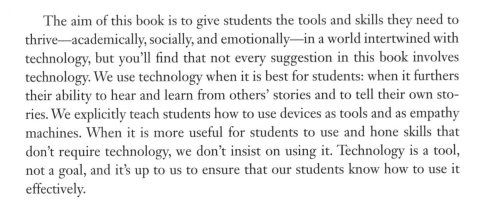

If nothing else children should leave school with a sense that if they act, and act strategically, they can accomplish their goals.

—Peter Johnston, 2004

The aim of this book is to give students the tools and skills they need to thrive—academically, socially, and emotionally—in a world intertwined with technology, but you'll find that not every suggestion in this book involves technology. We use technology when it is best for students: when it furthers their ability to hear and learn from others' stories and to tell their own stories. We explicitly teach students how to use devices as tools and as empathy machines. When it is more useful for students to use and hone skills that don't require technology, we don't insist on using it. Technology is a tool, not a goal, and it's up to us to ensure that our students know how to use it effectively.

Structures That Promote Agency

In order to actualize agency, we need to shift some things in our classrooms. We can't just keep adding and packing more and more into our days. None of us have a chunk of time each day or each week that we're looking to fill: each precious moment of instructional time is already in high demand. The level of instruction, support, and guidance that students need to develop the kind of agency we're aiming for can't be separate from our daily work—it needs to infuse that work. So the question isn't about fitting more in; it's about deciding what to amplify in our classrooms and what to let go of. What would add value? When we've thought about our students and the classrooms we've worked in, we've noticed that some practices have more impact than others.

We've also noticed that, at the core of their work, strong classrooms have a few consistent structures in place that inform their day-to-day choices. The ways in which we structure our instruction, our classroom time, and our classroom space also shape our students' experiences. If, for example, our lessons are predominantly whole-class direct instruction, in which students don't have opportunities for action or collaboration, how does that structure then shape us and our students? Does it position us as a teacher or as a font of knowledge? Does it position students as curious, independent learners? What does it require of us and of our students? What does it quietly teach our students about school and their place in it? Does it promote student agency or teach students to comply?

Our underlying beliefs are a kind of structure: they shape our choices and actions. If we believe that students are the most important factor in our classrooms, how does that shape the way we look for new classroom tools? Are we more likely to be drawn to the Next Big Thing and look for ways to try it out, or are we more likely to consider whether the thing is genuinely useful for our students before we think about using it?

We often don't notice when something has a strong and functional structure. Structures may be invisible. They may even be unintentional. But they are always actively shaping those who live and work within them.

Good structures set the stage for greatness and then slide back into the shadows.

With this in mind, we'd like to share seven structures that we've seen at work in strong classrooms, where students are actively reading the world, making connections, asking questions, learning from others' stories, reconsidering their own stories, and taking action. As you work through the ideas and suggestions in this book, you'll see that they are also steeped in these structures.

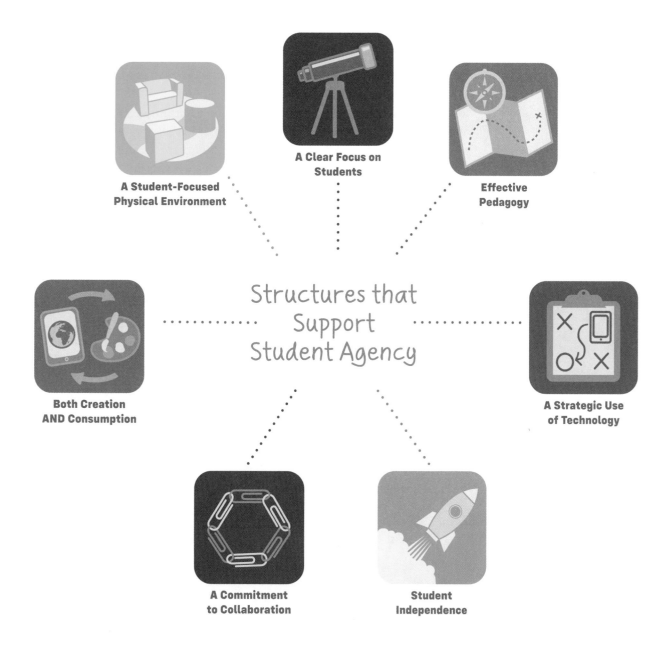

A Student-Focused
Physical Environment

A Clear Focus on
Students

Effective
Pedagogy

Both Creation
AND Consumption

Structures that
Support
Student Agency

A Strategic Use
of Technology

A Commitment
to Collaboration

Student
Independence

Teaching is heart work.

—JoEllen McCarthy (quoted in
Hertz and Mraz 2018, 3)

STRUCTURE 1
A Clear Focus on Our Students

Kids. That is why we are here.

If you are reading this book, you know about the challenges facing educational communities today. Public, private, or independent school, we are all feeling it. Adopt new technologies. Prepare students for the jobs of tomorrow. Raise test scores. Meet the needs of a changing student body. Find new outlets for funding. With the daily demands affecting the principal to the lunchroom staff and everyone in between, it's easy to get distracted by "all the things." But the only things that truly matter are the students who walk through our door. We are the primary advocates in our students' educational journey, and frequently we must push the pause button on the outside world and look to the microcosm of our own classroom to identify what really matters for children. When we keep this responsibility forefront in our minds, it becomes easier to make instructional decisions with clarity and confidence throughout the year.

How Can I Keep a Clear Focus on My Students?

To keep kids at the heart of what we do, we often ask ourselves:

► What do I know about this student?

► How have I built a relationship with this particular child?

► What might be happening in a particular child's life that is influencing what they are able to learn?

► What are students showing us they need today?

► How might we get a better picture of who students are beyond the walls of this classroom?

► Does this environment reflect students' passions and interests?

► Does the content reflect students' passions and interests?

► Have I shown students that I care?

STRUCTURE 2
Effective Pedagogy

Active Learning

Researcher P. David Pearson's work has taught us that the more active we can make the reading experience, the more students will comprehend and remember (Pearson and Johnson 1978). Building in ways for students to actively participate—annotating a piece of text, discussing ideas in a turn and talk, and leaving tracks of thinking with sticky notes, for example—provides kids opportunities to think, respond, interact, and learn.

Strategic Comprehension

Stephanie Harvey and Anne Goudvis' (2017) work on comprehension applies not just to reading but to all learning. The six strategic comprehension strategies at the core of their work are a tool kit for thinking:

▶ **Monitor comprehension:** thinking about our own understanding of a text, being able to stop and adjust our approach when comprehension breaks down.

▶ **Activate and connect to background knowledge:** being able to connect what we already know with what we are learning, including addressing misconceptions.

▶ **Ask questions:** asking questions to drive learning about, within, and beyond the text.

▶ **Infer and visualize:** considering what is not explicitly stated in the text, including building images and movies in our mind as we read.

▶ **Determine the most important information:** gleaning the most important ideas in a resource, sorting what's merely interesting from what's important.

▶ **Summarize and synthesize:** explaining the gist of a resource, bringing together the new and the known, combining learning from multiple resources, and explaining that learning in a clear and concise way.

As students have repeated opportunities to access, practice, and apply these ways of thinking, their ability to think critically grows in depth and breadth.

How Do I Know If My Pedagogy Is Effective?

Consider:

▶ Are students making progress in their skills and content knowledge? How do I know?

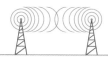

Join the Conversation:
A Curriculum Rooted in Thinking

"We can ensure that kids will be able to handle whatever curriculum we put in front of them because we've taught them how to think."

#ReadTheWorldNow

Hein.pub/RTW1.2

▶ Do students show curiosity and genuine interest in learning? What evidence do I have?

▶ Does our instruction emphasize the child's thinking process about content over specific pieces of content? For example, understanding a particular cause-and-effect relationship rather than memorizing names and dates.

▶ Is there more of an emphasis on process than on product?

▶ Are students able to independently transfer something that they learned in one class or setting to another?

▶ Are students engaged, responding, and interacting?

▶ Does the curriculum fit students' needs and strengths?

▶ Can students articulate what they are learning and why?

▶ Can students explain what they are working toward? Can they explain what goals they have set for themselves or with a teacher?

STRUCTURE 3
A Strategic Use of Technology

Often, tech in education is put in opposition with "the old way" of doing things. Yet, even though we now have access to some previously unimagined tools (who might have guessed, a decade ago, that it would be common for children to have access to age-appropriate video-editing tools?), our goals for our students are still the same: autonomy, agency, growth, curiosity, joy. Instead of throwing out the approaches that have worked for us in the past, we can say, "Yes, we write stapled-together books, AND we publish slide decks" or "Yes, we paint murals that teach, AND we record a song that summarizes learning" or "Yes, we have face-to-face book clubs, AND we collaborate online." Tried-and-true strategies and practices can still be of use, but with the help of technology, we can look beyond the walls of our classroom

Technology Can Take Us Further!	
YES! *Tried-and-True Instructional Practices That We Want to Persist*	**AND . . .** *Examples of How Technology Can Extend and Enrich Those Practices*
Students decode and comprehend text.	Students decode and comprehend text, images, video, graphics, augmented and virtual reality, and more, adding layers for interaction.
Students write and publish stapled-together books for the class to share.	Students create multi-touch books, blogs, graphics, and slide decks for the world to read.
Students compose short written pieces to summarize, reflect, or share new learning with the teacher.	Students practice summarizing and creating succinct micro-writing via email, blogs, and tweets, mirroring what they see in the real world, reaching an audience beyond the classroom, and providing opportunities for diverse feedback.
Students meet face-to-face in literature circles.	Students meet fact-to-face in literature circles and continue their conversations digitally between meetings, giving them opportunities for richer discussions.
Instruction happens in large- and small-group settings, as well as one-on-one.	The teacher uses video in the classroom and wherever students are connected to ▸ supplement small-group instruction ▸ personalize learning ▸ engage in video reteaching ▸ provide access to differentiated content and skill instruction.

and give students opportunities that are authentic, significant, and relevant in the world beyond school. In the chart below you'll see some of the ways technology builds upon the rich pedagogy of literacy instruction to support students.

Our work is also about helping our *students* see technology as a tool to be used strategically. Katie often thinks of the kindergartner who, with the air of an evening anchor delivering breaking news, tugged at Katie's pant leg, held up her tablet, and said, "Hey, there aren't any games on here!"

It's common for young children to come to school with the impression that technology is a tool for entertainment. If they have access to Siri, Alexa, Google Home, or other voice-activated technology at home, they might also see technology as a tool to get answers to straightforward questions like "How high can a serval jump?" or "How long does it take for the earth to go around the sun?" But it's rare that students come to our classrooms already seeing technology as a tool for collaboration and creation, for personal inquiry, or for widening their perspective on the world.

Children learn from our example in all ways, including how we use technology and how we allow them to use it. It's up to us to help students realize the full potential of the tools in their hands, to assist them to find meaningful purposes for those tools, and to learn to walk away from those tools when they're not helpful or when the tools are becoming harmful to their health or learning.

How Can I Use Technology Strategically and Teach My Students to Do the Same?

When planning for technology use, ask yourself:

- ▶ Which apps or tools will improve, amplify, or enhance the work that students are going to do?

- ▶ Which apps or tools will afford my students many opportunities to be creative across the year and the curriculum? (These types of tools are worth giving class time to so that students can explore and learn them well.)

- ▶ Which apps or tools fail to promote engaged and joyful learning, even if they are entertaining? How can the time spent with these be limited or eliminated?

- ▶ How will this technology make the work more authentic or connect students to an audience?

STRUCTURE 4
Student Independence

As teachers, we're responsible for giving our students a safe learning environment, sound instruction, and opportunities to learn. Unfortunately, some structures that we put in place to ensure safety, deliver instruction, and provide learning opportunities can have an unintended effect: teaching students to be complacent. After years in systems that require them to be quiet, still, and attentive or that provide instruction that merely asks them to take in information and respond to questions to assess their understanding, students can begin to equate success in learning with immediately doing what they are told, not asking questions, and ignoring their own interests.

Instead, we can prioritize building independence in our students. As we do, we'll find that our efforts are quietly revolutionizing our classrooms. When we begin with the expectation that students can and will learn to manage day-to-day functions, address challenges, troubleshoot, and take it upon themselves to help out when they can, then we are not only creating a learning ecosystem but also freeing ourselves to do the important work of teaching.

How Can I Help My Students Be More Independent?

▶ **Focus on topics kids care about and want to learn more about.**
Weave student interests throughout the curriculum. As our friend Smokey Daniels recommends, begin with the most interesting piece of the content first and turn the content into a question kids can't resist answering (Daniels 2017, 143). Or turn to inquiry, asking your students, at the start of a new unit, what *they* are curious about in relation to the topic you'll be studying together. A unit that focuses on students' questions about why we have seasons would easily address the same content requirements and standards as a straightforward, textbook-driven study of the structure of the solar system. And, in addition, it would show your students the importance of their ideas, curiosity, and connections—all of which fuel independent learning.

▶ **Give students time to make new skills and strategies their own.**
Acknowledge that it takes time for students to learn, develop, master, and apply new skills and strategies. Teach at a pace that feels energetic but does not rush students. Provide ample time (even more time than you think!) for independent practice while you kidwatch, confer, plan, and reteach.

This student-created chart is clear evidence that the teacher has instilled a sense of independence and community in her students.

▶ **Put the thinking back into kids' hands.** When researching or questioning, instead of telling kids the quick and easy answer, we help them build independence and take responsibility for their own learning with language like

- ◆ *I don't know. What do you think?*
- ◆ *Where can we go to find more information about that?*
- ◆ *Did you ask your turn and talk partner?*
- ◆ *Have you checked the specialist board to see if anyone knows a lot about this topic?*

Phrases like "talk that through" or "say more about that" are often the simple nudge kids need to gain independence. When we respond with "say more about that," we give a child an opportunity to refine their thinking. More importantly, the additional seven or eight seconds it takes a child to think something through gives the idea more depth and relevance than a teacher-provided answer, enabling them to retrieve, revisit, and reuse the ideas more readily in the future.

▶ **Step back from the front of the room.** Work alongside students as facilitator, coach, and listening ear, providing students just-in-time feedback to grow.

▶ **Value powerful learning over perfect learning.** Independent learning is messy learning. It is easy to assess things that are easily measured—the number of correct items on a test, the length of a piece of writing, the lack of errors in spelling and punctuation. However, the things that

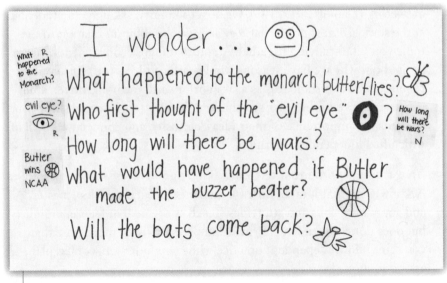

Encouraging and honoring kids' questions helps us craft customized learning experiences.

are easily measured are rarely the best indicators of learning and independence. Instead of prioritizing perfection, focus on the gains that students are making in directing their own learning, in collaboration, and in creative and critical thought.

▶ **Offer choices to students whenever possible.** When we present students with choices, what we are really saying is "I care what you think, I value who you are, and I value what you know about yourself as a learner." When given choice—in content to study, in how to work, in who to work with, in what to read—students are more willing to take on a task and to demonstrate improved performance. They are also more willing to accept challenging tasks (Patall, Cooper, and Robinson 2008). However, too many choices can have the opposite effect. We recommend presenting students with a structured choice, such as three to five options from which to choose.

▶ **Teach students how to succeed.** Independence can seem impossible when students rely on us for guidance and support with tasks, or when we find ourselves continually compelled to correct their behaviors. To help launch students toward independence, we can consider what our expectations are and whether we have taught our students *how* to meet our expectations. In some cases, this means being extremely explicit. We might walk a student through how to first set a device down on a table before pulling out their chair to sit, how to arrange their workspace and supplies for success, or how to quickly and efficiently get to work when they are released from a lesson or the carpet area. In short, try to anticipate areas where students will need to be taught the behaviors, skills, and strategies they'll need. And, if you find students behaving in ways that are counterproductive, take it as an opportunity to teach the necessary behaviors, skills, or strategies. Observe, listen, and ask so that you can understand the student's perspective and help them participate in the solutions.

▶ **Use visual aids.** Visual aids are helpful for reminding students of procedures and expectations. Instead of asking you what to do or how to do it, students can take responsibility into their own hands by referring to a written version of a procedure you've already introduced to the class. Hang charts in your classroom, make small versions of them for desks and notebooks, have students take pictures of them to access on their device, or turn them into bookmarks to keep these learning tools visible and at the forefront of students' minds. Be careful not to clutter the environment with too many visual aids: leave up only the most current and important ones for the learning at the moment. We frequently change things up, even making an old desk reminder a new color to capture students' attention and keep the classroom fresh and orderly.

Charts can provide scaffolding for tried-and-true strategies like turn and talks as well as for the use of technology tools.

▶ **Set a goal.** Setting goals in collaboration with students, mentoring students in reaching their goals, and celebrating achieved goals can help students in any number of tasks at school. Begin a whole-group, small-group, or one-on-one discussion about what students would like to work on and what accomplishing that goal will look like. Help students construct goals that are in student-friendly language, are concrete, and are attainable. Note that research does not support giving students tangible prizes for doing academic work (Schunk, Pintrich, and Meece 2008). Instead, we honor and celebrate student successes with a standing ovation, extra reading time, curating a musical playlist for the closing of the day, or free-choice inquiry time for the class.

STRUCTURE 5
A Commitment to Collaboration

Collaboration isn't kids working quietly and peacefully at all times—it can be noisy and it often involves some push and pull among members. True collaboration requires kids (and adults!) to be thoughtful, pragmatic, friendly, and flexible in their thinking and actions. Collaborators demonstrate independence, self-sufficiency, and care in their work and their relationships with adults and peers. They listen first, ask questions, and disagree with compassion. When things go awry, they have the skills and support to correct missteps and mend relationships.

These students are not just "good groups" or special in some way, and the schools where we have witnessed this work range from wealthy to high-poverty, in suburban, rural, and urban settings. What makes collaboration possible is not the location or the students, but all of us: the teachers. Building a culture of collaboration is a process that we launch at the beginning of the year and continue to emphasize, refine, and support until students leave our care. In collaborative classroom cultures we consistently see

▶ co-creation and ownership of the guidelines that dictate how students interact with each other and adults

▶ explicit instruction and support in when, how, and why we collaborate with others

▶ a culture of love, respect, reflection, and celebration that is encouraged by every student and staff member in the building.

Collaboration can supercharge the work that you are doing in your classroom: it ignites interest, adds a heightened sense of purpose to the work, and puts children in leadership and decision-making roles. But collaboration is even more powerful than what we see only in the classroom: the collaborative practices we teach leak into the hallways and playgrounds as students create self-sustaining groups and work together to solve problems and accomplish tasks.

How Can I Build and Support a Culture of Collaboration in My Classroom?

We find that the lessons about collaboration and how to work together are the ones we revisit most often. It's easy for kids to say the right thing, but it's not always easy for them to do the right thing in the moment.

▶ **Co-create guidelines and use them.** It's not unusual for teachers to begin a school year by establishing norms with their students—a list of rights and responsibilities, a classroom agreement, or a set of expectations. When done with care, this process can also lay the groundwork for a collaborative classroom.

Begin with a conversation about what collaboration can and should be, inviting students to help define what collaboration looks like, sounds like, and feels like. To help them see the connection between the climate of the classroom and the behaviors of the people in the classroom, ask them to consider some common scenarios:

When I'm reading, I want to feel . . .

When I'm solving a difficult problem, I want to feel . . .

When I'm working in a group, I want to feel . . .

When I'm confused, I want to feel . . .

Then ask:

What can someone else do to help you feel that way?

Other useful guiding questions to try include:

How do you want to feel when you walk in that door each morning?

What circumstances help you learn? Feel joyful?

What's something a teacher or classmate has done in the past that made your heart soar?

Invite students to jot ideas down in a notebook or shared digital tool like a Google doc or Padlet. Some teachers organize this information into a list of rights and responsibilities of collaborative work, adding in ideas that students might find helpful. Others might create a chart that lists the guidelines for collaboration and helpful language. If students have done work like this before, they might break into small groups and design their own format.

You may need to coach students away from writing rules or negative statements like "don't talk while the teacher is talking." This focus on negative behaviors may be something they've learned in other settings. However, our goal is to help them focus on their *emotions* so that you begin your year through the lens of empathy, with the understanding that our actions affect people.

Follow up the creation of classroom guidelines by starting to work on how students can support each other in following them. A T-chart like the one on the right will help students organize their thinking. Consider this something you revisit during the year as new situations arise and your students mature.

This early work that your students do will give you valuable information as to what they already know about collaboration and what you might teach them. For example, if students say that listening to everyone will help them feel like the group is respecting their thinking, we might also teach them to use specific and supportive language, make eye contact, and use nonverbal body language to validate each other's ideas. We also use an observation checklist like the one below to gather information about our students at the beginning of the year.

When . . . I want to feel . . .	So it would help me if . . .
When I work in a group I want to feel like I am being listened to.	we listened to everyone's ideas before making a decision.

Observation Questions for Collaboration Skills

- How does this student approach working in a small group? Do they . . .
  - tell other group members what to do or wait for someone else to take the lead?
  - listen before they speak or wait to talk?
  - complete the work quickly?
  - refocus themselves often or need assistance?
  - ask many questions or hold back if they are confused?
  - gather supplies right away?
  - wait to see what other groups are doing first?
  - disagree with members of the group?
  - look at group members when they talk?
- Does the student apply strategies taught in class?
- Does the student reference an anchor chart or prior lesson to enhance interaction? Build on the ideas of others? Solve conflict?
- How does the student transition from independent to collaborative work time?
- What helps this student do their best work?
- What else have I noticed about this student?

Once students have completed their ideas, have them share through a digital tool like Padlet so they can view and comment on each other's work.

Alternatively, you might ask students directly about collaboration with the help of a collaboration survey. We ask students to fill these out at the beginning of each school year. You'll also find several blank examples of collaboration surveys located in the book's online digital resources at Hein.pub/RTW-Resources.

Once you've gathered input from students—from a T-chart, from your own observations, from a survey, or from some combination of sources—you might pull the most salient points and draft a class set of guidelines for approval by students or work with the class as a whole to create the guidelines. Once complete, these guidelines can hang in the classroom, can be signed by each student, and can be revisited (or revised) during the year as needed.

▶ **Fishbowl a group conversation.** Students don't always come to our classrooms with an understanding of what respectful talk looks like or how to maintain that respectful talk when emotions are running high. The fishbowl strategy—holding a small-group discussion while the rest of the class observes—is a tool for helping students see the dynamics of a discussion while modeling different ways that conversations might go. Student observers might listen for specific language that helps move conversation in a positive manner or consider what language could have been used; notice ways participants disagree in a polite manner or ways they could have stated something more positively; or identify strategies that a group member uses when things aren't quite working, such as stepping back to take a breath. These lessons help our students know what good collaboration looks, sounds, and feels like. They also give students a chance to reflect on what they might have done or said differently in order to build a stronger discussion.

Fishbowls can also be used for digital conversations: the language of productive disagreement becomes even more essential in an online discussion where the absence of body language and facial expression muddies the waters of communications. You might guide your students to examine digital conversations to determine what is needed to communicate clearly, to discuss implied tone, and to identify language that is helpful in keeping the discussion on track and productive. Giving students opportunities to notice what does and does not work well in digital conversations is more likely to have an effect on their behaviors than simply giving them a list of rules to follow. For example, if students notice for themselves that one-word replies such as "yeah" do little to communicate what they are thinking and which ideas they agree with, they are more likely to elaborate in their own communications.

Collaboration Survey

1. What does it mean to collaborate?

2. What does it look like, sound like, and feel like when you're in a group that is collaborating well?

3. What does it look like, sound like, and feel like when you're in a group that is not collaborating well?

4. When you're in a group you like to (circle all that apply)

   - share your ideas
   - make sure everyone is working
   - let the teacher know when things aren't going well
   - listen
   - be helpful
   - help people work together
   - do your own thing
   - be with your friends
   - make new friends
   - organize things for the group
   - let other people organize things for the group

5. What is something that you've experienced in another class that was helpful to you either in becoming a better collaborator or in helping your group collaborate more efficiently?

6. Share a time when you were in a group that was collaborating really well. Why do you think that was the case? (This could be an in school or out of school experience.)

7. Share a time when you were in a group that was not collaborating well. Why do you think that was the case? (This could be an in school or out of school experience.)

8. Have you ever used technology tools to collaborate with a classmate? Please describe.

9. Have you ever used technology tools to collaborate with students in other schools or experts in the field?

10. How do you think collaboration using digital tools might look similar or different to collaboration face-to-face?

11. Do you have any ideas for how we can make our class a collaborating class this year?

For more examples of collaboration surveys, visit Hein.pub/RTW-Resources.

This co-created chart from a first-grade class outlines how to collaborate well. (Notice how students reference the Little Red Hen as an example of poor collaboration!) Charts like this hang in the classroom as a tool for students to use any time they gather to work with a partner or in groups.

▶ **Support effective group work.** Students' interactions in small groups get to the core of building a classroom that honors each student's experiences and expertise. Taking the stance of the lead learner in the room instead of group enforcer goes a long way toward communicating our respect to students. A few suggestions for supporting collaboration in groups:

- When approaching a group, use that line that has served us so well in reading and writing workshop: "How's it going?" Then, listen carefully. Ask questions, gather information, and carefully craft support in the way of lessons, scaffolds, and conversations.

- Have students fill out a Google form or online survey to share what they've accomplished, what they plan to accomplish in the next session, how they are feeling about their group, and what progress they are making on their goals.

- Have students do a quick "status of the class" using Padlet, an online bulletin board on which each student or group shares an artifact or reflection from the day's learning.

- Keep conferring notes so that you know whom you've talked with, who might need your help next, and what follow-up students are expecting.

STRUCTURE 6
Both Creation AND Consumption

For several years, "Creation, not consumption!" has been a popular refrain in the edtech world. In many ways, this has been a helpful guide in considering how to use technology in the classroom: look for tools that enable students to create, not products that treat children as consumers. *Creation* refers to students using digital tools for their own ends—sharing ideas, deepening learning, collaborating, inquiring, and connecting with an authentic audience. For the last several years, *consumption* refers to students using media passively—playing games or watching amusing videos for no purpose other than alleviating boredom, and completing automated lessons that are just as irrelevant as the worksheets they resemble. "Creation, not consumption!" has been a much-needed pushback against poor models of technology use.

Today, however, we see classrooms where making is out of balance with meaning, where creating does not seem to be connected to a plan, a purpose, or a goal. The push for "creating" can crowd out the need for taking in new ideas and information. So we now advocate for thoughtful consumption—consumption as a means to interact with the world—in addition to ongoing creation.

Consumption informs creation. Reading a news site, listening to a podcast on current events, or watching a short video about the solar system allows students to make connections between themselves, their school, and the world. At the same time, if we want students to consume critically, we have a tremendous opportunity—even an obligation—to teach them how to comprehend content presented across media. We can teach them how to go deeper with their *Inside Out and Back Again* (Lai 2011) book club and build background knowledge for the book's setting using Google Maps. We can guide them to an article on Newsela that presents a historical perspective of Vietnam. Then we can invite them to discuss their findings in a small group to refine their thinking. As with all subjects, we are not aiming for the use of technology; we are aiming for deeper learning, and using technology as a tool in our work.

Join the Conversation:
Consumption AND Creation
"We consume to be better creators."

#ReadTheWorldNow

Hein.pub/RTW1.3

How Am I Embracing Both Creation and Critical Consumption?

▶ What resources will my students be using this year? How will those books, articles, websites, infographics, videos, images, and podcasts give them opportunities to consume critically? How do they align with the skills and content my students need?

▶ What skills do my students already have for being critical consumers of ideas? How might they transfer those skills to digital media?

▶ What skills will my students need to critically consume digital resources?

▶ What tools will my students be using to "create"—to collaborate, to amplify their own voices, and to deepen their learning?

▶ How often am I asking students to consume? How often am I asking them to create? How often am I giving them a choice in how they do something? How is that working for my students? How do I know?

STRUCTURE 7
A Student-Focused Physical Environment

Take a moment to sit in your students' seats—literally. Take a minute to be aware of that perspective. Is it comfortable? Do you have access to the things you need? What would it be like to be a learner in this space? Now consider how your students use those seats—are they sitting in them for extended periods of time? Can they move around when they need to? Does this environment support them in learning?

The physical structure of our classrooms signals to students who owns the space. We convey that the classroom is not merely the teacher's room but collectively "our room" through design and use of space. Environment can tell students "I care about you. Let me know what you need. I respect your ideas. We will learn together. You matter."

A classroom that puts students at the center of its physical design looks more like a local coffeehouse than the formal classrooms of yesterday. Students may choose where to work based on their preference, their purpose, and the task at hand. High tables for standing are grouped in a back corner; desks are pushed into a pod of six or replaced with tables; kids stretch across the carpet armed with clipboards and sticky notes. Comfort becomes a priority, with couches, carpets, and squashy chairs making spaces for reading and working. Necessary materials—devices, paper, markers, pencils, texts—

Functionality Over Beauty

If you are cringing at the idea of a class-room redesign, remember that classrooms are learning environments that need to be functional; they don't have to be Pinterest worthy, and they don't have to be filled with fancy, expensive furniture. Perhaps a better place for many of us to start is with what we don't need. If we can create a clutter-free environment that honors the essentials—collaborative workspaces, tools for learning, lots of books—then we've taken the first and most important step. The rest we can build over time.

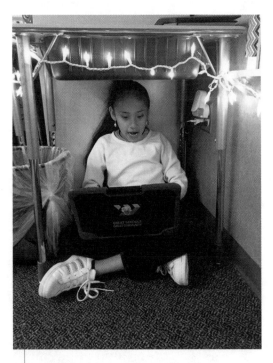

When recording audio, a child goes in her "studio" space. Working below the table minimizes sound interference in the classroom.

are easily accessible. Classrooms buzz as students discuss their work, travel around the space to independently access materials, and transition seamlessly between print and digital sources.

Moving to a flexible environment can feel like a big paradigm shift when we've spent so many years perfecting the art of the seating arrangement. However, recent research shows that optimizing the physical characteristics of kindergarten through sixth-grade classrooms improved academic performance in reading, writing, and mathematics by 16 percent (Barrett et al. 2015). By shifting working space from desks to high tables, to the floor, and more, we build in body breaks that improve focus and cognition. Teachers we've worked with have reported fewer management issues when moving to flexible seating, which they attribute to students' having choice and ownership over the classroom environment, as well as students' increased focus, which helps the class develop a peaceful and respectful working space.

Most importantly, flexible classrooms are successful because they go hand in hand with a change in pedagogy (Barrett et al. 2015). When we change our space, we change our mindset, helping us focus on instructional practices that are student centered and research based. Looking around a classroom space that is flexible, we can clearly see that if a teaching space is dynamic, our instruction needs to be dynamic too! We minimize whole-class instruction and find ways to meet with small groups, provide tabletop conferences, and teach responsively. In doing so, we have more time to assess on an individual basis and use the feedback students give us today to plan for tomorrow's instruction. An environment that allows students to move with ease increases collaboration, invites small-group conversations, and promotes student-led research. Flexible spaces provide students with choice, choice amplifies engagement, and engagement drives students to seek, access, and effectively use new knowledge.

How Can I Make My Classroom's Physical Environment Student Focused?

Involve your students. If we want to be student focused, our first step is to involve the students in the decision-making process. Survey them, allow them to design portions of the classroom, and ask them what works and what doesn't.

Kidwatch. What are students telling you with their behavior? When are they engaged? When are they not engaged? How do you know? Take time to do this kind of kidwatching across the year. What worked in August might not work in March when legs are longer and bodies are bigger.

See it through your students' eyes. Ask a coach or administrator to come in and teach your class so you can be a student. Are you comfortable? Can you access what you need without the teacher? Can you see what you need to see? Can you find collaborative spaces and private spaces for when you need them? Are there times when you have choice and times when you are challenged to collaborate with someone new?

Classroom layouts, seating options, and adjustable learning environments can support both digital and analog learning.

WRITE WITH US

⏻ **What do you believe about the role technology can play in improving learning opportunities for your students? If it helps, think about *one* student in particular.**

⏻ **Write about a time when you saw, either in your own classroom or someone else's, a positive impact from students' technology use. What factors caused that experience to be positive?**

⏻ **Find a group to share your thinking with. Share your responses, and listen thoughtfully to theirs. Come to a consensus about something you might try together, learn, or study to deepen your understanding of the role that technology might play in your instruction.**
Jot down your new learning here.

⏻ **Based on what you've noted, what is one goal you can set for yourself that will support positive uses of technology in your classroom?**

⏻ **Bonus round: Discuss the questions above with a few colleagues from school. What new ideas did you hear? What reinforced beliefs you already held? What made you think of things in a new light?**

⏻ **Share your ideas. #ReadTheWorldNow**

2 *Reading Today's Texts*
Comprehension and Thinking in a Digital Age

Sun shines through the window, casting long shadows as students sit in small groups around the classroom, some grabbing their books and others grabbing tablets. As Mr. B works his way around the room to confer with students, he keeps glancing at two boys on the carpet whose body language reveals that they are struggling to find engagement with the day's work. It is not the typical getting up, talking, and fiddling avoidance behavior, but rather flicks of the fingers, tense bodies, and stolen glances around the room.

Mr. B reflects, as we all do during these moments, "Maybe I shouldn't let them read on the tablets. They are too distracted. But the app they are on offers a wide variety of books they are interested in and that they can access." Many of us have found ourselves in Mr. B's shoes, grappling with how to best engage our readers, which tools will best meet their needs, and how to give them the instruction and support they need to use technology in a way that will amplify the work they are doing.

What Do We Now Need to Teach That We Didn't Need to Teach Before?

It is easy to make assumptions about the knowledge and experience students are coming to us with, for example, that students already inherently know how to use technology as a tool for learning. Yet Common Sense Media (2015, 21) reports that while seventy-eight percent of tweens spend their time on devices for consumption-based activities (viewing videos, watching TV, playing games, browsing websites), only three percent of their time is related to creative activities (digital art, coding, writing). In short, students today come into our classrooms familiar with some aspects of mobile devices. They know how to use them as a tool for entertainment. They may know how to use them as a tool to communicate. But they don't necessarily know how to use them as a tool for thinking.

So students might, at first, appear to be the mythical "digital natives" we've heard about: it may seem that they understand and can navigate technology effortlessly. But, upon closer inspection, we see that their expertise is often

> **Learn how to learn. That needs to be the norm of education moving forward. Jobs will change but learning is forever. That's how we prep for the future.**
>
> —Dr. Anne-Marie Imafidon, 2018

Join the Conversation:
Digital Reading in the Classroom

"The reading experience is now so complex because it varies by format. . . . There are so many more combinations of how to read."

#ReadTheWorldNow

Hein.pub/RTW2.1

> **Digital reading experiences must be part of the opportunities we give students on a regular basis. If not, we're discounting much of the reading they will engage with in the future.**
>
> —William L. Bass II and Franki Sibberson, *Digital Reading*, 2015 (4)

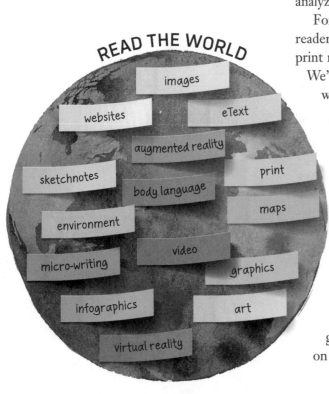

limited to technology that provides entertainment. Students still need instruction, coaching, and guidance when it comes to learning, reading, and creating in digital spaces. They are ready and willing to learn about new tools and even to support teachers in learning about tools, but they need to be taught how to use devices in a way that amplifies positive learning experiences.

Take a moment to visualize the last website you viewed. Think deeply about what it looked like. If you're unable to gather a clear picture of a site in your mind, we invite you to engage in a moment of digital distraction and put down your book to take a look at CNN, ESPN, Amazon, or your favorite social media site. Go!

Chances are the website you visited opens with an image or a short video clip. If you take a look at web design and media content, you'll notice a shift away from text boxes on a page and print intended to be read from top to bottom to layouts that are dominated by images and short video clips. In fact, in many places, text is a click away and the viewer has to link to long-form print via a caption or headline. This visual layout asks the reader to use classic nonfiction features—captions, headings, titles—and depend on them as a signal to read on. Furthermore, we read the visuals and use them to decide what content we pursue. These visual messages are layered with information and are constructed to send a host of messages to the reader about bias, intent, values, and persuasion—evidence students must analyze to determine the purpose in a media message (Center for Media Literacy, n.d.). Once you start looking, you'll find examples all around that indicate we need to teach kids to read beyond text—images, video, graphics, and more—and critically analyze the message to comprehend deeply.

For the past fifty years, educators have studied how kids become effective readers in print text. We've crafted minilessons to support a diverse range of print readers, and we continue to refine these lessons on an ongoing basis. We've provided students time and choice with a variety of texts because we know this increases their ability to read. But have we done the same with text on screen? Images? Infographics? Video?

While the student-centered practices behind strong instruction are just as powerful when working with technology, minilessons for print don't always translate to building strategic on-screen readers. In some cases, attempting to apply skills honed for print to digital media without support from teachers may cause more confusion to the reader (Ciampa 2014). Therefore, we need to craft lessons based on our observations of students, on the areas where understanding breaks down, and on evolving technologies. In short, we need to redefine what it means to read: the mere act of reading words in a digital medium is far more complicated than previously thought.

In print reading, we teach the characteristics that define various genres as well as the structures and nuances of those genres, focusing on specific strategies needed to access and comprehend the information presented. It's common practice that, even for emergent readers, we take note of genre and begin to build a mental map or checklist of what to expect from that genre. This mental mapping supports readers in comprehending increasingly complex texts as they progress through their educational careers.

Yet, with devices, we tend to group all forms of digital reading under the umbrella category of "reading on-screen." However, there are many formats and permutations of eText: even more than there are for print. With digital texts or eTexts—words, images, and graphics in non-paper-based formats (Mills 2016)—students need to not only navigate the subtleties of the traditional print genres but also take into account the delivery method. Anne Mangen's research suggests that reading eText varies by format (e-book, PDF, social media feed, etc.) as well as the device that it is delivered upon (e-reader, laptop, tablet, etc.). In short, reading a PDF on your phone is a different reading experience than reading it on your laptop or tablet device (Mangen and Kuiken 2014).

Similarly, reading an e-book provides a very different experience than reading a PDF or a social media feed, and again that experience varies across devices. We now have significantly more formats in which we must access and interpret new information. Thus, Mangen (2016) concludes, "The future of literary reading in a time of increasing digitization is too multifaceted, complex, multilayered to be studied entirely within disciplinary boundaries." The dynamic nature of digital text is so variable and complex that we must teach it in all subject areas, not just reading.

As technology provides countless new ways to access information, it also requires us to identify new strategies that will help us acquire and build knowledge. One path forward, according to Maryanne Wolf, director of UCLA's Center for Dyslexia, Diverse Learners, and Social Justice, is for young readers to develop a biliterate brain—learning the needed skills and dispositions for paper and digital reading in tandem—much in the way children who are raised to speak two languages develop their skills (2018).

While some of the research in this burgeoning field illuminates new understandings about how our brains interact with and respond to varied digital reading situations, much of it confirms what we have already observed about digital reading: students need explicit instruction in both the skills *and* habits of reading on devices, students need ample time and opportunity to practice applying skills to varied digital reading scenarios, and students still need robust reading instruction in print texts to further deep reading skills. Yet, startlingly, the majority of educators have not had professional development geared toward applying existing literacy strategies to this new reading format (Schugar and Schugar 2018). Above all, our students need educators who are researching and observing, while keenly applying all they know about teaching and learning to help them navigate these new mediums and act as tech mentors in our connected world. The Try It lessons in this chapter are designed to help you on your own journey of rethinking reading today.

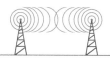

Join the Conversation:
An Expanded Definition of Reading

"We have so much input coming in. We want to be able to help our students synthesize all of that input into a way that makes sense."

#ReadTheWorldNow

Hein.pub/RTW2.2

In general, the lessons build upon each other. However, the lessons do not need to be used only in the order presented. You can use the *Try This When* . . . notes and the comments at the beginning of each lesson to determine which lessons to use and when to use them.

It's important to note that we often use the term *read* interchangeably with the term *view*. When we read, there is always a thinking component. Therefore, "reading" media other than text also reminds us that there is a thinking component: we don't just look at images and video; we consider, we analyze, we question, we connect, we synthesize . . . we *read*!

Several of the lessons also emphasize digging beyond the text itself to understand who has written it, why, and what perspectives or biases they might have. In the past we've reserved this skill for older grades, but new research and the inflow of digital content suggest it is now vital to understand authorship of text and media, even at a very young age.

These lessons are by no means an exhaustive list; we hope that they will be an entry point into this work and an inspiration for you to write your own lessons. You'll find a blank lesson planning page located in the book's online digital resources at Hein.pub/RTW-Resources.

Let's get to work. As Debbie Miller (2018) says, "What's the best that could happen?"

This printable tool can be downloaded at Hein.pub/RTW-Resources.

WRITE WITH US

When we look at the vast number of opportunities available for learning, we believe it's the best time to be a student and the best time to be a teacher! Today we have more options to hook kids into thinking than we've ever had before. And as the world around us changes, we have to be more responsive teachers than ever before.

To do that, we need to spend time thinking about our lives as the chief learner in the classroom as well as notice and understand what our kids are showing us and what they may need next. With a colleague or coach, or independently, take a few moments to think about the following.

⏻ How do I approach digital reading? What preferences, habits, or strategies do I bring into the classroom? How might this influence what my students think or do with digital reading?

⏻ When and where do I see and use digital media in my life?

⏻ What opportunities does digital media provide me? How can I bring those opportunities into the classroom for my students?

⏻ What challenges does digital media present in my life? How can I prepare my students for those challenges?

⏻ Share your ideas. #ReadTheWorldNow

About This Chapter

This chapter will help you help your students transfer what they already know about reading and interacting with print texts to new media like images, websites, e-books, and videos. We've taken care to include scaffolds such as sample teaching language to help you along the way.

THINKING THROUGH TEXTS

It's up to us to ensure that our students have exposure to, instruction in, and practice with using digital texts—in independent reading, in lessons, in small groups, in read-alouds, and in researching. In this section, we suggest a few introductory lessons for helping our readers become thoughtful and critical readers of various kinds of digital texts.

TRY IT

APPLYING READING STRATEGIES TO IMAGES AND MEDIA

In these lessons, we teach students to apply the same skills they use in reading to the new media and resources that exist in a digital world such as images, videos, infographics, or podcasts.

TRY IT

RESPONDING AND CONNECTING USING VISUAL TOOLS

Here, we connect students' comprehension and thinking to creation, make students' thinking visible, and help students build a portfolio of work that demonstrates their growth over time.

TRY IT

THINKING THROUGH TEXTS: *Orient Ourselves to Digital Texts*

TRY THIS WHEN . . .

- you introduce students to a new medium of digital texts

- you observe students struggling to orient themselves to a digital text

- you have concerns that students will be distracted by a digital texts' features.

This lesson offers students opportunities to explore digital texts, consider how they might approach these texts differently from—or similarly to—print texts, and identify strategies that assist them in increased comprehension.

WHAT TO DO

Present students with a digital text (e-book, article, website, etc.) and ask them to discuss how the digital text is similar to and different from print texts they have read before. For instance, students might notice that an e-book has a cover, illustrations, and text. In addition, they might also notice that it's difficult to tell how long an e-book is, or that items on the screen or interactive features may be distracting.

A common challenge that teachers we work with lament is how easily distracted students are and how quick they are to design strategies for masking other activities they might be doing instead of reading, like playing games. This challenge is not unique to children; many adults we know face similar distraction challenges when working on devices. While there are many ways to police student's device use, policing does not build skills or promote learning. We advocate teaching students skills to anticipate, understand, and address possible roadblocks to engaged working time.

Ask students to consider if they will need to approach the digital text differently than they might approach a print book, and gather their ideas on a chart. Give students time to put their own ideas into practice and reflect on what additional strategies they might need to use. Create a class anchor chart to hold on to the students' ideas.

Helpful Language

What do we notice?

What do we wonder?

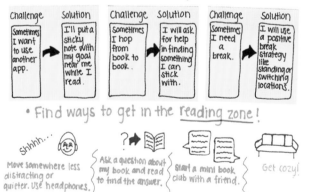

This chart, created with a fifth-grade class, shows a combination of student insights and ideas suggested by the teacher. When posted in the class, it serves to remind students of strategies they might try when reading an e-book. It can also be a source of minilesson ideas if the teacher notices that students need more support with some of the strategies.

OUTCOMES AND WHAT TO LOOK FOR

We expect students to consider a text before reading and develop a holistic understanding of what skills and strategies they might need to use. Can students

- ▶ examine a text to understand the genre, layout, structure, and features?
- ▶ identify similarities and differences between print and digital media?
- ▶ anticipate what strategies or skills they will need to engage in order to comprehend and enjoy a text?
- ▶ identify personal barriers or challenges they might face when reading digitally and setting goals to overcome them?
- ▶ show understanding of how app or website features may help or harm comprehension when they are reading on those platforms?

FOLLOW UP

Revisit the charts with students in the coming days as they practice digital reading. Charts for digital strategies scaffold and support students as they work to build skill fluency, just as traditional anchor charts do for literacy and the content areas. Encourage students to reference these charts as needed and to add to the charts as they identify new challenges.

THINKING THROUGH TEXTS: *Use Web Features Effectively*

TRY THIS WHEN . . .

■ students are beginning to use websites (perhaps at the beginning of the year)

■ students encounter new features on websites

■ you have concerns that students may be distracted or confused by web features.

Students will encounter a variety of elements on websites as they read and research online. In this lesson, we teach them to apply what they know about informational text features to help them understand what they are reading, as well as understand when features are unhelpful or distracting. This lesson is adapted from *Connecting Comprehension and Technology* (Harvey et al. 2013, 63–71).

WHAT TO DO

This can be taught in a whole- or small-group literacy lesson. Show your students a variety of websites they might typically access for reading or research. What features do they notice? Do they know how to interact with all those features? Give students time to explore the various features of the sites in small groups and consider which of the features are helpful and which (if any) are distracting. Ask students to develop guidelines for what to do if they encounter those features on another website. To the right is a chart that one third-grade classroom collaborated on after exploring some of the students' favorite sites.

OUTCOMES AND WHAT TO LOOK FOR

Kids will familiarize themselves with a variety of digital text features that aid or distract reading comprehension. Knowing what to look for when encountering digital text will assist students across the year each time they are online. Can students

▶ explain which parts of a website are important to their reading task and which ones aren't?

▶ effectively navigate a website using links, headings, and search functions?

{Using Web Features Effectively}

How do we navigate text online?

Look for title → CLICK → read on

Look for image → read words below image to see if you want to read on

Watch intro video → push play ▶
Remember a video doesn't tell the whole story! ① Read on. ② Ask "what's on the other side of that video?"

	Helpful ☺	Hurtful ☹
search	• gets you good info on a kid site	• open search takes you to info that doesn't help you find what you need
tags	• organizes info into simple, big ideas	• leads you down wrong path
font	• easy to read clear	• hard to read distracting
comments	• fun to hear others thinking	• can be distracting or off topic
pop-ups	• provides new idea or fact	• tempting toys, stores, or other sites but not for school

Charts like this offer scaffolds for students as they work, freeing teachers from tech support duties so they can interact with kids in a way that pushes thinking.

Helpful Language

What do you think you need to know about the way this website is laid out before you begin?

What do you see that looks familiar here?

10 FEATURES WE USE ON THE WEB

1 → WEB ADDRESS
Tells you what website you are on, let's you know if the site is credible

2 → TITLE
Gives you the gist of what you're about to read.

3 → VIDEOS
Tells a story of gives information using pictures, moving clips, sound, and music

4 → PICTURES
Helps us visualize what we might want to read about

5 → CAPTIONS
Gives more details about videos and photos

6 → TEXT LINKS
Might tell what a word means or take us to another article. (Be careful!)

7 → LEARN OR READ MORE LINKS
Shows us articles or pages with related topics that we might be interested in.

8 → SEARCH BAR
A place to type in key words if we are looking for something specific.

9 → DISTRACTIONS
Ads, games, and other articles that take us away from focusing on our task.

10 → COMMENTS
A place where people give their thoughts or opinions.

Students in a third-grade classroom worked together to brainstorm these ideas in order to create this "bookmark" infographic.

▶ engage with a body of text, images, or video of a website while keeping their purpose in mind?

▶ say why a website might be a worthwhile resource or why it should be abandoned (too many ads/distractions, etc.)?

FOLLOW UP

As kids have more time with devices across the year, they will access increasingly diverse and complex digital texts. Remind students to use the resources in the room—charts, bookmarks, and other artifacts—to support them as they interact with new features. Revisit the lesson and add new strategies and noticings, ensuring that the lesson is presented in a way that not only supports students in the current text they are in but is transferable to any text they might read. Remember, we teach readers and thinkers, not specific resources.

THINKING THROUGH TEXTS: *Analyze How Digital Features Work Together*

TRY THIS WHEN . . .

■ you notice that students are missing key parts of a digital resource, or are not pausing to reflect on how key elements work together

■ you want to scaffold students into understanding more complex written text by first gathering key ideas from images, videos, or infographics.

Once students have developed an understanding of different digital features and how to approach them as readers, we focus on how they interact to tell a specific story. Just as we teach students to synthesize the components of an informational text (blending knowledge gained from text, images, and other nonfiction features), we can help them make meaning by synthesizing a text's digital parts.

WHAT TO DO

Share a website or online magazine that offers a combination of text and videos or multimedia digital text with students. Using a thinksheet like the one to the right, model and engage students in guided practice on how to determine what the most important information from each element is and how those elements work together. We might prompt students to consider this last point by asking questions like

▶ What information does the picture/graphic/text add?

▶ How does the video/image help us form a mental picture of what's happening here?

▶ What is our brain doing when we read the titles and subtitles? How does that help us be more efficient readers?

▶ Which features let us know if we can trust this information?

You'll find blank thinksheets located in the book's online digital resources at Hein.pub/RTW-Resources.

DIGITAL FEATURE THINKSHEET

Feature	What I learned	Why this feature was important

This printable tool can be downloaded at Hein.pub/RTW-Resources.

Helpful Language

What new information can we learn from this feature? How does that information add to our understanding?

Why might the author have included this?

Does this feature tell the complete story or is it biased in some way?

OUTCOMES AND WHAT TO LOOK FOR

We are looking for students to be mindful readers of digital text, to understand that it is complex and has many features and elements that require time, thought, and analysis. Do students

▶ stop and notice what elements are present, be they text, video, images, additional links to reading, infographics, or other features?

▶ stop to read, view, explore, and discuss each element?

▶ gather important information as they interact with each of the elements?

▶ compare and synthesize the information in the different elements?

▶ understand that stopping to synthesize elements is something accomplished and thoughtful readers do?

▶ consider how an image or video might affect their understanding, opinions, or thoughts about what they are reading?

Here is an example that a fourth-grade class did collaboratively, using Google Docs, before setting off to try it on their own.

HOW DO WEB FEATURES WORK TOGETHER?
Website: *National Geographic Kids*, "Chipmunks Wear Mini Spy Gear"

Feature	What we learned	Why this feature was important
Title	The article will be about something chipmunks wear. Spies are people who watch other people in secret.	It told us what the article would be about.
Subtitle	The thing they wear is telling us about how they live. This takes place in Canada. They are rodents.	Gave a little more information because the title was a little confusing.
Video	They wore tiny microphones around their neck. The people spying are scientists. They don't seem to mind. They recorded different kinds of sounds they make. They sound like birds.	Helps us get a picture of what was happening. We could listen to the chipmunks like we were scientists.
Published Date	This article was published in 2015.	Tells us when it was written, if it is current.
Article	Located in Green Mountain Nature Reserve. Scientists are studying how chipmunks communicate. The world's smallest digital recording device. Scientists also made fake threats to hear how they would respond. They can have different personalities.	Gave us more specific details about when, where, who, and how. Added expert quotes.
Photo and Caption	Chipmunks wear different-colored tags so you can tell them apart.	Showed us a photo so we could study a chipmunk.

THINKING THROUGH TEXTS: *Stop and Jot About Digital Texts*

TRY THIS WHEN . . .

- you introduce a digital article or video for the first time
- you notice that students are not actively engaging with digital texts
- students are copying long passages of information as opposed to quickly jotting key ideas and stopping to think and wonder.

We often ask students to stop and jot down key information, thinking, and questions as they read. This active literacy practice works just as powerfully with digital texts. When we teach students to gather, synthesize, and reflect on thinking, we are teaching them to be thoughtful, active readers, regardless of the medium.

WHAT TO DO

There are many ways that students can interact with digital texts using technology tools. However, we often find that the simplest way is to ask them to use the same types of structures we use for print text. Many students find that switching between resources and tools such as a website and a note-taking app is taxing, so unless they have the ability to write or record directly on the article, we suggest a paper stop and jot with a digital text. Thinking frames or thinksheets with two or three columns, like the ones found in *The Comprehension Toolkit* (Harvey and Goudvis 2005), are especially helpful as they offer some guidance for students while avoiding a question and answer format.

While researching volcanoes on Wonderopolis, fourth-grade students annotated their new learning and wonders using a two-column thinksheet. Pulling from the text, images, and video on the site, students documented new learning and asked questions, which they will then follow up with as the inquiry unit continues. As always, the focus is on student thinking and not the tool.

Select a high-interest and accessible text or video for your students to practice on, such as an informational digital book or a daily wonder from Wonderopolis. You can either create a class chart to collaborate on or provide each student with their own copy of the thinksheet. Model for students

Helpful Language

When I'm reading on a screen, I take special care to make sure I'm stopping and gathering my thinking. Watch how I apply all that I know about being a thoughtful reader to this article I found on the internet.

Aha! That seems like an important idea. I'm going to stop and jot it down. Now, what do I think about that idea?

I notice as I'm reading that I have some questions. I'm going to write them here. If you have any questions, will you write them on your page too?

When I need to jump-start my thinking, I sometimes use a prompt like This makes me think . . . or This seems important because . . .

Let's look back over our notes. What is this article mostly about? What are the big ideas the author wants me to know?

The printable tools in this Try It can be downloaded at Hein.pub/RTW-Resources.

LEARN-THINK-WONDER THINKSHEET

What I learned	What I think about what I learned	What I still wonder

Three-Column Thinksheet

LEARN-WONDER THINKSHEET

I Learned	I Wonder

Two-Column Thinksheet

how you stop as you read to jot key ideas and thinking. Have students practice independently or in partners.

OUTCOMES AND WHAT TO LOOK FOR

Students should demonstrate that they can apply reading and writing strategies to digital texts in order to better understand them. Can students

- ▶ notice when they've encountered an important or interesting detail in the text and stop to jot it down?
- ▶ write thoughts, reactions, or comments about what they've read?
- ▶ record questions about, within, and beyond the text?
- ▶ review their stop and jots in order to determine the big ideas of the text?
- ▶ explain what they've read and learned to someone else?

FOLLOW UP

If students are struggling to write down thinking or questions about what they are reading, then they may benefit from more time to talk with a partner before stopping and jotting. You may also choose to work with students in small groups or individually to scaffold thinking and generate more sentence stems or prompts for them to use as they write and talk. Be sure to note whether students are using their stop and jot strategy efficiently and effectively as they work. Then, offer appropriate instruction and coaching. Consider the level of support a student might need, from a simple verbal reminder to a specific structure to follow.

Tip

At the beginning of the year, teach students how to make two- and three-column thinksheets using a blank piece of paper, or keep teacher-created thinksheets handy. Then, students can independently access the supports they need when they need them. Throughout the year, introduce new ways to use thinksheets, including

- I learned / I wonder
- What the text says / My thinking
- Text feature / Purpose
- Questions / Where I can go to find more information?
- I learned / I wonder / Wow
- See / Think / Wonder
- Questions / Where I can find more information? / New learning

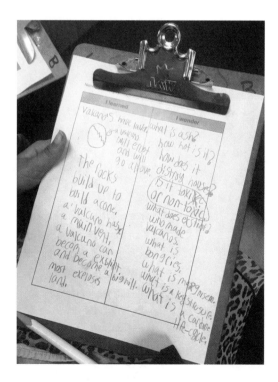

TRY IT!

THINKING THROUGH TEXTS: *Talk About Digital Texts*

Helpful Language

Listen in as I discuss this text with some of your classmates. What do you notice us doing?

What are some strategies we use to read print texts that we could apply to digital texts?

I notice that . . . [Here, name the positive behaviors you see, such as listening to one another and then responding to each other or talking through what you've learned and what you wonder.]

Hmmm . . . this is a challenging article. What other reading strategies might we need to use to help us understand what the author is saying here?

TRY THIS WHEN . . .

- you introduce digital texts to students near the beginning of the year
- you need to scaffold a challenging digital resource
- you notice students copying a lot of information from digital resources without taking time to process it.

Teaching students to transfer active literacy skills to digital texts supports their comprehension of those texts. Using talk strategies supports student understanding and furthers their learning whether they are reading a digital book, article, or website.

WHAT TO DO

If you're introducing talking about digital texts to the class for the first time, this can be a whole-group lesson. If you're using (or revisiting) this lesson in response to a particular issue, consider whether it would be more effective to use the lesson in small groups or with the entire class.

If students aren't used to working in partnerships, refer back to Chapter 1 and teach students how to talk with a partner.

Choose one of the strategies from the charts below as the focus of the lesson, keeping in mind that you can teach the others later with the same lesson format.

Stop and Talk

- Preview the text, checking to see how long it is.
- Plan some stopping points.
- Read to the stopping point independently.
- Turn and talk with your partner:
  - What was this about?
  - What did you learn?
  - What was confusing?
  - What do you wonder?

Read Together

- Read the text together, taking turns.
- Stop to reread, discuss, or wonder.
- Finish the text and discuss:
  - What was the author trying to say here?
  - What important ideas did we learn?
  - What questions or clarifications do we need?

To begin, invite a few students to help you demonstrate this strategy using a short article, website, or excerpt from a digital book.

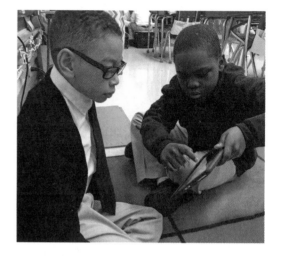

After your brief demonstration, ask the class to share what they noticed worked well about the discussion. Then, give them an opportunity to practice in partners while you listen in and support as needed. Students can either continue with the same text or use a new text. Remind students that this strategy can be used to help them any time they are reading a text—digital or print.

Finally, ask students to debrief at the end of the lesson and share how the strategies they used supported their thinking and partner work. This conversation should also leave room for students to identify challenges or gaps—ways in which the strategy could have been improved or a different strategy might have worked better. For instance, some students might reflect that reading together is a more effective strategy if the text is challenging or they need to support each other a great deal, whereas other students might note that stop and talk is a strategy that honors both partners' need to think and read on their own.

OUTCOMES AND WHAT TO LOOK FOR

We are looking for students to be able to use discussion as a way to help themselves understand digital texts and to transfer print text discussion skills to digital media. Can students

- identify a strategy for working with a partner that will complement the thinking work they need to do?

- effectively preview a text to identify natural points (such as paragraph breaks and new sections) to stop and talk?

- use sentence stems, prompts, or the language of reading strategies (*I'm inferring that . . . , I predict . . . , I wonder . . .*) to have a thoughtful discussion?

- listen and respond to their talk partner in a thoughtful manner?

- demonstrate active literacy strategies while interacting with digital texts?

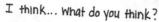
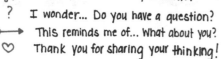

Digital Buddy Reading

Sit and read together.

Stop, think, and talk.

Use kind words for thinking.
I think... What do you think?
? I wonder... Do you have a question?
↔ This reminds me of... What about you?
♡ Thank you for sharing your thinking!

Second-grade students contributed their ideas about how to read with a partner for this chart. Partners took turns modeling what it looked like to share a device, discussing where to stop and talk and using the language of thinking.

FOLLOW UP

Provide students ample time each week to practice reading and discussing digital texts. Richard Allington (2002) identified *volume* (the more you read, the better reader you become) and *response* (the best way to understand what we read is through meaningful conversation) as foundational tenets of becoming a proficient reader; we hold on to these principles with digital work as well and structure time for kids to practice doing this work. As a next step, we also provide kids "choice" digital reading time. Often we guide kids to digital text that relates to a unit of study; however, decades of reading research has taught us that kids become better readers when they have a choice in the text they read. The same is true for e-reading. Structure time throughout the week for kids to engage in choice reading on a set of classroom-approved websites. As of this book's publication, a few of our favorite sites are Tween Tribune, Wonderopolis, Newsela, Science News for Students, Epic!, and Scholastic News.

THINKING THROUGH TEXTS: *Understand the Author's Point of View*

TRY THIS WHEN . . .

■ students are familiar with reading and interacting digitally and are demonstrating thoughtful reading strategies with digital texts

■ you are modeling with a text and want to demonstrate to students how you question text

■ the text has implicit bias or a viewpoint that you want students to be aware of.

Texts, images, and media that we encounter online frequently hold various levels of bias from individual authors. Using real-world digital texts in the classroom exposes students to a much wider array of voices than using publisher-produced texts designed to accompany a boxed curriculum. This is why it's important to use materials from varied sources and offer ample opportunities to practice understanding what story an author, photographer, or artist is trying to portray. This lesson focuses on how authors often reveal their point of view or bias in the language they use.

WHAT TO DO

Begin by sharing an article, image, or video digitally. Ask students to read and discuss the article in partners or small groups, then set a focus for re-reading. For example, you might ask students to focus on the language that that author has used. We might also ask students to consider what ideas the facts or quotes presented support, notice whether the author seems to be repeating ideas, mark the tone in a piece as positive or negative, and/or read another text where the author clearly has a differing viewpoint. Students then revisit the article and use Padlet to note specific words or phrases that reveal how the author feels about the topic. Once groups have contributed their ideas, ask each group to create a copy of the class Padlet and organize it, adding their thoughts and interpretations. Then, have group members discuss what they can infer from these notes about the author's point of view. Finally, have groups consider: Does the author's point of view affect the way the author explains the ideas? Does the author's point of view affect the way we, as readers, feel about the topic?

Helpful Language

When we read, it's important that we understand what the author thinks about a topic. This can help us see if they are sharing the whole story in a fair way.

Look just at the words the author uses. How do those words make you feel?

What words, phrases, ideas, or feelings seem to repeat?

OUTCOMES AND WHAT TO LOOK FOR

Students should be able to look for clues that show what an author thinks and compare the author's view to their own thinking, as well as understand that there may be other points of view not shown or written about. Can students

▶ notice language that tips readers off to an author's viewpoint? (This might be emotional or inflammatory language or "I" statements that signal the author is writing an opinion.)

▶ think critically while reading by asking questions like *What is the author's point of view?* and *Is the author's point of view affecting my point of view?*

QUESTION THE TEXT

Who wrote this?
What do they want me to think?

FOLLOW UP

The idea that we should question what we read is one that we want students to carry with them each day in school and beyond. We can continually revisit this approach to reading as we encounter new resources and media by modeling critical thinking about the how and why behind a text during read-alouds and lessons. We can also remind students to consider these hows and whys in the resources they encounter. Some teachers find that a quick visual or meme—like the one shown here—posted in the classroom, taped into notebooks, or used as a device lock screen can help remind students of key teaching points.

Use words and phrases to understand an author's point of view.

Read the article with your group. Then go back and post a note with key words and phrases that show what the author thinks of the topic.

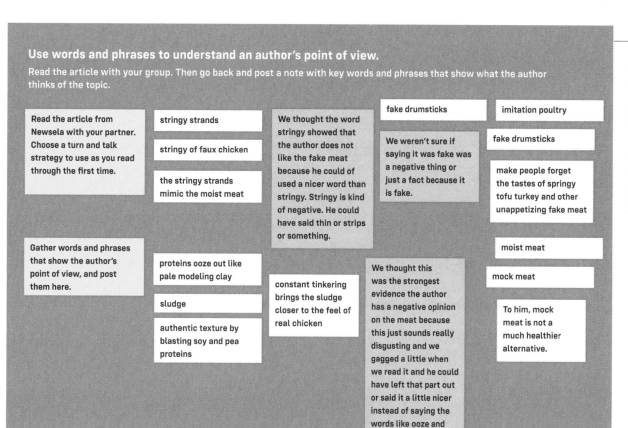

Read the article from Newsela with your partner. Choose a turn and talk strategy to use as you read through the first time.

stringy strands

stringy of faux chicken

the stringy strands mimic the moist meat

We thought the word stringy showed that the author does not like the fake meat because he could of used a nicer word than stringy. Stringy is kind of negative. He could have said thin or strips or something.

fake drumsticks

We weren't sure if saying it was fake was a negative thing or just a fact because it is fake.

imitation poultry

fake drumsticks

make people forget the tastes of springy tofu turkey and other unappetizing fake meat

Gather words and phrases that show the author's point of view, and post them here.

proteins ooze out like pale modeling clay

sludge

authentic texture by blasting soy and pea proteins

constant tinkering brings the sludge closer to the feel of real chicken

We thought this was the strongest evidence the author has a negative opinion on the meat because this just sounds really disgusting and we gagged a little when we read it and he could have left that part out or said it a little nicer instead of saying the words like ooze and sludge.

moist meat

mock meat

To him, mock meat is not a much healthier alternative.

This image reflects the work of a small group that has identified key language from the article, sorted and organized that language, and shared their thinking and interpretations.

WRITE WITH US

⏻ **Which (if any) of the Try Its in this first section get at something you'd like to work on with students right away?**

⏻ **Which (if any) do you feel that you'll need to work up to? Why?**

⏻ **If you find yourself concerned about potential barriers, what are those barriers?**

⏻ **What would it take to get around or through those barriers?**

⏻ **Which colleague(s) will you enlist to try and reflect on these lessons with you?**

⏻ **Share your ideas. #ReadTheWorldNow**

APPLYING READING STRATEGIES TO IMAGES AND MEDIA:
Evaluate Infographics

TRY THIS WHEN . . .

- students are encountering infographics for the first time

- you want to launch a unit of study

- you're including an infographic in a text set.

Infographics are succinct, engaging, and highly visual ways to present students with information and hook them on a topic of study. They are prominent online and are used for many different purposes: marketing, advertising, raising awareness, entertainment, and education. Because they are ubiquitous and their purpose might not be immediately apparent, it's important that students learn to apply their critical literacy skills to infographics.

WHAT TO DO

When introducing infographics to students, start by projecting one for the class. If students have devices, give them access to the infographic so they can look at it up close and zoom in on parts as needed. Ask students to activate their background knowledge, notice the various elements of the infographic, and wonder. You might ask them to notice what seems familiar, how they can tell what the infographic will be about, and analyze how they might read the infographic differently than a traditional left-to-right text. Give students time to look closely and share their thinking in pairs about the infographic layout, encouraging them to annotate infographics just as they would any other text or media. If digital markup isn't feasible, try giving students printouts of the infographic, taped to the center of a piece of chart paper, so that students can annotate around them.

Icons give us the gist of a section of text, data, or other images. They are like picture subtitles.

Charts help us understand how many or how something might be broken into parts.

Healthy Snack Choices

Numbered lists show us possibilities or an order.

Infographics use icons like this to show how many people are affected. This is one way to show a ratio using pictures.

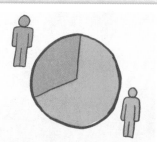

Nonfiction Features
Sometimes we see familiar features like pictures, subtitles, captions, and text boxes.

Katie uses a chart like this when introducing students to working with infographics. Zooming in on the different elements helps students consider how each part contributes to the overall story or information.

Helpful Language

What do you notice about this infographic that looks familiar? Do you see any features like titles, subtitles, or captions?

What surprises you about this infographic? Is there anything here that confuses you?

What do you notice? What do you wonder?

How might we read this infographic?

Who created this? Why do we think they might have created it?

Next, offer students several different infographics to compare and contrast. There are many resources for infographics in books and online, most of which should be carefully vetted before bringing them into the classroom. One need only do a quick internet search with a topic in mind and the word *infographic* to find a wide variety of options. There are also websites like Daily Infographic (www.dailyinfographic.com/) that offer a steady stream from which to choose. Again, read these with a careful eye before using with students. A few options to start with are

▶ Kids Discover (www.kidsdiscover.com/infographics/)

Infopackets featuring infographics can be accessed with a free account.

▶ "What's Going On in This Graph?" (www.nytimes.com/column/whats-going-on-in-this-graph)

From the *New York Times* and the Learning Network, this feature provides weekly graphics and visuals each Monday for students to closely read and analyze. Throughout the week, classrooms around the world engage in discussion via the comments section of the site. On Thursdays, the site reveals the origin of the graph and explains what data the graphic represents.

▶ ChooseMyPlate.gov (www.choosemyplate.gov/infographics)

This site offers a wide variety of health-related infographics.

As they are becoming increasingly popular, infographics can also be found in many informational books at the library and perhaps even right in your own classroom. We recommend starting with

▶ *Animals by the Numbers* by Steve Jenkins

▶ *Information Graphics: Animal Kingdom* by Simon Rogers and Nicholas Blechman

▶ *Infographics for Kids* by Susan Martineau and Vicky Barker

▶ *By the Numbers*, *By the Numbers 2.0*, and *By the Numbers 3.14*, published by National Geographic Kids

Engage students in comparing the infographics' features, looking at (and possibly researching) who created the infographics, considering reliability and validity, or building knowledge around a topic in order to launch a unit of study.

> ### Tips for Reading Infographics
>
> - Look at the title; think . . . what is this about?
> - Skim the whole thing; understand the parts.
> - Dig in—use a strategy like writing or talking.
> - Read the small print. Who made this? Why?
> - Gather the big ideas and your questions.

OUTCOMES AND WHAT TO LOOK FOR

Depending on grade level and how you situate this lesson, you may be looking for students to simply demonstrate that they can apply literacy strategies to this new medium or you may be looking for them to take a more analytical approach to authorship, reliability, and credibility. Can students

▶ identify common text features to help them situate themselves in the infographic?

▶ synthesize information from text, icons, images, graphs, and other elements to get the big idea of the infographic?

▶ identify who created the infographic and what sources they used?

▶ infer what the author's purpose is in creating and sharing the infographic?

▶ analyze the infographic for bias and/or tone?

FOLLOW UP

Build students' fluency with infographics across the school year by asking them to engage with increasingly challenging samples. Or ask students to do a genre study, identifying elements of successful infographics, and have them create their own infographics.

TRY IT!

APPLYING READING STRATEGIES TO IMAGES AND MEDIA:
Identify Students' Strategies for Reading Images

TRY THIS WHEN . . .

- students are working on developing a close reading stance

- you want to develop the class' background knowledge and/or quickly build interest regarding a particular topic

- you need to quickly situate students in their thinking

- you want to offer an access point—regardless of reading ability—into a topic.

Visuals have always been a powerful educational tool for meeting the needs of all students: striving readers and emergent bilingual students can interact with a visual on equal footing with peers with more developed literacy or English language skills. Visuals can also pique curiosity and build a narrative about an event, topic, or issue. In fact, nearly 80 percent of the information we process is visual. Yet students are rarely taught how to read images critically. And, as our digital communications become increasingly more visual, this need becomes more urgent.

WHAT TO DO

Project or share an image with students—either one you've selected to go with a lesson or one from a read-aloud book. Use prompts from the Helpful Language box to engage students in discussion and discovery about how to tune in to or approach an image for close reading. We frequently pull from the language of print reading as we introduce this strategy, guiding students to notice the *characters* and *setting*, identify the *key details* that help them *infer*, and cite specific *features* or *text evidence* that inform their understanding. We also introduce design elements such as color, tone, mood, and artist's perspective as new lenses for viewing and comprehending a visual text. At the end of the viewing, ask students to share how they interacted with this photo. Comments like "I studied the faces in the photo" or "I looked at the setting and tried to determine where it took place" are terrific strategies students can employ as they read images in the future. Gather students' ideas on a chart as a reference tool.

Helpful Language

What do you notice first? Where do your eyes go first?

Now, slow down and spend some time really looking. What else do you see?

What story elements can we look at in this image? Is there a setting? Are there characters?

How do the elements make you feel?

If we were investigators, how could we get all the little details of this image? Let's zoom in and look really closely to see what we can find.

Let's try thinking about this image from the point of view of the people or characters inside it.

What else do you see?

Is there anything you already think you know about this image?

[In response to a student's comment, ask,] What do you see that makes you say that?

OUTCOMES AND WHAT TO LOOK FOR

Students should be able to demonstrate careful and close reading of images as a result of this lesson. Do students

▶ spend time with an image, looking beyond their first impression or idea?

▶ transfer key ideas and terms from literacy—such as setting, characters, and conflict—as a way to orient themselves to an image?

▶ look at the different parts of an image, considering elements like color, emotion, mood, and composition?

▶ look at an image through varying lenses to consider the different ways to think of an image?

▶ zoom in to look closely at the parts of an image, then zoom out to look at it as a whole?

To Read a Visual Image

Slow down and look closely.

What do you notice? What do you wonder?

Take another look and reread the image. Look at the little details.

What more can you find?

Position yourself as the artist. What story is the artist trying to tell?

How do YOU read images?

☑ I study the **background** to figure where this story takes place. — Dante

☑ I look at their **faces** + **clothing**. — Amea

☑ Usually I say "whoa" at the big idea in the picture then look for **little details**. — Jamila

☑ **Slow down**! You have to look for the good stuff. — Tim

☑ I look for **feelings**. How is a person feeling in that picture? — Asis

☑ **Act like a detective**! Ask what, where, and why? — Jamarcus

☑ Think! What makes sense? — Precloria

This chart captures sixth-grade students' personal strategies for reading a photo to gather information. When we co-create personal strategy charts with students, kids have the opportunity to hear what strategies their friends are using, and then try those strategies themselves. Creating a chart with kids is also a quick formative assessment that helps us see what the students' understandings are and how they are applying strategies. Once the chart has been created, it gives students a process or procedure to follow in order to accomplish a goal.

FOLLOW UP

It's tempting for students to do a quick glance at an image and then move on. Remind students of how to tune in to an image, revisiting the chart as needed.

Ground student responses to visuals in the language of *see*, *think*, and *wonder*, as this structure engages them to use text evidence to support their thinking. Offer students a chance to interact through whole-class discussion, shared inquiry, stopping and jotting, turn and talks, or digital chats. Have students explore other related images in small groups or with partners using a three-column See/Think/Wonder thinksheet, sentence stems for a digital discussion, or large paper for a gallery walk.

Some students may benefit from vocabulary development such as word walls or word study around the language of discussing an image. Select an image or bank of images for students to view and interact with. Begin by modeling and engaging students in guided practice with one of the images. Prompt students with language frames to encourage them to apply new language (*I see . . . , I think . . . , I wonder . . .*).

A seventh-grade student captures her thinking in a See/Think/Wonder thinksheet as she analyzes an image.

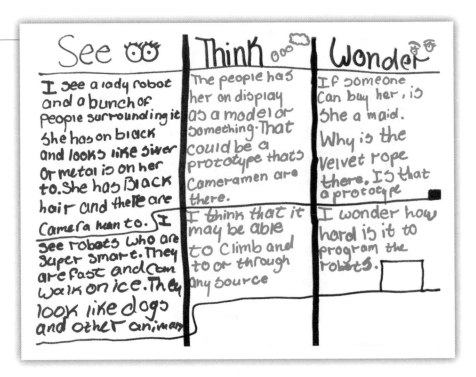

APPLYING READING STRATEGIES TO IMAGES AND MEDIA:
Read Images Using Reading Strategies

TRY THIS WHEN . . .

- you want to help students make an explicit connection between the strategies they use to read text and the strategies they use to read an image

- you're working with a challenging text or read-aloud (using the image to clarify or expand on the text's topic or content)

- you want to help all students build background knowledge and discussion skills free from reading ability constraints.

The comprehension strategies that we use for reading are equally effective when we are learning from images. As kids view an image, they infer what's going on in the image and draw upon their background knowledge to make sense of what they're seeing. Questions pop into their heads as they wonder, "What's going on in this picture?" In this lesson, we teach kids to notice and actively use comprehension strategies as they view an image.

WHAT TO DO

Remind students of the strategies they use when they read, and refer to any charts you may have from reading workshop to support them. If you do not already have an anchor chart for reading strategies, a chart like the one on the next page may be helpful; however, this lesson will be most powerful if it explicitly connects to reading strategies you have already taught students. Tell them that today they are going to be mindful of how they apply reading strategies to images and reflect on how those strategies help them better understand images. Model for students how you apply these strategies to reading an image: *I'm inferring . . . because I see. . . Class, did you see how I used my inferring skills to learn more and think about this image? Now you try.*

Place students in small groups of three and provide them with an image or bank of images—these might be images related to a unit of study or high-interest images you've found. Have students work to notice how each of the strategies contributes to their understanding of the image and jot a few ideas down. For example, they might write something like "We noticed that we synthesized when we were connecting this image with the book we read in class" or "We asked a lot of questions. We answered some by talking further but not all of them."

Helpful Language

Which strategies do you notice yourself using with this image? Why do you think that is?

I hear you asking a lot of questions. Does this image make you curious? Can you answer any of those questions with the image itself?

Which parts seem important about this image? How can we tell?

ACTIVE LITERACY STRATEGIES
STRATEGIES I USE TO MAKE ME A MORE THOUGHTFUL VIEWER

ACTIVE LITERACY STRATEGIES

STRATEGIES I USE TO MAKE ME A MORE THOUGHTFUL VIEWER

ACTIVATE AND CONNECT
What do I think I already know abuot this image? What does this remind me of?

INFER MEANING
What do I think is going on here? What do I see that makes me think that?

DETERMINE IMPORTANCE
What seems to be the most important elements of this image? What is in the foreground? What do I notice first?

ASK QUESTIONS
What do I wonder about this image? What more do I want to find out? What am I curious about?

SUMMARIZE AND SYNTHESIZE
Overall what seems to be the big idea here? How does that build on what I already know? Or other images I've looked at?

MONITOR COMPREHENSION
What is confusing? Unknown? How can I understand?

Harvey and Goudvis's Active Literacy Strategies (2017, 16–19) can help us to structure our instruction in reading images.

As students work, prompt them to consider strategies they haven't tried yet. Bring students together to share their learning and discuss the strategies they felt were most helpful to understand the images. Reiterate that whenever we read (text, image, media, or other resources), we are always using all our active literacy strategies to build meaning.

OUTCOMES AND WHAT TO LOOK FOR

Students should be able to spend time with an image, looking carefully at both the details and big picture to spark thinking. Do students

▶ carefully observe the image, determining what is important and noticing various parts and how they work together?

▶ infer context or emotion based on what they see?

▶ ask questions about the image, making connections and demonstrating intellectual engagement with the image and across images?

▶ compare and contrast images within an image bank or draw conclusions about how multiple images might be related?

▶ revisit an image multiple times as they build their knowledge about the context of an image in order to gain new meaning?

▶ consider each other's interpretations and viewpoints of the image?

▶ summarize their findings across images when appropriate and determine the most important information in the image set?

APPLYING READING STRATEGIES TO IMAGES AND MEDIA:
Use Images to Generate Questions

TRY THIS WHEN . . .

- you want to hook students on a new read-aloud, concept, or topic (often at the beginning of a lesson, unit, or read-aloud)

- students need a scaffold for complex texts or ideas

- you want students to generate researchable questions to hold on to as the learning unfolds

- students need a new lens or perspective on the content they are learning (often in the middle of a unit, lesson, or read-aloud)

- students are developing vocabulary, especially content-specific or topic-specific vocabulary.

Using images to help students ask questions provides an opportunity for students to engage their intellectual curiosity and develop questions for further study or to anchor their reading. Images can help students situate their thinking within a narrative or story of the people in the image and offer a personal entry point into units.

WHAT TO DO

Begin by finding a rich, useful image. If you are using this lesson to support particular content—a text, a topic, or content-area vocabulary, for example—use an image that gives or alludes to this information. For example, a photo from a historical event is likely to have more embedded information (the location, the people involved, the action, the effects, the emotion) than a formal portrait of a historical figure. We often find that images with people instead of just items or landscapes (though they can be useful as well) help students begin to build a narrative of events, issues, or topics.

For this session, it's best to select an image that will pique student curiosity. Is it unfamiliar, confusing, or discrepant in some way? Does it convey strong emotion or a snapshot of a story that students might find especially intriguing? Does the image make *you* curious?

Project the selected image for all students to see, asking students to generate questions either individually or with partners and then share with the class. Encourage them to write down their questions if it feels helpful.

Third-grade students work in partners as they see, think, and wonder about images.

Next, invite kids to share the questions they have about the image. Record student questions on a chart, wonder wall, or digital medium. One effective format to try is the Question Formulation Technique (Right Question Institute, n.d.), which offers guidance for producing, categorizing, prioritizing, addressing, and reflecting on questions (www.rightquestion.org). Another terrific resource is *The New York Times'* "What's Going On in This Picture?" feature. Each Monday the *Times* posts a thought-provoking image and then walks students through the Visual Thinking Strategies online or via their blog post (nyti.ms/2j8eoam).

OUTCOMES AND WHAT TO LOOK FOR

Students should be able to ask many questions based on an image and evaluate those questions. Do students

▶ ask multiple questions about an image?

▶ ask increasingly complex questions, appropriate to their background knowledge, about an image?

▶ build on each other's questions?

▶ understand or identify which questions will have quick answers and which ones will require more reading, discussion, or research?

▶ identify where they might find answers to some of their questions?

FOLLOW UP

Revisit the image as students gather answers to their questions from the piece you are reading, as your unit unfolds, or in their own research. Do these answers bring new understandings or interpretations to the image or topic? What questions do students have now that they know more? When we encourage students to question, they often surprise us with the depth and complexity of questions they ask. Some of these questions will be answered through a natural reading or inquiry process, while others will not. We often set aside flexible time for students to follow up on these questions during the week or at some point in the unit. We must also share with students that not all questions can be answered quickly and easily. When this happens, we look for the opportunity to seek more information about a topic and model that living a curious life is not only about finding the answers but also about continued questioning and ongoing learning. Ultimately, we want kids to be information seekers.

APPLYING READING STRATEGIES TO IMAGES AND MEDIA:
Read Video for Understanding

TRY THIS WHEN . . .

■ you introduce video as a piece of text in the classroom

■ students are missing or misunderstanding key elements in videos

■ students begin to work with videos independently in the classroom.

Video allows students access and an entry point to content that they may not yet be able to decode or comprehend in print, thus inviting students to think and wonder at a higher level. Using video in the classroom is especially powerful when you want to "hook" kids into thinking, wondering, or pursuing a topic for additional research. Yet, while students know how to use video as a tool for entertainment, they often do not have experience in using it as a tool for thinking, making this lesson essential when using video as an information medium. Instead of pressing play and watching a video in its entirety in silence, students can read videos with the same critical eyes that they use when reading.

WHAT TO DO

Find a short video clip (two to three minutes) that connects to an upcoming unit. In grades K–2, aim for videos that are closer to two minutes than three. Ask students to consider what they're learning and what they're wondering before viewing. Then, play the video for the class.

Remind students that often when we read a text that has a lot of information, we go back and reread it again. We also go back and reread video so that we can collect any additional information we missed during the first viewing, look to answer a specific question, or view the video through a different lens.

Provide students with a two-column thinksheet titled "I learned / I wonder." Explain that the thinksheet is a way for them to record their thoughts as they watch the video. Begin playing the video again. After thirty seconds or a minute, pause the video to think out loud as you fill in your own thinksheet, jotting or drawing your new learning and noting questions. Invite students to turn and talk about what they saw you do. Chart student observations, leaving blank space at the bottom to add more strategies as you continue this work in subsequent lessons. If helpful, use some of the sample language in the Helpful Language box and in the chart on the next page. Then, ask students to do the same with their thinksheets as they watch the rest of the video.

Helpful Language

When we reread video, we listen and look for new information and wonders. We also listen for answers to questions we had during the first viewing.

What do you want to clarify or understand better when you reread the video?

If students have access to the video on their own devices and you'd like to give them practice in rewatching strategies, let them work with partners or in small groups to review the video together as necessary.

OUTCOMES AND WHAT TO LOOK FOR

Students should be able to identify facts or ideas that signal new learning and ask questions about the video and its content. Do students

▶ ask multiple questions about the video clip?

▶ identify information that they didn't know before and document it in drawing or writing?

▶ rewatch a section or the entire video to find answers to their questions or gain additional understanding?

This chart serves as an example for the types of charts we might create with our students during a lesson. When we involve students in the process of creating the chart with us, it becomes a teaching tool they have ownership in. Adapt the language as needed to fit your students' developmental needs.

Rewatch with a Purpose

- Read the text together, taking turns.
  - I learned . . .
  - I wonder . . .
- Decide what you want to look for as you rewatch.
  - I want to better understand . . .
  - I want to answer the question . . .
- Rewatch the video and talk with your partner.
  - This time I noticed . . .
  - Something I saw that I didn't see the first time was . . .
  - At first I thought . . . , but now I think . . .

FOLLOW UP

You may want to continue this series of lessons by working with students to identify video features and their purposes to aid in comprehension. It may be helpful to pinpoint specific strategies or protocols for different genres of videos, perhaps even giving students an opportunity to inquire into how viewing these different genres varies. Do we watch a video that tells a story differently than an informational video? What should our viewing stance be when watching a TED Talk? A public service announcement? A historical video? A video of a scientific phenomenon? An advertisement? Propaganda? This also gives you an opportunity to discuss with students how they can determine what genre a video is and activate the strategies they need to read it effectively.

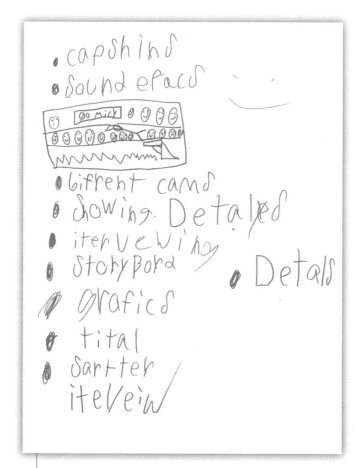

In this work sample, a fourth-grade student identified features he noticed in a documentary that provided information to the viewer. As a follow-up, the class studied the purpose of each of these features.

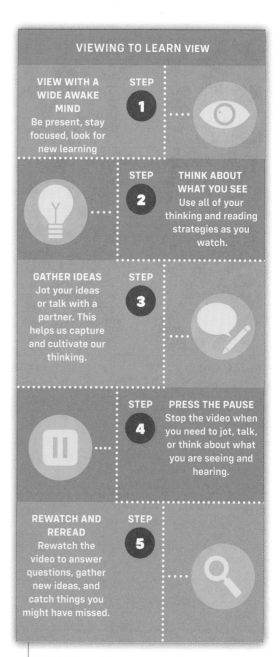

VIEWING TO LEARN VIEW

VIEW WITH A WIDE AWAKE MIND
Be present, stay focused, look for new learning
STEP 1

STEP 2
THINK ABOUT WHAT YOU SEE
Use all of your thinking and reading strategies as you watch.

GATHER IDEAS
Jot your ideas or talk with a partner. This helps us capture and cultivate our thinking.
STEP 3

STEP 4
PRESS THE PAUSE
Stop the video when you need to jot, talk, or think about what you are seeing and hearing.

REWATCH AND REREAD
Rewatch the video to answer questions, gather new ideas, and catch things you might have missed.
STEP 5

This infographic was created on Canva by a group of fourth graders—with teacher assistance—to show the strategies they identified during the lesson.

TRY IT!

APPLYING READING STRATEGIES TO IMAGES AND MEDIA:
Inquire Using a Multimedia Tech Set

TRY THIS WHEN . . .

☐ you have already introduced how to read images and annotate digital text

☐ you launch a new science or social studies unit or you want to parallel a book club or literature study with short, informational text

☐ you need to address a current event and print materials are not available.

Digital media offer a wide range of information, perspectives, and voices and are often more current than the print texts that have traditionally been used in classrooms. For students to be able to make meaning from digital media, they need guidance and practice in comprehension across these diverse texts.

WHAT TO DO

Organize a workflow for students using your Learning Management System (LMS) or a digital site that students can access, such as a website, Google Slides, or Padlet. In it, build a simple View/Read/Respond structure. This will guide students to engage in image study to gain background knowledge, read to learn new information, and then to merge their understanding of image and digital text. Provide the following in the sections listed:

View

Select three to four images for students to see, think, and wonder about. We frequently find quality photos on photosforclass.com, pics4learning .com, or a reputable news source like *The Washington Post*. You might explore the first image as a class, reminding students to use all they know about images. Then, have them continue in partners.

Read

Find at least two articles or pieces of short text so students have a choice in what they read. Wonderopolis is a good source for informational blog posts, and Newsela has a variety of informational texts. Have students read independently, in partners, or in a small group.

Respond

Invite students to respond through writing, via small-group conversation, or with a video tool like Flipgrid or Seesaw. This section is for students to reflect about what they've discovered, merging what they read and viewed. When appropriate, ask students to read or view the reflections of classmates and respond or continue the discussion.

OUTCOMES AND WHAT TO LOOK FOR

In this lesson, we want students to be able to apply strategies in multiple media as well as synthesize those media for understanding. Can students

▶ establish context and background knowledge by first viewing images?

▶ apply previously learned strategies for viewing images?

▶ demonstrate the ability to stop and talk or jot about digital texts?

▶ explain how the images and text work together to tell a story?

▶ explain their thinking and new learning using a digital tool?

▶ respond to each other's thinking and new learning using a digital tool?

FOLLOW UP

Use this structure repeatedly with varied texts to build students' autonomy in interacting with multiple texts. Once the format is familiar, you can increase the complexity of texts and topics while continuing to provide a predictable format for student interaction.

Another option is to vary the workflow for student thinking to accommodate other forms of media and response, such as adding a written conversation piece or a video.

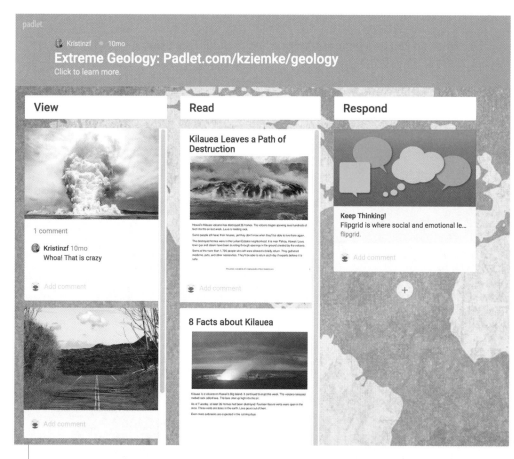

This Padlet structures the launch of an inquiry into the Kilauea eruption in May 2018.

WRITE WITH US

⏻ **Where in your curriculum might students benefit from using a variety of media resources?**

⏻ **Which Try Its might you plan to use to support how they'll interact with those resources?**

⏻ **What do you and your students stand to gain from using digital tools?**

⏻ **Which of the lessons in this chapter can you use in the next few weeks with students?**

⏻ **What will you need to have in place before you attempt a particular lesson?**

⏻ **Share your ideas. #ReadTheWorldNow**

RESPONDING AND CONNECTING USING VISUAL TOOLS:
Record Students' Thinking Using a Video Tool

TRY THIS WHEN . . .

- you are ready to introduce some variety in the ways students can respond for formative assessment
- you need to assess student understanding in a one-directional conference
- you want to build fluency in students' speaking skills.

Asking students to respond to reading spurs students' thinking and provides formative assessment. But do these responses need to be written? Recording student responses as videos for the class offers students an authentic audience and can present us with a different lens through which to view and understand how kids interact with text. Video recordings have the added benefits of not limiting students based on their writing ability and of serving as powerful documentation tools to track growth.

WHAT TO DO

From book reviews to student-made math tutorials, video response can range from very structured to open-ended. We've found that the natural and authentic way that students respond when given a more open approach with a few scaffolds in place gives us the clearest view of students' perspectives.

The easiest way to explain what a video response looks like is to show students examples of video responses. If you have student examples from another classroom, use those. If not, record your own mentor examples. As you show students the models, notice what the speaker did. Pay attention to both the presentation (making eye contact, using body movements, speaking clearly and loudly) and content (giving examples from the text). Students will naturally attend to presentation, but may need coaching to listen for content. We can also help students by recording live in front of students or showing videos where we may make "mistakes" or reflect on things we forgot to say. Response videos are not "final products" but merely a snapshot of thinking and learning in progress. When discussing videos with students, emphasize the importance of their ideas, not just their final presentation, and encourage a casual tone over a more formal planned recording.

The Tips and Video Response Checklists on the following pages are distillations of the processes we've seen classes use to create video

The chart in this kindergarten classroom is not fancy; Kristin made it on the fly during a demonstration lesson on how to use iMovie. Nonetheless, this anchor chart supported students, and within a few minutes a student accessed the chart as the lesson progressed. The scaffolds and support we place in the classroom don't have to be perfect in order to be powerful for students.

Helpful Language

I see . . . [Here, name the positive behaviors you see, such as *you are rewatching to see if you said what you wanted to say* or *you are deciding to work with a partner to help you get started.*]

You shared many details about your learning.

What is the most important thing you want viewers to know?

Room 302's Tips for Recording a Check-In Video

Remember: The purpose of a check-in video is to share your thinking about a text. It's not supposed to be perfect.

° Review what you read; what is important to say?

° Give a quick overview of what you read (title, main ideas).

° Spend most of your time talking about your thinking.

- This article made me think . . .
- One important thing I learned was . . . , and that made me think . . .
- Something interesting I read about was . . . because . . .
- Something I'm now wondering about is . . . because . . .
- I'm inferring that . . . because in the article . . .
- One of my favorite quotes is . . . because . . .
- A theory I have developed is . . . My evidence is . . .
- I'd like to know more about . . .
- This connects to . . .

° Leave by posing a question or a comment that gives your viewers something to think about or respond to.

° Rewatch to make sure you've said what you wanted to say and your technology works.

This example, from a fifth-grade classroom, supports students in crafting meaningful video responses to something they've read.

responses; they are included here to give you an idea of what might be helpful to emphasize in your modeling. As always, your students will likely feel more invested in this process if you co-create these kinds of guiding charts with them rather than posting our examples in your classroom.

Give students an opportunity to practice recording their own video responses, alone and with partners, depending on age and comfort level. Then, students can receive positive feedback from the teacher and peers on what they did well.

Once students have learned the process for video response, student videos should not be events that require lots of preparation and recording time.

If students struggle to get started or have difficulty recording themselves, try the following:

▶ Guide students to choose a few sentence stems from the chart to get started.

▶ Help students prepare by suggesting that they mark a few of their own notes (or pages, or parts of the article) that they want to share.

▶ Have students practice and record with a trusted friend, or have the friend record them. Some students are uncomfortable recording into a front-facing camera.

▶ Allow students some time to prepare what they want to say in writing ahead of time. Gently wean them from needing to write a script to using a short bulleted list of topics to cover.

▶ Assist students by providing sentence stems or an organizational structure.

▶ Allow students to record short videos or video segments that can be combined into a longer response.

▶ Allow students to show a still image of the text while they speak if they are nervous about being on camera.

OUTCOMES AND WHAT TO LOOK FOR

Students should be able to record a brief video that demonstrates their thinking, their application of comprehension strategies, or another literacy skill. Can students

▶ determine key ideas and details to include in their video?

▶ give examples from the text or resource to support their thinking?

▶ show awareness of their audience when they record?

▶ speak loudly and clearly?

▶ use given language, sentence stems, or other supports to record their video?

Video Response Checklist

° I spoke in a loud voice.

° I looked at the camera.

° I shared something I think about this book.

° I gave an example from the book.

° I ended with a question or comment for viewers to think about.

° I thanked my viewer.

FOLLOW UP

As a follow-up to this lesson, after we've built a strong classroom community (see the next Try It, titled "Comment Productively and Kindly"), we can teach students to offer each other feedback. We first model what appropriate feedback looks like and sounds like. Then we frame feedback as a tool for growth. Use language like *Can we give* [student's name] *some "positives" and some "pushes"? What did you see* [student's name] *do well? What would you encourage* [student's name] *to do next time to make it even better?* Inviting kids to unpack a student work sample actively engages them in learning strategies that will improve their own video content. Once feedback has become an established routine in the classroom, you might move students to self-assessment using a class-created checklist.

How often you use this strategy is dependent on the number of devices you have available, the age level of your students, and what platforms you are using. We find that variety and choice play an important role in keeping this strategy fresh, useful, and efficient. For example, in the fifth-grade class that presented the video check-in tips shown earlier, students used short video responses once or twice a week, keeping most responses to two or three minutes. Most responses were intended for—and responded to by—peers, with the teacher making choices about which ones to use for formative assessment and when and how to give students feedback. This feedback ranged from video or audio recordings made in response by other students and the teacher, quickly written comments, micro-rubrics/checklists, or in-person conversations. In cases when video responses were to be used for summative assessment, students were given notice in advance.

RESPONDING AND CONNECTING USING VISUAL TOOLS:
Comment Productively and Kindly

TRY THIS WHEN . . .

- students begin to use video responses as a tool to document and share learning

- you want to enable or allow students to make digital comments on each other's work

- you notice students leaving a string of short and general comments (like "good job")

- you want to showcase that digital publication is often a two-way conversation.

Peer feedback gives students opportunities to have digital conversations, build on each other's thinking, and consider fresh viewpoints and ideas. In this lesson, we establish clear guidelines that maintain a supportive and productive classroom culture. Students learn the classroom expectation: to give each other respectful, kind, helpful, and thoughtful comments that further conversations and support comprehension.

WHAT TO DO

Begin by sharing a variety of examples of digital comments with students as a genre study. You might use digital comments from previous years' student work—names removed, of course—or you might create your own examples. Comments may be text, audio, or video, depending on the tech tools that your students will be using. Include a range of comments for students to explore, like the ones listed in the chart on the right. Ask students to view all the comments and rate each on the following criteria:

▸ Are the comments **clear**?

▸ Are the comments **kind**?

▸ Are the comments **helpful**?

▸ Are the comments' suggestions **possible**?

Example Comments for Students to Analyze

- I really liked your video.

- This was good, but you should talk louder.

- I read this book too and I enjoyed it. What was your favorite part?

- This is too short.

- Something you said about this picture got me wondering: Do you think . . . ?

- You were very detailed and gave some good examples from the article. One question I had was . . . ?

- I learned a lot from your video. Do you know how . . . ?

- I don't agree with this.

- You make a good point but I would like to offer another idea.

Helpful Language

Before you comment, think about what types of comments you'd like to receive.

When we comment, we want to say more than just "good job." We want to tell the person what they did that went well. For example, "Maria, when you shared that quote from the article, I could really understand your point of view."

Use your comments to start a conversation about the ideas the person has shared.

Ways to Start a Comment

- I agree with you because...
- What I liked about you post is...
- When you <u>wrote</u> < quote from their said writing or video> it made me think...
- Thank you for sharing, can you tell me more about...?
- I really enjoyed your video/post. One question I have is...

This chart, designed for a minilesson for second and third graders, supports students in getting started with a productive comment while modeling kind and respectful language.

Comment Checklist

☐ I watched the person's video carefully and listened to all they had to say.

☐ I thought about what the person said.

☐ I left a comment that pointed out something positive the person did.

☐ I left a comment that asked a question to clarify or continue the conversation.

☐ I made a connection or shared my own thinking about this topic.

☐ I used kind and respectful language.

This infographic chart synthesizes the ideas that students came up with during a class discussion about commenting. The images included are more than decoration—they support young readers and present information in a memorable way, offering visual cues for what to do!

Have students discuss and reflect on the comments. What do they notice about specific comments? What kinds of comments would they like to receive?

Co-created checklists and guides (like those shown here) can also help scaffold students as they begin to comment on each other's work. If the checklist is done on chart paper, we ask students to take a photo with their device or we photograph it and provide miniature copies for students to use as they comment.

OUTCOMES AND WHAT TO LOOK FOR

Students should be able to read and respond to each other's thinking and work in a way that supports each other and the deep thinking we want them to do. Once students begin leaving comments on each other's work, can they

▶ show active and careful listening?

▶ point out specific elements of a classmate's work that are effective or that they connect with on a personal level?

▶ disagree using respectful language and clear reasoning?

▶ extend the discussion by responding to the classmate's work in a way that prompts conversation about meaningful topics and ideas presented?

FOLLOW UP

Use commenting on a regular basis and establish a protocol for commenting:

▶ Make commenting an enjoyable time in the classroom. Play soft music, and have students make use of flexible seating.

▶ Allow students to watch videos with partners and comment together after talking.

▶ Students do not need to receive comments from every classmate on every piece of work. Establish commenting groups or circles so that all students receive comments from those in their group. Rotate groups frequently so that students can establish relationships and learn from everyone in the class.

▶ Use comments—either your own or others'—as a launch point for small-group discussion.

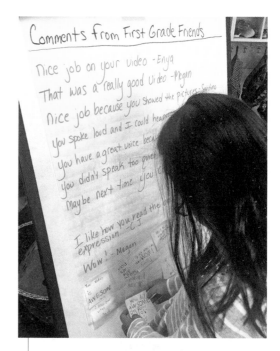

First-grade students brainstorm what to say before their first experience with commenting.

TRY iT!

RESPONDING AND CONNECTING USING VISUAL TOOLS:
Micro-Write to Summarize and Share Learning

A classroom Twitter account gives students oppotunities to experience and practice short-form writing.

Helpful Language

What are the big ideas that need to be shared?

Think about how you can communicate that message in only a few words.

Start by writing something and then go back and see if you can make it a little clearer.

If you're stuck, ask a think partner for help.

TRY THIS WHEN . . .

- you need to gather a short formative assessment or reflection on learning

- students need practice summarizing or synthesizing their thinking

- you want students to build fluency for writing succinctly

- you're working to include more writing opportunities across the curriculum.

Much of the writing we do today is short—especially the writing we do with technology: email, text, tweets, Instagram posts, and more. Yet writing short effectively is often more difficult than writing an extended response because students must be able to summarize succinctly. Giving students opportunities to write short strengthens

- ▶ their knowledge of the content: there's no room for vague statements in micro-writing

- ▶ their ability to revise: short work requires ongoing revision

- ▶ their word choices: precise words save space.

As with all types of writing, students need time to practice this genre in order to build fluency and proficiency as short-format writers.

WHAT TO DO

Using a piece of short text (narrative or informational) or a picture book, model how you would summarize the big ideas of the text into a six-word story. If you're teaching this lesson the first time, we suggest you write on chart paper and draft a summary that is a bit longer than the six-word limit. Count the words with students and explain how you want to revise it so it is just six words. Ask students for feedback on where you could minimize the text or replace a string of words with a single, more precise word. Model for students how you draft and revise both on paper and in your head. Once you've written your six-word story, ask students to reflect on what you did. Write student reflections on a chart so that students can apply the same techniques when drafting their story.

Then, invite students to summarize another text in six words. We typically begin this practice in a notebook or with a sticky note (the size of the paper helps students keep it short) and invite students to buddy up with a thinking partner as a scaffold for revision. Ask students to brainstorm their revisions first and then distill them into their six-word summarization. For example, while reflecting on a book about Ruby Bridges, one third grader jotted down her ideas—"never-ending, devastating, segregation, trapped, broken, not belonging"—and then wrote her six-word summary: "Segregation seems like it's never-ending." Later you can take this practice online using a digital bulletin board, backchannel, or classroom Twitter account to build an audience for student writing.

OUTCOMES AND WHAT TO LOOK FOR

Students should be able to generate a six-word story (or maybe a five- or seven-word story) as they attempt this new format of writing. Ultimately, we want kids to learn how to communicate their thinking succinctly and build fluency over time. Once kids have engaged in micro-writing, can they

▶ communicate a message with only a few words?

▶ revise their work to make it clearer?

▶ evaluate word choice to enhance their writing?

▶ build new vocabulary as the content becomes more specific?

> **Tip**
>
> Six-word stories have gained popularity online. To find mentor tech examples to share with students, search for #6wordstory or #sixwordstories on social media.

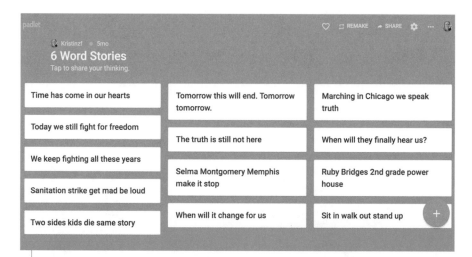

Fourth-grade students engage in micro-writing to share their reactions during a study of the civil rights movement. In just a few words, kids share their current understandings with their peers. Simple digital bulletin boards like Padlet are a terrific way to publish for an audience beyond the teacher.

FOLLOW UP

There are many possible variations on this practice and many opportunities for kids to write short in every subject across the day. Katie engages her students in this practice with a simple prompt: *Tell me the story of your learning in 140 characters* (the length of an old-school tweet). Additional variations on this practice could include

▶ Write an eight-word book review.

▶ Write a math micro-story your friends can solve.

▶ Invent a hashtag that describes the author's message in a picture book.

▶ Create a headline to summarize an image or video.

▶ Write a tweet from a book character's perspective.

Very short written responses can provide helpful writing practice—and that practice can add up as we ask students to write multiple times across subjects. This increased writing time in reading, science, technology, engineering, art, music, math, and community building or social emotional learning can add up to paragraphs, even pages, of additional writing. As students increase production, they become more fluent micro-writers, attuned to making every word count.

RESPONDING AND CONNECTING USING VISUAL TOOLS:
Sketchnote to Respond to a Podcast

TRY THIS WHEN . . .

- you notice students need to practice listening comprehension skills

- you want to introduce podcasts as a new multimedia literacy

- you need to engage students in sketchnoting as a way to organize information.

In a world that is increasingly visual, listening comprehension is often neglected, yet it is essential in effective communication and in building empathy and compassion (more on that in Chapter 4).

Recent research tells us that sketching or nonlinear note taking—a helpful way to capture ideas when listening—results in increased comprehension and retention (Pillars 2016). Podcasts provide a wealth of opportunities to practice listening comprehension from a wide range of voices across genres and content areas. When we combine sketchnoting and podcasting, we introduce students to a new response option to capture their thinking and a new medium for learning.

WHAT TO DO

If students have used sketchnoting before, you might begin this lesson by revisiting their previous work or any charts you've created. If the idea of sketchnoting is new to them, show a variety of examples—a quick Google search will yield many—and discuss what they see and how the medium is different from other ways they've been asked to gather learning and thinking before. For younger students, you might draw a circle on a piece of chart paper and ask, "What can you make with a circle?" Students of any age will respond with ideas—a ball, a pizza, a tire, a snowman! Draw those items on the chart as students provide suggestions. Repeat the practice with a square. Discuss how most sketches and drawings are a series of shapes used together, and how even simple images can convey ideas.

Explain to students that you'll be using writing and sketching both to remember ideas that you hear and to note your own thinking. Play a small portion of a short podcast for the whole class to hear. After a minute, pause the podcast and begin to sketch and label as you think aloud about the podcast. Then invite kids to turn and talk about what they saw you do. Ask for a few students to share their observations. Next, ask students to join you and invite

Helpful Language

It sounds like this podcast is going to have two distinct parts. I'm going to consider that as I start to think about how to use my space on the page.

Watch how I listen closely to try and find the most important ideas for my sketchnote.

Hmmm . . . how might we use a picture or quick sketch to represent that information?

Are there one or two important words we need?

What colors might best work with this information? Should I switch colors to emphasize something?

Wait, I need to listen to that again!

them to pick up their notebook and draw and write their thinking as they listen to the podcast. Let them know you'll press Pause after a minute or so of audio so they have time to draw and write their thinking. Do this several times throughout the podcast, modeling how to pause and play the podcast. Release students to continue this work at their own pace once you've seen that they are ready.

These are our current favorite Podcasts to share with kids. If you're looking for a podcast to start with, a short snippet of one of these is a great place to begin.

▶ *Wow in the World* by NPR

▶ *But Why: A Podcast for Curious Kids* by Vermont Public Radio

▶ *Tumble Science Podcast for Kids*

Katie used this sketchnote about sketchnoting to launch this lesson with a group of fourth-grade students.

Students in Michele Giovanelli's fourth-grade class use sketchnoting to gather key ideas from a video.

OUTCOMES AND WHAT TO LOOK FOR

In this initial lesson, we are looking for students to be able to engage their listening comprehension skills and represent their understanding using sketches and words. Can students

▶ listen carefully for the main ideas and details of a podcast?

▶ represent information using pictures (quick sketches) and words?

▶ connect or organize information using boxes, circles, lines, and arrows?

▶ use their sketchnote to talk about what they learned, sharing key ideas, thinking, and questions?

FOLLOW UP

Sketchnoting can be a powerful tool for students to gather, make sense of, and share information. However, like anything else, it is a skill that takes time to learn. You may wish to spend more time on helping students explore different media (paper versus digital), structures, and art skills. This is where we recommend connecting with your teacher librarians, art teachers, coaches, and any other support staff who can help your students synthesize the skills needed to master this genre. Older students might use their understanding of text structure to play with formatting their sketchnotes in a way that mirrors the structure of the podcast, video, or article.

TRY IT!

RESPONDING AND CONNECTING USING VISUAL TOOLS:
Create an Infographic to Summarize Learning

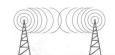

Join the Conversation:
Authentic Genres

"We need to think, 'How will my students benefit from this? How will they be enriched by this?'"

#ReadTheWorldNow

Hein.pub/RTW2.3

Helpful Language

Let's take a tour through this creation tool today. Which layouts seem like they would really show your ideas well?

Skim through your notes and look for words, phrases, or big ideas that we might turn into little icons or symbols.

Are there any facts or numbers that would lend themselves to a graph or pie chart?

What structure do you want to share your information in? Is it in a sequence of first, next, last? Or maybe cause and effect? If it doesn't have a clear structure, how could you separate the information into chunks or sections?

Think about all you've learned during art class about using space. Do you have any empty spaces on your infographic? How could you fix that?

What color scheme might work best here?

Let's make sure to list our sources at the bottom!

TRY THIS WHEN . . .

■ you want students to summarize and synthesize their learning

■ students would like to create a preview of key ideas in a longer piece of writing or research.

Sometimes we want students to synthesize information in a professional way in order to share it with a wider audience. Digital infographics offer a concise and visual way to communicate information. They also prompt the student to determine the most important information or evidence to include, and to support readers with images, data, and text. Websites and apps like Canva, Piktochart, or Slides enable kids to make infographics quickly and easily as they offer a variety of predetermined layouts to choose from. Younger students might collaborate on a class infographic, with partners or small groups each taking on a small section of the infographic like a diagram, graph, or label.

WHAT TO DO

Students should have several experiences reading infographics before they begin creating their own (see the Try It titled "Evaluate Infographics" earlier in this chapter). Begin this lesson by providing students with a few examples of infographics, perhaps from designers such as Steve Jenkins, Chip Kidd, and Nicholas Blechman. Seeing a variety of structures from a variety of designers will give students more options to consider for their own work.

Choose a topic on which students have already compiled information from a unit of study, short text or video, or personal inquiry project. Have students consider the information that they would like to include: What is important? What can be shown with pictures, icons, or graphs? What should come first, second, next, and last? Many times, students will find a layout that seems to work well and then go from there; for example, some topics lend themselves to a sequential layout while others may have a hierarchy or categories as organizational features.

Lead students on a tour of the tool itself. What does it enable them to do? What are its limitations? Model thinking through several options that you might use and why those may or may not work. Give students time to explore and play, then share what they've learned or discovered with the class.

Support students as they work by using small groups or conferring as needed. Prompt students to gather feedback from their peers during or after creating the infographic, considering questions like *What works well? What isn't clear? What questions do you have?* and *What else might I add?*

OUTCOMES AND WHAT TO LOOK FOR

The goal of this lesson is to help students create infographics that clearly summarize and communicate key ideas that they want to share. Can students

▸ create a thoughtful design that clearly communicates information and/ or ideas?

▸ include all the needed elements of the infographic?

▸ make well-reasoned decisions about content and design, such as what to include, how to include it, and what information can be shown graphically?

▸ seek out and accept feedback from peers and teachers?

FOLLOW UP

Whenever students create, give them an opportunity to share their work with the community circles they are part of. This gives students an audience they have a genuine connection to, and it enables them to receive feedback on their efforts. We might have students post their work on a blog, class website, or LMS. In other instances, this work can be printed, in full color, and displayed in the classroom and hallways. If students have created the infographic as a way to hook an audience to read a longer piece of writing, view a video, or listen to a presentation, a QR code can easily be added. Perhaps we are nostalgic, but we feel that students should be able to take tangible artifacts of their digital work with them when they leave our classes, and thus we make time to ensure that they and their families can access and archive their creations across the year by including them in portfolios, printing them, or sharing files.

Things to Think About When We Make Infographics (Primary)

- What sources will I use to find information?
- Do I plan to draw my graphic or use shapes and icons?
- Which mentor models will I use as a guide? Will I make a graphic in the style of Steve Jenkins? Chip Kidd? Nicholas Blechman?
- What words will I need to help the viewer understand?
- Who is my audience?

As you teach the lesson and coach students in their work, build your own class chart to capture questions to consider when building an infographic. Post the chart for students' reference. If you notice points of confusion regarding infographics after this lesson, target a particular question on the chart and use it as the core of a minilesson, providing modeling and practice for students.

Things to Think About When We Make Infographics (Intermediate)

- Did I choose a layout that communicates my information clearly?
- Did I find icons, pictures, or graphics that will help my reader understand?
- Did I include a title and subheadings?
- Did I make sure that I wrote just enough for a reader to understand my ideas, but not so much that the reader will be overwhelmed?
- Did I choose a color scheme that went with my topic?
- Did I include resources?
- Did I proofread my infographic to make sure that everything was just right?
- Did I get feedback from at least two classmates before finalizing my design?

You might also consider using infographics as a way to assess student learning. Kathy Schrock (2018), educational technologist, has created a fantastic resource page and video presentation for how to use infographics as a creative way to assess students (www.schrockguide.net /infographics-as-an-assessment.html).

This infographic was created by first-grade students during an inquiry into extreme weather. Working in a small group of three, students collaborated to create a diagram, determine the most important information about hurricanes, and research additional facts. Students used a drawing app to create their diagram and made the graphics and text in Keynote.

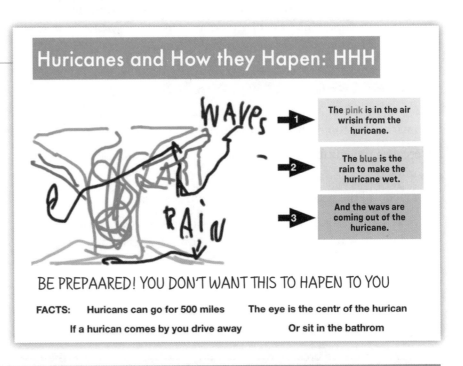

As part of a research workshop, eighth graders made this infographic by surveying students in the school and representing their findings in a visual format.

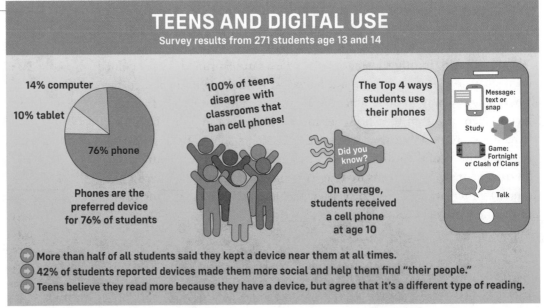

WRITE WITH US

As you use the Try Its in this final section of the chapter with your students, ask yourself:

⏻ **What are you noticing about your students that you hadn't before?**

⏻ **What strengths are they showing?**

⏻ **What new opportunities for growth are you seeing?**

⏻ **Share your ideas. #ReadTheWorldNow**

3 *Critical Reading*

Developing an Empathetic Stance Through Connected Literacy

The otherwise-chatty group of fifth graders sat silent for a moment.

"Can that really happen?" one of them asked. "I mean . . . this story, could this happen in real life?"

The small book club group had been reading *Out of My Mind* by Sharon M. Draper, a story about a nonspeaking girl with cerebral palsy named Melody whom everyone assumes is also cognitively impaired. When Melody is given a communication device, a whole new world opens and those around her realize that she has a great deal to say. This book, which has both been lauded and come under criticism for its treatment of a character with a disability, was part of a carefully selected set of books for students to choose from. None of the students in the book club had any close relationships with anyone who had a disability like Melody's. They struggled to merge what they were reading with their own limited personal experiences. They looked at each other, unsure how to continue the conversation.

"It's just a story," one said, "I don't think it can happen." This comment launched a spirited debate between them about the plausibility of the plot of their book. The teacher finished with the students she was sitting with and quietly sat just outside the circle of the group to listen in. As they came to a stalemate in their debate, the students turned to her.

"How's it going?" she asked. They all started to talk at once. Then, Annalisa pulled her hair behind one ear and summed up the conversation. "We're arguing about whether something like this could happen in real life."

"It's a good question," the teacher responded. "I think there's someone you should meet." She grabbed her laptop and pulled up the Twitter profile of Jordyn Zimmerman (@jordynbzim), a young autistic woman who lived the majority of her life unable to communicate. Jordyn did not have expressive language skills, and schools projected her intellectual ability based on the way she communicated. Instead of including her in the standard school curriculum, Jordyn was instructed to do simple tasks like touch her nose. As with Melody, the main character in the book, access to an assistive

Empathy is about finding echoes of another person in yourself.

—Mohsin Hamid, 2012
(quoted in Leyshon 2012)

91

communication device revealed Jordyn's true intelligence and potential. A video on her website showed Jordyn today, a student at Ohio University communicating clearly about her advocacy work for autism and inclusion.

"I want to tell you that Jordyn has autistim, which is very different from cerebral palsy. What Jordyn and our main character Melody have in common is that they both use assistive technology to help them communicate," the teacher explained.

"So if we just give everyone a tablet, they can talk?" one student asked. The student looked expectantly at the teacher.

"It sounds like we have some big questions here and we need to learn more. We can't really know what someone else's experience is like until we know their story. I think we need to hear some more stories. Let me do a little gathering for you and let's meet again tomorrow."

As we give our students opportunities to become more informed citizens of the world, they will inevitably encounter situations and experiences that are unfamiliar to them. These situations and experiences can also be unfamiliar to us, and it is OK to be honest about what we still need to learn and where we need to grow. In the example above, the students were initially at a loss, making decisions about whether or not the character's situation was possible based only on their own guesses. It was only through examining multiple stories and accounts that they were able to learn more and contextualize what they had read. The work of this chapter is to ensure that students have the tools and strategies they need to learn with empathy rather than jumping to conclusions or making assumptions.

What Do We Now Need to Teach That We Didn't Need to Teach Before?

The values and goals of strong instruction are not new: we respect children; we meet them where they are academically and socially and help them to grow; we encourage a sense of agency in our students; and we aim for them to become independent learners, readers, writers, and thinkers. However, technology now offers us both new challenges and new opportunities in relation to these values and goals.

We live in a world where any human with a device can record events and share their story wide and far (Jenkins 2006). We can access countless texts, primary source documents, images, video clips, and other resources. We no longer need to depend on a textbook's homogenized single story: technology makes it possible for us to gather as many stories about a topic or event as we can. Whereas previously we may have read one article about a current issue, technology now allows us to access multiple stories from every side and angle. In fact, in many ways, our society *demands* that we do so as there are limited resources that seek to tell stories in a truthful and unbiased manner. For better or for worse, journalists and publishers are no longer the

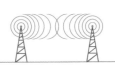

Join the Conversation:
The Power of Story

"We've moved from papyrus to print books to video to tablets and devices, but *story* is something that will endure regardless of the device or the medium."

#ReadTheWorldNow

Hein.pub/RTW3.1

gatekeepers of news and history. Citizen journalism has empowered people to bring awareness to issues and perspectives that mainstream media haven't covered or won't cover. At the same time, it has given a voice to sensationalism, radicalism, hate, and untruth. Media outlets tell us repeatedly that Americans are more divided than ever. Now is the time for educators to step forward and challenge that tendency.

As technology pulls us into a truly global society, we are confronted with the need for future-forward teaching. This is especially obvious when studying the social sciences: most social studies curricula focus on students' understanding of their role within their family unit, school, town, and state. They do not emphasize making consistent connections to the world beyond the students' own community. Without those connections, students don't learn how the world that comes to them via technology relates to the world in which they go to school. The decontextualized bits of information that reach them from communities other than their own can lead to misunderstandings, mistrust, and division rather than an understanding of the rich variety of ways that people live, work, and interact. This does our students a disservice and has lasting, divisive effects on our country as a whole. Instead, we could be using technology to bring the world into our instruction, in the service of what the National Council for the Social Studies defines as global education, which "focuses on the interrelated nature of conditions, issues, trends, processes, and events" (NCSS Board of Directors 2016).

But the effects of technology in our students' lives are not limited to their understandings of those who are distant from them. For the children who fill our classrooms today—the children who are now entering the stages of development when they begin to make sense of the world beyond themselves—technology is shaping the only reality they've ever known.

Young learners are on a constant quest to make sense of new information. They view themselves in juxtaposition with others, integrating new information about their peers into their existing schema (Piaget 1974). School is, for many children, the first time that they are tasked with learning in a large-group environment where "we" becomes an important factor in learning, competing with the "me" focus students have had until this point. Inevitably, we see elementary-age children gravitate toward those who fall in line with their own identities or binary preferences: we like the same things; we have the same hat; we look the same; we are the same gender (Ziv and Banaji 2012). We also see this tendency toward binary thinking at work whenever we pull up alongside a reader to confer about a book and are met with a definitive "I like it" or "I don't like it." And, when these same children are given technological tools without further guidance, those same binary preferences persist in their online preferences: a cute cat video may lead them to thousands more cute cat videos, but not much else.

Our role as teacher can reinforce these lines of division or break them down. The way we speak to, interact with, and manage students—whether intentional or unintentional—can reinforce these divisions and ask students

Empathy is the one human capacity that allows us to link minds and hearts across cultures and generations to transform our lives.

—Michele Borba, psychologist, 2016 (xii)

to place themselves into a category that may make them uncomfortable. We can push students to think beyond a knee-jerk reaction to a book; introduce them to a new perspective; give students an opportunity to share their own stories and identities; and help them interact with, befriend, appreciate, and respect those who are different from themselves: all of these align with where they are on their developmental journey. We curate materials to ensure students can access multiple voices and stories. And, when we use technology thoughtfully and critically, it has the potential to be a powerful ally in this work. We share stories with our students so they can better understand others and themselves, and experience the wisdom of empathy.

Sadly, it's not unusual for educators who emphasize children's growth as humans to be met with pushback. Perhaps you've heard a colleague state that teaching empathy is not in their job description or that there isn't enough time for social-emotional learning in the already-packed school day. Yet research has shown that "profound" empathy—the connection that develops "through close and frequent interaction" (Cooper 2010)—improves not only personal and social development, but academic development (Durlak 2018). Additionally, researchers have tracked organizations and seen gains in financial performance, growth, innovation, and productivity as a result of diversity in their teams, whether in terms of race, gender, or beliefs (Phillips 2014). As these diverse environments become more prevalent and valued, empathy is needed to ensure that all members of the community thrive. Empathy and the act of adding more voices to our learning aren't "soft" skills; they're essential skills.

We could try to limit students' access to technology. But would that help them make sense of the world around them? To be critical thinkers and independent learners? To be resilient, empathetic humans? Or would it leave them powerless and unprepared when they eventually do encounter different perspectives or even untruths? Instead, we can look at this moment in their development and in our culture as history in the making. We can help our students develop well-researched, well-reasoned ideas and dispositions based on multiple perspectives. We can embrace this moment that gives students opportunities to grow both their empathy and their critical thinking. We can teach the skills our students need in the world today. Rather than fearing the devices that bring these stories, we can put them to use as empathy machines—tools that give students opportunities to build bridges rather than barriers.

Story: The Path to Empathy and Compassion

Discussing empathy as a concept can feel distant to children—and even to adults, at times. Yet we've found that empathy can be grounded in day-to-day life when we consider it in conjunction with *getting to know each other's stories*.

> Courage. Kindness. Friendship. Character. These are the qualities that define us as human beings, and propel us, on occasion, to greatness.
>
> —R. J. Palacio, 2012 (304)

When we listen to others' stories with our whole selves—whether the stories are self-contained anecdotes or the unfolding narratives of their lives and cultures—we are opening ourselves up to empathy. When we help our students stand in the shoes of those whose stories they hear, we are encouraging compassion. And, when we listen closely to the stories our students tell us about themselves, we are both practicing and modeling empathy. Whether it be the third grader who recently told Katie that he loved a book because the protagonist had also lost his father; the seventh graders who told Kristin, in the wake of the Ferguson verdict, that "it's cool that you're listening, and I appreciate that, but you're never going to know what it's like to be us"; or the fourth grader who took pride in being a responsible uncle to his niece and nephew, these glimpses into who our students are all help us see the stories of their lives.

As you listen, consider:

▶ **Am I getting who this student is?** What do I know about this student beyond the data points? What do I know about them as a person? Their family and cultural background? How they interact with peers in different situations? How they view their identity? Might that identity shift in certain situations?

▶ **Do I understand this student's situation?** Can I see what is happening from their viewpoint? Can I put myself in their shoes? Do I have a full picture of what they are bringing to the learning exercise, whether it be personal experience, background knowledge, or social strengths or concerns?

▶ **How am I offering support, options, and alternatives that will help move this student forward?** Have I listened to what *they* think they need to move forward?

▶ **Does the student believe that I am here to listen and help?** Do they believe that I understand who they are, where they are coming from, and what they need and that I care?

(Adapted and reprinted with permission from "How to Really Understand Someone Else's Point of View" by Mark Goulston and John Ullmen. Hbr.org, April 2013.)

One more reminder of the importance of understanding others' stories: the questions above are adapted from items that originally appeared in a *Harvard Business Review* article (Goulston and Ullmen 2013) about being more successful in business ventures. Empathy is not a mere pleasantry; it's a skill for every domain of our lives.

Preparing to Do This Work

The first step in embracing the work of empathy in our classrooms is to proactively cultivate the type of classroom community where this work can flourish. The mindsets, beliefs, and understandings that we bring to school each day determine whether we see a charged moment in class as a problem or as an opportunity for learning, whether we see a disagreement as a chance to deepen understanding or as a threat. Before we embark on the work of fostering empathy and compassion in our classrooms, let's consider who we are and what we believe. As our friend and colleague Sara Ahmed has written about the work of social comprehension, "If we want to teach students to be compassionate, complex thinkers, we must first muddle through this work ourselves . . . The more we are able to be introspective upfront, the more comfortable we may become with the *discomfort* of powerful discussions that can move all of us to new levels as learners and critical thinkers" (2018, xxvi).

Ask yourself:

▶ What do I need to learn more about if I truly want to try to understand and have empathy for my students?

▶ What do I need to learn more about if I truly want to try to understand and have empathy for a wider array of people?

The answers to these questions will give you an idea of where to focus your attention as you begin the work of learning more.

Building an Environment of Trust and Respect

The environment you create with your students communicates that you and your students trust, respect, and care for each other. A healthy classroom environment supports your students every day, whether nothing out of the ordinary happens or a tense situation arises. This environment nurtures both in-class interactions and those you will ask students to have digitally, thus beginning the process of creating more empathetic digital communicators.

Here are a few ways to foster a strong, student-focused classroom community:

▶ **Begin the year with expectations that support trust and respect.** This can mean co-creating or discussing classroom norms, such as *In this classroom, we challenge ideas, not people* and *We use language that shows respect for others.*

▶ **Consistently model and nurture language and behaviors that reflect respect for everyone involved—even when there is a disagreement.** The following language frames can be equally helpful for you and for your students. You can use them in your own teaching, and teach them directly to students in a minilesson.

- *I hear what you're saying, and I'd like to offer a slightly different perspective . . .*

- *I think we might also consider . . .*

- *One perspective we haven't considered yet is . . .*

- *I wonder what would happen if we looked at this a different way . . .*

- *I respectfully disagree because . . .*

▶ **Kidwatch.** Pay attention to who is doing most of the talking and who isn't. Observe body language. Who seems to feel safe in the classroom? Who doesn't? What changes can you make to help all students feel that they belong to the classroom community?

▶ **Listen.** Educator and author Cornelius Minor (2019) considers listening to be teachers' "superpower." He writes: "The ability to listen will not make teaching easier. It will not take the painful parts away, but listening can give us our children back. If we listen to what children and communities are saying, and we respond accordingly, we can be ourselves again. We can be people" (11). He explains that there are three parts to listening to our students: actively listening to our students in the moment (whether they're telling us something in words or through their actions), considering what we've heard in relation to our own work and impact, and making "active and longstanding adjustments" in response (16–17).

Learn More Using Professional Development Tools

There is a wealth of strong resources designed to help teachers have a better understanding of the students they teach and of how they can best support those students. Take the time to find something that feels helpful to you and work through it thoroughly. Diving into these resources with a partner, a team, or even a large group can magnify their power.

These are a few of our favorites:

▶ *Being the Change: Lessons and Strategies to Teach Social Comprehension*, by Sara Ahmed (2018), teaches both adults and students the skills that make up social comprehension: exploring our identities, listening, being candid, becoming better informed, finding humanity in ourselves and others, and facing crises together.

▶ *We Got This. Equity, Access, and the Quest to Be Who Our Students Need Us to Be*, by Cornelius Minor (2019), emphasizes listening deeply to our students and using what we hear to reenvision our classrooms, our curriculum, and our communities.

▶ *Game Changer! Book Access for All Kids*, by Donalyn Miller and Colby Sharp, (2018) provides tools and information to increase access and work toward equity through literacy.

What assumptions am I making based on bias?

ability

age

race

labels

Bias

SES

gender

apperance

religion

What biases might be affecting my instructional decisions?

Project Implicit

▶ **Teaching Tolerance** has a website that contains free anti-bias resources, including classroom tools, videos, podcasts, and more (www.tolerance. org). Teaching Tolerance's downloadable Let's Talk! resources are an excellent starting point for exploring the organization's offerings.

▶ *Child Trauma Toolkit for Educators*, by the National Child Traumatic Stress Network (2008), is a free downloadable PDF that includes clear explanations of the psychological and behavioral impact of trauma, examples of situations that can cause trauma, signs of trauma in students, and suggestions for educators: www.nctsn.org/resources/child-trau- ma-toolkit-educators.

As you look for your own professional development resources to broaden your understanding, be mindful of the voice and experience of that resource. Ask yourself: Does the author (or authoring organization) have firsthand, lived experience on the topic?

Learn More by Turning to an Expert

Look to see who, in your school community or in your professional network as a whole, has been speaking out about anti-bias-related topics or leading anti-bias staff development, and follow them online or join their in-person workshops or gatherings. This will put you in a community with other people who have similar aims and are in similar situations.

If you're thinking of asking an expert for help with a particular situation, be respectful of their time and work first. Make an effort to educate yourself and to learn about information they've already made public before reaching out to them: they may have already answered your question in a public document, chat, or video. Think before you ask.

There is a difference between people who are marketing themselves to help—an author, speaker, or consultant—and people we work with. When we, as humans, encounter situations beyond our own experiences, we are often tempted to seek out someone whom we perceive to have had that experience based on some aspect of their identity—race, religion, gender identity, history, or ability. It's important that we stop and think. Has this person offered to help educate us in this situation? People are often unfairly asked to speak for an entire identity group in situations like this. They have their own unique story that they might wish to share, but we need to proceed with care.

Prepare for Difficult Discussions

There is one loose end we would like to perhaps begin to try and tie up, although we acknowledge this is difficult work. That is, how to navigate those hard moments in the classroom, moments that occur with increasing frequency given the world and times we live in—moments that might arise from inviting students to read and learn about experiences that are different from their own. We've all experienced a moment with our students when things take a sudden turn into uncharted territories: a conversation moves to a charged topic, a student makes a comment that exposes a bias—or a truth—that makes other students uncomfortable. These types of moments in classrooms are not new or unique to this digital culture we live in; however, technology has our students connected more than ever before, even at a young age. While we can't know what each day will bring, we can be prepared with a few strategies so that we don't need to fear the unknown. There is no way to avoid all conflict in the classroom, but the more we maintain a constant and empathetic focus on our students, the more we'll be able to support them when these situations do arise. These are a few strategies that have worked well for us:

▶ **Remind students of the classroom discussion norms they created.** Set the tone before conversations take place. If you hear disagreement turn toward disrespect, remind students of your classroom agreements.

- *Before we start, let's take a moment to revisit our discussion norms. What will be easy for you to stick to today? What might be challenging? Jot that down on a sticky note and keep it with you.*

- *It sounds like emotions are running high. Let's stop to breathe and revisit our guidelines before continuing.*

- *I'm hearing us get to a place of disagreement. Let's pause for a moment to consider our words.*

▶ **Give students time to focus.** Give the class a few minutes to collect their thoughts privately on an index card or publicly but anonymously via a quick digital survey. You might ask students:

- *What are you thinking or feeling right now?*

- *What words or phrases come to mind when you consider this topic?*

- *What is something you'd like to say about this topic?*

▶ **Ask more; tell less.** While we teachers often feel that it is up to us to have the right words for every situation, usually the best response is to listen and learn. You might show respect and care for a student by asking:

- *Will you say more about that?*

- *Can you help me understand?*

- *What would you like to do with that feeling (or thought, or new thinking)?*

▶ **Be honest when you need time to process.** If you find yourself overwhelmed in the moment, it's OK to say to students, "I need some time to think about that. Let's take a moment to finish what we were working on, and then we can pick up this conversation again tomorrow."

When things get <u>TOUGH</u>

① Stop and breathe
- you <u>can</u> handle this.
- Stay calm
- Consider options

② Kidwatch
- What do I see? How are they feeling?
- listen, honor emotions, acknowledge

③ Take a minute... ☺
- pause to write or turn & talk
- "I see we have strong feelings about this... let's take 'a minute.'"

④ Debrief
- with Students
- with Colleagues or myself

This page from a teacher's notebook reflects her learning during a staff workshop on difficult conversations. Each staff member was asked to develop their own step-by-step strategy for what to do based on a variety of strategies presented, their own comfort level, and their current class of students.

Then, be sure to pick up the conversation again no later than when you'd promised.

▶ **Let an important issue change your plans.** If you find that the class is needing to talk through something or to learn more about something—a scary recent incident in the news, for example—be willing to set aside your lesson plans to go on that journey with them. Saying "I can see that this is important to you—let's do some research together now" conveys to students that their concerns matter and that you are there for them.

▶ **Keep families in the loop.** There are times when a classroom discussion or event might warrant a follow-up with families. We find this especially true if students are discussing something that they may have a lot of questions about or feel the need to do more research on. Teachers we've worked with have used a simple format like this one to structure emails or notes to families:

- *Today in class students discussed . . .*

  Give a brief and factual account of what occurred.

- *This was in response to . . .*

  Note whether the topic came from a classroom resource, from service work, or from the students directly.

- *Some topics and questions that came up were . . .*

  Share the topics and questions that students had.

- *If you'd like to follow up at home, you might . . . or I have attached a resource for you to read or discuss with your child if you wish.*

  Give parents a simple resource or questions to follow up on if you think it's appropriate.

- *I have asked students to . . .*

  Be clear about what your expectations are for students.

WRITE WITH US

⏻ **What do you think of when you think of empathy?**

⏻ **Think back to a situation when you've felt empathy. What did it feel like? Was it challenging to be empathetic? How? Did empathy benefit you and the others in the situation? How?**

⏻ **Consider: How might the digital devices in your classrooms be used as "empathy machines"?**

⏻ **Share your ideas. #ReadTheWorldNow**

About This Chapter

The lessons in this chapter give specific, practical suggestions for centering empathy and understanding others' stories in your classroom. We begin with a Try It that is not for your students but for you. It is about taking the time to carefully analyze and reconsider the texts you share with your students. This work will not only result in a stronger offering of texts for your students, but also help you fine-tune your focus on multiple perspectives and the resources you use to teach. Then, we move on to lessons about shifting perspectives and responding and connecting to others.

PREPARING OURSELVES AND OUR RESOURCES

If we want our students to cultivate their ability to take perspectives into account, we must consider the perspectives we are sharing with them.

SHIFTING PERSPECTIVE

Empathy, the ability to place oneself in another's shoes on an emotional level, begins with perspective taking: the ability to look at situations, resources, and relationships from another person's point of view.

RESPONDING AND CONNECTING

Students grow when they hear stories that challenge or broaden their own perspectives. We can help students actively listen, process their feelings, and respond authentically.

TRY IT!

TRY THIS WHEN . . .

- it's the beginning of the school year and you're planning for instruction, or getting ready to spend district funds or grant money

- you or your students are organizing the library and you're beginning to notice some gaps

- you've reflected on your student population and realized that not all students are finding texts that they can relate to on a personal level

- you have readers whom you're seeking to make connections with

- you're seeing instances when students do not understand or value different cultures, at home or abroad

- you're evaluating your classroom library and resources and would like to involve students in the process

- you're planning for a unit of study and looking for new texts

- you've been using a textbook or the same small set of resources for students year after year.

Join the Conversation:
The Resources We Put in Front of Our Kids

"Many of our students come to school and they do not see themselves reflected in the books and resources that they're picking up."

#ReadTheWorldNow

Hein.pub/RTW3.2

"Kids read what we bless," says educational researcher Linda Gambrell (quoted in Miller 2012). And so, we have a special responsibility to ensure that the texts we "bless"—the texts that we share in read-alouds, include in our classroom libraries, mention with love in our classrooms, and include in content-area studies—are giving students, in Rudine Sims Bishop's words, both mirrors (representations of the realities that students live in) and windows (representations of perspectives and situations outside students' immediate realities). Bishop writes:

> We are realistic enough to know that literature, no matter how powerful, has limits. It could however, help us to understand each other better by helping to change our attitudes towards difference. When there are enough books available that can act as both mirrors and windows for all our children, they will see that we can celebrate both our differences and our similarities, because together they make us all human (1990).

The texts we place before our students send messages. Students who are given a wide range of both mirrors and windows (Bishop 1990) learn that their own experiences and interests are valid and that multiple perspectives are valued. These texts help shape our classroom communities to support curiosity, inquiry, and understanding, and provide sliding glass doors for kids to walk through to become a part of the world created by the author (Bishop 1990). They let students hear voices and stories that might otherwise be lost in a homogenized (and typically Eurocentric) version of history. Additionally, having access to texts that provide both mirrors and windows is an important factor in students' choice of their reading materials: when students have both texts they choose to read and time to read those texts, their reading skills grow (Krashen 1993; Allington and Gabriel 2012). In contrast, students whose in-school reading is based on a classroom library of randomly donated or aging texts, of read-alouds primarily from a list of so-called "classics," and of textbooks are less likely to see true representations of themselves or others in their reading.

WHAT TO DO

In this Try It, we'll work through the three steps of reconsidering the texts you expose students to:

1. Evaluate the texts that are currently in your classroom or curriculum.

2. Plan a collection that supports your students and their learning.

3. Procure new texts.

This process can help us become more mindful of equity in the texts we use, but it is only the first step. Our students and our changing world require us to continually reflect on and adjust our resources. Thus we view it more as a recursive cycle with which we analyze and adjust our resource collections on a rolling basis.

Evaluating the Texts You Place Before Students

Begin by considering all the ways in which you make texts available to students. In our experience, the main conduits tend to be

▶ the classroom library

▶ read-alouds

▶ book club or literature circle sets

▶ author studies

What does *diversity* mean?

Merriam-Webster's online dictionary tells us that *diversity* means "the condition of having or being composed of differing elements" (n.d.a). As educator Chad Everett explains, "using the word diverse to describe texts . . . creates a default position, because one must ask diverse for whom or diverse from what?" (2017). No book is a "diverse" book—it can provide only one author's story.

With this in mind, working for diversity in the texts you offer students is not about finding a few new titles. It's about rethinking the collection as a whole to ensure a wide array of different voices are represented, without a single perspective or narrative taking precedence. We must also consider the nature of representation. Donalyn Miller and Colby Sharp point out, "In too many books, the diverse qualities of the main characters, their families, or their communities are at the heart of the conflict or problem that must be overcome. Children and adolescents should not always encounter messaging that what makes them diverse is negative or a source of conflict" (2018, 62)

Providing our students with windows and mirrors is not work we can accomplish in one meeting or even one school year. It's a commitment throughout our lives.

A Note to Principals and Administrators

This work takes time, thoughtful conversation, funding, and your support. We encourage you to set aside staff development or meeting time to do this work with teams and be a part of the conversations. This not only sends a message that it's something you and the school value, but it also keeps you in the loop of what is happening in classrooms so that you can address questions from parents if they arise.

▶ anchor or mentor texts (whole-class novels)

▶ content resources (such as textbooks or trade books) and primary sources

▶ digital books or articles

▶ websites.

Each of these presents texts differently. A classroom library makes texts available to students and (we hope!) offers them choices about which texts to read and which not to read. Read-alouds, book clubs, author studies, and anchor texts give you a shared experience as a class, but they offer students no choice. They also send a message about what is valued and worthy of our time. The same is true of content-area resources and primary sources, but they also bear an additional weight: the voices they include or don't include and the stories they tell or don't tell have the potential to affect a child's understanding of content areas—the facts of history, for example, or the stories behind science—in addition to the powerful potential to affect children's perceptions of what is valued and what is not.

Decide which collection of texts you'll address first—perhaps your classroom library or your trusted go-to read-aloud collection. You might decide to take on the collection in which you think you have the greatest need or to begin with an area that seems easier to manage. Whichever you choose first, know that you'll need to repeat the process for *every* collection to ensure that students are consistently getting access and exposure to both mirrors and windows.

Once you've decided on a collection, look for a team to help you: involve colleagues like grade-level teammates, librarians, coaches, or mentors. If you are unable to do this work with others in your school, consider using your social media community to solicit feedback. These will be the people you turn to for second opinions and for suggestions. As you consider who to rely on, ask yourself: Who can give you a perspective on texts that you don't already have?

Gather the texts in the collection you're working on. Try to have all the physical and digital texts on hand. Lay them out so that you can spend some time considering them, with the same care and attention you might consider works at an art gallery.

Chances are these texts have ended up in this collection for different reasons. Perhaps they are leftovers of another teacher's past, or are tied to a specific author or genre study or unit. Or perhaps they're personal favorites, gifts, or recommendations from students in years past. We often accumulate many resources in our teaching careers. On the surface, that might seem to be a good thing: It's better to have too much than too little, right?

However, if the texts you're offering students are not helpful as mirrors, windows, or sliding glass doors; if they perpetuate damaging misconceptions; or if they crowd the shelves so that kids can't find the books they'll connect to, they are doing more harm than good.

Begin by looking at each text separately. Ask yourself: Does this text perpetuate stereotypes, misconceptions, or single stories? If there is something about this text that you find legitimately helpful to students, consider how you will present the text in a thoughtful and sensitive way. How will you address potential misconceptions or stereotypical portrayals head-on? Can you provide ample time and attention to discuss the problematic points, and perhaps bring in other texts to counter them? Ultimately, you might decide that whatever learning this text might spark is outweighed by the potential for the text to do harm. In that case, it's in the best interest of your students to remove this text from your collection and find another text to replace it. And, of course, if you find any texts with information or language that is largely out-of-date, it's time to retire them; there is likely a better option available.

Evaluating Classroom Libraries and Read-Alouds

Now that you've looked at each text individually, use these lenses to assess your classroom library or read-aloud collection. (If you're working on a set of content-area texts or primary sources, skip to the corresponding section in this Try It on page 111.) Notice that the following questions ask you to consider your collection *as a whole*—the goal is to consider the effect of the entire collection.

▶ **Authors**

As a whole, is this collection authored by people with an array of experiences and backgrounds: different nationalities, abilities, races, religion, sexual orientations, languages, gender identities, and family configurations?

- Whose voices are missing? Consider aspects of identity such as gender, race, and socioeconomic status.

- What stories and perspectives are represented by the authors in your collection?

- Whose stories aren't being told?

- Which voices in this collection would resonate with particular students in your class?

- Who on your team might help you consider the questions above from a new perspective?

The Danger of Single Story

In her TED Talk "The Danger of Single Story," author Chimamanda Ngozi Adichie says, "Show a people as one thing, and only one thing, over and over again, and that is what they become" (2009). Simply bringing stories with a diverse array of characters into the classroom is not enough: If our students read only stories about a group of people that are really the same story over and over again, what do our readers learn about that group? If our libraries contain only books about families that feature a mom, a dad, and two kids, what does that signal to students whose families may look different? If the only books in our classroom library that feature African American characters are about slavery or civil rights, what does that say to students?

#OwnVoices

#OwnVoices is a social media hashtag started by Corinne Duyvis with the purpose of sharing literature in which the main character and the author are from the same marginalized group. As novelist and editor Kayla Whaley explains, "There's a long history of majority-group authors (white, abled, straight, cisgender, male, etc.) writing outside their experience to tell diverse stories. Sometimes the characters and stories they create are wonderful! But many times, they're rife with stereotypes, tropes, and harmful portrayals" (2019). In #OwnVoices books, the author has their own lived experience to draw from when writing the character.

▶ **Characters**

As a whole, does the collection center on (not just include) characters with a wide range of identities: different nationalities, abilities, races, religions, family configurations, languages, sexual orientations, and gender identities? Are these characters written by authors who have elements of identity in common with their characters? (See #OwnVoices.)

- Whose voices are missing? Consider aspects of identity such as race, gender, and socioeconomic status.

- What stories and perspectives are represented here?

- Whose stories aren't being told?

- Which characters in this collection would resonate with particular students in your class?

- Who on your team might help you consider the previous questions from a new perspective?

▶ **Character representations**

As a whole, does the collection represent a full range of characters within a particular group, rather than portraying characters of a particular race, gender, or socioeconomic group in one consistent way? (For example, a particular race is not consistently shown as the "bad guy"; a particular gender is not always shown as braver or smarter; a particular group is not consistently linked with certain traits, such as wealth or poverty.)

- Do these stories represent a group of people in multiple ways, or do they reinforce a single story or stereotype?

- Which character portrayals in this collection would resonate with particular students in your class?

- Do the protagonists / main subjects of the texts represent a wide range of groups, or are some groups seen more in the roles of supporting characters?

- Who on your team might help you consider the previous questions from a new perspective?

▶ **Sources**

Are the collection's informational texts from varied and reputable sources?

- Do the books and resources all come from one publisher or multiple publishers? Do the publishers show evidence of working toward more equitable coverage?

- Does the collection offer access to primary sources—such as blogs, podcasts, letters, images, or videos—that feature stories of the people?

- Do many of the resources come from respected organizations with a history of research and attention to equity, such as the Smithsonian Institution?

- Who on your team might help you consider the previous questions from a new perspective?

▶ **Perspectives**

For any given issue or event that the collection's informational texts address, are there a variety of voices and perspectives represented?

- Do the voices represented go beyond "winners" and "losers" to help students develop a rich understanding of the complexity of these issues?

- Are voices presented in a personal way? (That is, through images, letters, videos, and other primary sources that tell the story of a person instead of generalizing to an entire population.)

- Who on your team might help you consider the previous questions from a new perspective?

If you find yourself unable to give a resounding yes to any of the previous boldfaced questions, use the follow-up questions to pinpoint where your collection needs attention. If you're unsure about how to answer a particular question, or if you'd like more specific guidelines, Lee & Low Books' Classroom Library Questionnaire (bit.ly/2lZOcCy) is a helpful guide to evaluating read-alouds as well as classroom libraries.

Remember that you have another expert resource available to you: your students. Involving students in reflecting on books and resources lets them know that the teacher is listening and that kids have a voice in the classroom

Seventh-grade students generate a digital list of stories that are missing from their classroom and school. With the help of the school librarian, the students and teacher sought stories that matched their list to bring into the classroom library. Later, students used this chart as an idea board for their own works of fiction.

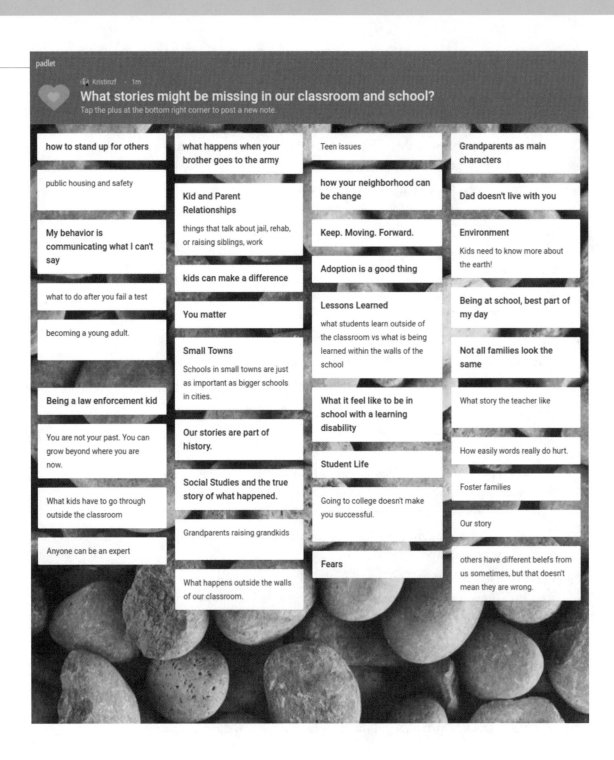

design, structure, and experience. We start this work with our youngest learners by asking them what types of books they would like more of and what stories they wish they could read about.

Depending on the age of your students, you might choose to use conversations, surveys, written feedback, or even a "suggestion box" located somewhere in your classroom. Establishing an ongoing system that is visible and easily accessible is preferred as students may not always be able to sit down and list in one sitting all the stories they wish they had. We might launch by saying something like *Readers, I know that there must be stories or characters you wish you could read about. What stories do you think are missing from our classroom? What would you like to read about? What are you wondering about that you would like to read about? What book do you wish you could pick up right now?*

Evaluating Content-Area Texts and Primary Sources

Now that you've looked at your texts individually, consider them using the following lenses. Note any instances where your response to the boldfaced questions falls short of an unconditional yes. Then, use the follow-up questions to pinpoint where your collection needs attention.

▶ **Perspectives**

Are your materials offering a range of perspectives rather than one consistent side of the stories they convey?
Does the diversity of perspectives include not only differences of opinion but also differences in language, race, gender, and socio-economic status? Is this true of all the issues and topics that the collection addresses?

- If the materials do not represent a diversity of perspectives, which perspectives are not represented?

- Are some perspectives given much more attention than others? Which perspectives are overrepresented? Which are underrepresented?

- Who on your team might help you consider the questions above from a new perspective?

▶ **Bias**

If a text has a clear bias, is there an instructionally sound reason for including the text? When you use a biased text with students, do you address the bias with your students and pair the text with other texts that offer different perspectives?

A Note About Responses from Families

Every child, regardless of race, religion, gender preference, sexual orientation, or ability, deserves to know that their family and their existence are worthy enough to be represented in our rooms. Yet we sometimes don't offer every child that opportunity for fear that some people might react negatively. Here are a few questions to consider if you hear concerns:

- **Is a *concern* the same thing as a *problem*?** Often, we teachers are expected to smooth over parental concerns and keep the peace. Rather than assuming that a concern or question from a parent demands an immediate change, could you begin a conversation with the parent about why you and the students are reading a wide range of texts?

- **Are you really alone in this?** Let your peers, supervisors, and administrators know what you are doing and urge them to join you. Having the support of your staff and administration at the outset can make the process easier.

- **How can you get families on board before an issue arises?** Early in the school year, communicate to parents that your classroom values learning about a wide array of people and experiences. If you anticipate or see the early signs of a negative response, a thoughtful face-to-face or phone conversation can address many parent concerns and help them understand the value and importance of a resource.

- **How can you keep a single concern from affecting the work as a whole?** Work out alternatives when necessary, but don't sacrifice the education of the whole class because of a few loud voices. Those who are most in need won't often speak up.

Do you have strong reasons to believe that any biased texts you use with your students do not perpetuate single narratives, stereotypes, or misconceptions?

- How will you ensure that any biased texts that you use are not harmful to your students? (That is, how will you ensure that they are not perpetuating stereotypes or misconceptions?)
- Who on your team might help you consider the questions above from a new perspective?

▶ **Accessibility**

Do your materials represent a wide variety of levels and offer multiple access points for students?

- Which levels are well represented? Which need more representation?
- Are there digital texts with read-to-me features available?
- Do the texts include students' home languages?
- Who on your team might help you consider the questions above from a new perspective?

Planning a Collection That Supports Your Students and Their Learning

At this point, you've considered what you might remove from your collection and the areas in which your collection needs to grow. The real work comes in attempting to fill in the gaps, as we can almost all be assured that there will be gaps: after all, there are so many unique stories to tell! As we source content that speaks to children across the learning continuum, we intentionally seek stories—not just books or print materials, but multimedia resources that will engage kids to inquire, research, read, respond, and think. Our aim is to ensure that our students are engaging with stories that inspire their minds and touch their hearts. Here are some suggestions for finding the titles your classroom library needs:

▶ **Cast a wide net.** Request catalogues (if you are in the United States, reach out to international publishers as well), ask for samples, scour the internet, connect with professional organizations, reach out to your online professional community, and get friendly with your local librarian.

Resource/Link	What You'll Find and How It Helps
American Indians in Children's Literature bit.ly/2heiHQC	AICL offers recommendations of books by or about American Indian as well as key perspectives on how indigenous peoples are portrayed in books that we may be using or wish to use in the classroom.
Bank Street Center on Culture, Race, and Equity bit.ly/2KDmyGl	The site offers a free interactive resource guide, *All Hands In*, which includes lesson ideas as well as links to strong videos for classroom use.
¡Colorín Colorado! bit.ly/2ml1mdr	This bilingual site for educators and parents offers book lists by topic, including many featuring Latinx and indigenous characters.
Disability in Kidlit bit.ly/1yKXoFm	Resources on this site detail the realities of disability as opposed to the popular media portrayals that are often inaccurate. Content is sorted by disability, genre, and more. The site includes articles, book reviews, and book lists.
Facing History and Ourselves bit.ly/2ml1wBz	This site offers lessons, texts, and instructional strategies for helping students engage with critical historical and civic content.
Geena Davis Institute on Gender in Media bit.ly/2uRkNKW	Teaching resources and videos on this site can help students see gender bias at work in their own lives.
Lee & Low Books bit.ly/2m5fR4X bit.ly/2kJnl8i	These sites offer book lists that focus on "contemporary diverse stories that *all* children could enjoy," reflection tools, teacher resources, and informative blog posts (Lee & Low Books 2019).
Teaching Tolerance bit.ly/1yxFWGr bit.ly/2lVCdWF	Teaching Tolerance offers a variety of resources, texts, and strategies for addressing issues of social justice in the classroom.
We Need Diverse Books bit.ly/2kqBf4h	Resources at this site can help educators and librarians find high-quality books featuring diverse characters and story lines.
Social Justice Books bit.ly/2wt6yM1	This site provides a variety of book lists organized by interest, including the LGBTQIA+ community and gender identity.

▶ **Follow equity-minded educators.** Twitter, blog posts, and social media can be great resources for finding new texts. Educators such as Val Brown, Shawna Coppola, Travis Crowder, Tricia Ebarvia, Chad Everett, Laura Jiminéz, Aeriale Johnson, Autumn Laidler, Jessica Lifshitz, Donalyn Miller, Anna Osbourn, Ken Shelton, Franki Sibberson, Dana Stachowiak, and Julia Torres (to name a few) often share current recommendations online.

▶ **Check out equity-minded organizations.** There is a wealth of free resources and text recommendations available online through organizations. See the table on the previous page for a few of our favorites.

▶ **Ask your students.** If students are able to assist in looking for titles or resources that would address these missing stories, have them do so. Taking part in researching by reading blogs, looking at book lists, and visiting libraries further empowers them to be an active part of their own education. Challenge students to build a wish list that you can share when seeking funding.

▶ **Think digital.** Digital tools can be a cost-effective way to address gaps in our physical text collections, but we must ensure that students can access them seamlessly. Take time to explore the resource as if you were a student, or ask a group of students to pilot the tool for you. If you are unsure of what digital resources exist, reach out to your librarian or technology coordinator.

▶ **Be on the lookout for series.** Finding a great text is wonderful. Finding that the great text is part of a series can be even better: it may lead you and your students to more great texts.

Once you've compiled a list of potential texts, preview them. Do they meet the needs that you identified for your collection? Loop in your team for second opinions and insights as necessary.

Procuring New Texts

So, what happens when we realize we need more texts? In a perfect world, school districts would prioritize well-stocked resource sets and classroom libraries. That may not be your reality. We recommend building an order wish list and reaching out to your local PTO or education foundation to see what grant opportunities are available for resources. Additionally, DonorsChoose.org is a fantastic organization that makes it easy to write grants for books and classroom materials. You may also want to reach out to a local company to see if it will hold a book drive to procure texts from your list. Lastly, don't forget about your school and local libraries. A librarian can help you build sets to address gaps while you are working on acquiring more books. Some local libraries offer book bags that you can rotate through the classroom as a supplement. If you are an administrator, setting aside money for every classroom teacher and librarian to purchase texts *every* year can greatly advance the work of equity, inclusion, and empathy building in your school.

Building resource sets takes time, but with an ongoing dedication to providing texts that promote equity, you'll be steadily enhancing the titles you offer your students.

FOLLOW UP

Ensuring that our students are hearing *all* the voices they need to hear in the texts we offer needs to stay on the front burner of our teaching stove. The work we've done in this Try It is not the end goal, but a step that is part of a continual process of becoming and remaining reflective and aware of the stories our students are holding in their hands and the stories that we are presenting in class.

WRITE WITH US

⏻ When you think about the work of building your toolbox and reconsidering the texts you share with students, what feels exciting?

⏻ What strategies do you use to show respect and care when stepping into a student's reading life?

⏻ Where do you feel hesitancy or worry about this work?

⏻ Jot down three things you might do to address these barriers.

⏻ Share your ideas. #ReadTheWorldNow

SHIFTING PERSPECTIVE:
Ask Questions to Understand the Author's Perspective

TRY THIS WHEN . . .

■ you want to highlight how the author's perspective affects the message, information shared, or ideas in a resource

■ students are working with text sets that offer perspectives from different sources and authors.

There are many facets of an author's perspective that we might explore in a literacy classroom. However, we are most concerned with students' ability to accurately identify, analyze, and critique an author's viewpoint in order to further their own critical literacy skills. The internet's omnipresence has given almost everyone the ability to self-publish, widening the possibilities for children, citizen journalists, and marginalized people to share their own stories, ideas, and perspectives. This access has also paved the way for problematic writing, videos, and other forms of digital content to be shared widely. Today's students need to develop a critical position very early in their learning careers. We can build students' skills in understanding who is sharing the information, why that person is sharing the information, what their background and beliefs are, and what they hope the reader will come away with. We find that introducing the simple mantra of "question everything" early on supports students when they encounter more subtly biased sources later in their career.

WHAT TO DO

Present students with a text, video, or image and a chart of focus questions that help students consider a text's author, purpose, and potential biases. The charts on the right show some questions that have worked well for us, but you may wish to brainstorm your own questions with your class. Ask students to keep these questions in mind as they read or view and to jot down comments when they notice evidence that reveals the author's perspective.

We find that it's most effective when students have an immediate basis for comparison, so we recommend offering resource sets that include examples of texts with minimal bias (no text is completely without bias!) as well as biased or intentionally persuasive texts.

Questions We Ask About Authors

- Who is this person? What is their background?
- Does this person have authority?
- What else has this person done?
- Is this author benefiting from sharing this information?
- What story is this author trying to tell?
- Who is the audience the author is creating for?
- What does this author want us to do? Make something? Buy something? Believe something?

Ask questions to understand an *author's* perspective

☐ What do I already know about this author?

☐ What does the author know about this topic? *Look* · author's note · bio · publisher · website

☐ How do we think the author feels about this topic? How can we tell? → What Words do they use? What pictures do they use? What music do they use?

☐ What can we learn about this topic from the author?

Keep questioning !!!

A chart that you co-create with students as you work through this lesson will serve as a guide and reminder when they work independently later. Kristin created this example while working with a fourth-grade class.

Helpful Language

What do we already know about this author?

What information does this author have? What information might they not have?

Are there places in the text where the author is trying to make you think or feel a certain way?

Do you notice any words or phrases that reveal what the author thinks?

Does this text feel objective or biased toward a side?

What other ways might someone write about or explain this information?

Might there be another way to look at this information?

How does this text compare with . . .?

For audio and video: What kind of music is the creator using? What kind of mood do you notice?

What genre of writing is this? What is the source?

How does knowing this piece might be biased inform how you read it?

Is this a trustworthy source?

It's important to note that not all biases are equal in their ability to harm; some biases come with inherent power based on gender, race, socioeconomic status, or other factors. When we evaluate our resource sets, we must be intentional to dedicate ample space and time to explore the voices and stories of those who have historically held less power and also minimize or eliminate resources that reinforce systemic issues of inequality and racism. For example, in an attempt to present all sides of an issue, we can inadvertently reinforce one side if that side is already the predominant viewpoint or narrative and holds power over students in our classroom.

Look for a variety of genres and media relating to your topic— articles, videos, and infographics. The way in which you approach this study will depend on the age of your students and their familiarity with the concept of bias. You might try these strategies:

▶ Present one resource to the whole class. Model your thinking process as you use the questions in the charts on the previous page to determine who the author is and what their bias may be. Then ask students to practice this skill in small groups with a selected source or sources. Students might then report back to the class on what they found and what evidence in the resource supports their thinking.

▶ Select three sources of varying bias and explore each one as a whole class, charting observations and specific evidence like the language the author has used, before releasing students to practice more independently.

▶ After doing some guided practice with the class as a whole, have student partners explore a range of resources and then rank them from least to most biased, or place them on a continuum from bias toward one argument to bias toward the opposing argument. The goal in this work is not the end product but the reasoning that the partners use to consider bias. As they work, listen in to assess what they are noticing in the texts, and consider examples you might share with the class as well as models and areas in which students may need more practice.

Once students have had an opportunity to work with texts while focusing on bias, gather them back together to consider how knowing an author's bias might affect how they read, think about, and interact with the material. We pose the following questions for students to wrestle with through shared discussion and reflection:

▶ *How does knowing an author's bias affect how you feel about the resource?*

▶ *Can we use a resource if it has bias?*

▶ *How might you read a resource that you know will likely have bias, such as an opinion piece?*

To give students wide and varied practice, look for ways to use all types of texts, including those that are specifically designed to be opinion pieces. Op-Eds, blogs, and letters to the editor all offer excellent opinion or argument writing samples for students. Point out how these texts differ from texts that aim (or claim) to be unbiased, such as news articles, when you introduce them. We often ask students to reread, discuss, and revisit their thinking about particular texts once a bias has been clearly identified. Revisiting texts with a critical stance gives students opportunities to grow ideas and reevaluate their initial reactions and takeaways.

OUTCOMES AND WHAT TO LOOK FOR

This lesson asks students to take a critical stance as a strategy for approaching a resource. Can students

▶ work together to brainstorm critical questions they might ask about an author?

▶ read or view with these questions in mind?

▶ analyze information with these questions in mind?

▶ discuss and critique the resource using their critical stance?

▶ ask follow-up questions to "fill in" information or perspectives that might be missing?

FOLLOW UP

Rally students to be aware of perspective and potential bias in *any* resource they encounter, whether it be an article, informational text, infographic, video, image, data set, graph, or advertisement. You might even choose to extend this lesson by asking students to use paper and marker or digital tools to create reminders for themselves—like those shown here—to put on device lock screens, tape into notebooks, or hang on the classroom wall.

Photo by Rolands Zilvinskis from Unsplash. Reproduced with permission.

SHIFTING PERSPECTIVE:
Think from Another Perspective

TRY THIS WHEN . . .

- your class is exploring debatable issues and/or you notice that there are strong viewpoints

- you notice most of the students are considering only one perspective on an issue or topic

- you want students to consider a perspective that differs from their own.

Learning to see an issue from someone else's perspective is perhaps one of the most essential skills we can help students internalize: it serves as a way to bridge differences and bring understanding into debate or discourse. While learning to see from another's perspective is often used during conflict resolution or social-emotional instruction, it also helps us read and understand texts.

WHAT TO DO

Use this lesson with a text set that presents a debatable issue. As always, think beyond print texts: include texts such as videos, audio recordings, infographics, and photographs. Bringing in new topics—Should we be eating bugs? Are robotic exoskeletons for able-bodied people a good thing?—can ignite new thinking. Look for high-interest topics with multiple valid sides that offer fresh ideas to consider. Don't use a topic that is already a contentious area of debate in your school, in your community, or across the country for this introductory lesson: those topics are more likely to yield rehashes of arguments students have already heard than to yield fresh thinking at this point in your work. Save those topics for when your students have already become experts at thinking from another perspective. We find inspiration in our favorite online reading and viewing sources for kids, our own reading lives, and the world around us.

Allow students some time to read through the sources you've gathered and to consider what they think and feel. With younger students, instead of independent reading, we use two or more read-alouds. Students of all ages may find it helpful to use a three-column chart to write down information, questions, and reactions for each source text.

Once students have had some time to critically read the various sources, pose a debatable question about the text set. Ask students to spend a few minutes considering their own viewpoints, listing at least two or three reasons with evidence from the texts. Younger students can whisper talk, draw, write, mentally rehearse, turn and talk to a partner, or use a tool like Flipgrid or Seesaw to capture or share their ideas. In addition to using these options, older students might also jot down their ideas independently. Have students gather in groups with those of like-minded opinions and ask them to share their ideas. When working with older students, we might point out that this is very similar to the social media echo chambers that we create, in which we find our own ideas affirmed time and again. Or ask students to arrange themselves in a human continuum with the strongest advocates of one idea at one end, the strongest advocates of the other idea at the other end, and everyone else positioning themselves according to their feelings between the two ends. Encouraging students to take a stand based on their opinion rather than argue for an assigned opinion, or even an opposing opinion, keeps this work closer to the real-world experience of appreciating others' perspectives even if they differ from your own.

Next, ask students to find someone (or a pair of students, depending on how many students are on each side) who believes differently than they do. As students move into partnerships, their goal is to listen and understand, not to debate. Each partner should have ample time to explain their viewpoint using calm language and "I statements." For younger students, it can sometimes be helpful to use a talking stick or a physical object that signals whose turn it is to speak. At the end of the discussion, each partner should acknowledge the other's viewpoints and share any changes in thinking they had as a result of the discussion. You might find that a quick protocol with sentence stems, like the Switching Perspectives chart on this page, to be helpful.

Finally, ask students to once again reflect either in writing or through discussion: Did their thinking change? How? What did they learn from this process? Primary-grade students might see that there are multiple sides to every story and, based on a specific situation or context, what feels "right" may vary. Older students might reflect on when they might consider different perspectives or opposing views in arguments they encounter: When do they need to set aside their instinct to argue and instead turn on their listening skills?

Phrases We Sometimes Use to Reflect

- At first I thought . . . , but now I'm thinking . . .
- I still believe that . . . However, I can see why someone would think . . . because . . .
- Now that we've talked, I'm wondering about . . .

Switching Perspectives

Sentence stems like these can be helpful while wrapping this lesson up, to help students practice using respectful language when sharing viewpoints other than their own. We've found these to be useful with students of all ages.

- I think . . . because . . . [evidence + personal experience]
- My partner thinks . . . because . . .
- When I take the other side, I see that . . .

OUTCOMES AND WHAT TO LOOK FOR

This lesson asks students to step outside what they believe and try to understand another perspective. Can students

▶ listen patiently and reiterate what someone with an opposing view has to say?

▶ consider an opposing perspective with the aim of understanding it better?

▶ state whether/how hearing another perspective affected their thinking?

FOLLOW UP

Once you've introduced this strategy with a relatively safe topic, use it any time a source of potential disagreement or an opportunity for discourse arises in the classroom. This strategy both honors the way that students think and feel and offers them support and structure for listening to others, reflecting on others' ideas, and allowing themselves to change their own thinking if they wish. This strategy can also be transferred to reading any time students have different interpretations, ideas, or reactions to a text.

SHIFTING PERSPECTIVE:
Tune In to Others

TRY THIS WHEN . . .

▪ students are reading a text that calls for examining different perspectives of characters or people

▪ you want students to consider individual characters' or individuals' perspectives.

This Try It asks students to consider how other people think and feel or believe. By having students then compare those interpretations with their own thinking, we are helping them understand that they, too, have a perspective as they experience history and make sense of events.

WHAT TO DO

Using the framework below, ask students to consider a text from differing viewpoints. You might read the text aloud and complete the chart together during and after discussion, or ask students to work in small groups. Each column represents one person or character who is important to the text, so the frame you use for your chosen text can have as many columns as needed.

My Perspective	Fred Korematsu's Perspective	The People Running the Camp's Perspective
How do I feel? What do I think?	How might this person/character feel? What might they think?	How might this person/character feel? What might they think?
I feel sad and frustrated that we took American citizens and put them in internment camps. I feel angry that the court was so racist. I don't think giving him the medal made it better, because the people lost so much. I think this is happening today. People are still judging others based on race and ethnicity. If I had been a Japanese American in an internment camp, I might not have wanted to be in America anymore.	I think he felt scared but also rebellious. He hid instead of going to the camp. I think he felt like he hadn't done anything wrong and he could fight it. He took his case to the Supreme Court. I think he felt very disappointed and betrayed when he lost his case.	I think some of the people running the camp felt like they were doing the right thing, but maybe some of them didn't and they didn't stand up for the Japanese Americans.

This chart was started with a sixth-grade class reading Fred Korematsu Speaks Up by Laura Atkins and Stan Yogi. Students then continued to add their own thinking and feelings as they read.

Students in Bridgette Hurst's fifth-grade class consider perspectives while viewing "If You Fall" by Tisha Deb Pillai.

What I feel...

- I feel like babba is a very helpful person.

- I am thinking that babba wants to make Lila smile :)

- I feel like babba and Lila have a strong connection, and a good friendship!

- I also think that a lot of things are very hard to come to and pay for.

- I also think that Lila always wants her mom to be with her.

- I am seeing that Lila is not always happy with her mom if she can't go to "EVERYTHING".

- I also feel like it is important that Lila learns to do something by herself and not with baba.

- What I think is that parents should be able to be with their kids but they also have to have a job to pay for things in their family.

↑ My thinking

What the character feels...

- Babba is always there for Lila!

- Babba wants to be an awesome parent he trys to make her mom come to.

- Also babba wants her to learn how to do things on her own.

- Babba wants the most attention on Lila as he can give her.

- Babba is next to and with Lila always.

- The character also feels bad for Lila at many times.

- Lila was feeling very happy when baba put up the painting because, she really loved his paintings!

- Lila finally learns to do something by herself without babba when she rides her bike by herself.

- Lila is happy when both of her parents are together and with her.

BABA (point of view)

Helpful Language

Let's think about how the people [characters] we are reading about might think and feel at this moment. Put yourself in their shoes.

What other perspectives might be worth exploring to help us better understand this issue?

Let's take a minute to reread and really think from this person's perspective.

What words or phrases in the text are informing our thinking here?

I think the character feels . . . because the text says . . .

[For younger students]: Read the faces of the characters. How can you tell what they are feeling? What do you see that makes you say that?

Also Try

Short films, such as Jacob Frey's animated short *The Present* (bit.ly/2Ouo8Jp) or Daniel Martínez Lara and Rafa Cano Méndez's *Alike* (bit.ly/2mEZM1E), can also offer opportunities to tune in to others' perspectives.

Students might also continue to add columns for other individuals as they consider who else may have a differing opinion on the text. For example, when students are reading a text about Japanese internment in World War II, the chart might first address the people named directly in the text, but students might go on to consider the viewpoint of President Roosevelt, military personnel, or other interested parties.

Once students have had an opportunity to consider the different perspectives in a text, work through three sharing rounds as a class. Invite volunteers to first share what they felt and thought, then what the characters felt and thought, and, finally, what they noticed about the work of considering their own perspectives separately from the perspectives of others. How did they feel? What challenged them? Were there points when they realized they had to rethink something? If so, what happened?

Remind students that, while we can draw conclusions and do our best to empathize, we can never truly know what it is like to live from another person's perspective: unless we have a direct quotation or other specific, clear evidence, we cannot be certain about what a person or character feels or thinks. However, we can do our best to try to understand others' perspectives and grow our own empathy by listening carefully to others. In real-life interactions, this means listening with the aim of learning, not passing judgment or making assumptions. In texts, this means paying close attention to what we learn about a character. In conferences or small groups, continually direct students back to the text when they make an assertion, asking them to point out specific words or phrases that are informing their thinking, to interpret images, and to connect to other texts they've read to ensure that their inferences are grounded in evidence, not their own perspectives or assumptions.

For primary-grade students, we might begin this lesson with a picture book read-aloud and ask them to draw characters or faces and use speech bubbles and captions to show what they think and feel. This can be completed as a class, with students sharing verbally or on sticky notes, or in small groups, with partners, or independently.

OUTCOMES AND WHAT TO LOOK FOR

Students should be able to demonstrate that they can use literacy, empathy, and critical thinking to consider and tune in to others. Can students

▶ identify the different viewpoints within and beyond the text that are relevant to the reading?

▶ effectively place themselves in the place of a person or character, drawing on text evidence and personal experiences?

FOLLOW UP

We can follow this lesson with a reflection where students consider how tuning in to how others might feel and comparing that with their own feelings and thoughts enriches their understanding. For example, students might take a moment to reflect and jot down how considering others' perspectives challenged or changed them. Once students have become familiar with this strategy using texts, the same strategy can also be used for real-world conflict resolution.

SHIFTING PERSPECTIVE:
Build Our Empathy Vocabulary

TRY THIS WHEN . . .

- you notice students could use support in having more empathetic responses in social or academic settings

- you are moving into studying a topic that may be sensitive for some (or all) students

- you are deepening students' ability to understand and/or write about emotions in characters.

Equipping students with language to identify and express their emotions helps them better evaluate how they are feeling in any given situation, as well as observe and connect with others' emotions. Encouraging students to connect their own daily emotions to those of characters or people they may read about helps them understand themselves better and respond to others with compassion.

WHAT TO DO

Select a picture book that names different emotions to launch the lesson (see the box on this page for ideas). If you're working with older students who are not used to seeing picture books in class, take this opportunity to remind them that picture books are often far more complicated than they might seem, and that everything from the word choices to the illustrations in a strong picture book is highly intentional.

Read the book with students and use it to begin a chart of emotion words for students to use during lessons and discussions. Ask students if they have any additional words beyond those in the book that they would like to add. Discuss, act out, or invite students to tableau (Steineke 2009) the words to build a common understanding of their meaning.

Give students an opportunity to practice using the words right away by viewing a short video with a range of emotions. Our favorites for this work include

- ▶ *The Pits* by Mike Hayhurst (bit.ly/2mqUgUZ)

- ▶ *Luxo Jr. [Pencil Test]*, a Pixar wireframe by John Lasseter (bit.ly/2m0vE59)

- ▶ *If You Fall* by Tisha Deb Pillai (bit.ly/2kSMnXO).

Helpful Language

What emotions do we see in this text? Have you ever felt that way? Show me what that looked like.

What might be some clues that someone else is feeling this way?

What other emotions can we add to our chart?

Why might it be important to understand how a character or person is feeling?

Picture Books for Discussing Emotions

These are a few books that work well with this lesson:

The Feelings Book by Todd Parr

I Am Human: A Book of Empathy by Susan Verde

I Wish You More by Amy Krouse Rosenthal

In My Heart: A Book of Feelings by Jo Witek

Say Something by Peter H. Reynolds

Physical Response to Emotion

wide eyes → surprise, fear, question

eyebrows down → mad, angry

circle mouth → surprise, new learning, wow!

squiggle mouth → confused, nervous, unsure

tears → sad, joy, scared, worry

arms crossed → mad, scared, protect me, stay away, cold

A first-grade classroom uses picture books as mentor text to identify facial expressions and the body's physical response to emotions. They refer to this chart as a tool for interpreting how characters and classmates may be feeling. Helping kids identify how a person is feeling is foundational for productive face-to-face interactions.

Ask students to view the video in pairs and to stop the video periodically to discuss it, jotting down the different emotions that the characters feel as the video progresses. Then, ask students to identify the clues that helped them identify the emotions in these characters—a movement? a sound? a posture? a pause? You might note the types of clues on a chart to help students consider others' emotions as they read, view, and discuss.

When the chart is complete, review it with students. Ask: *Do these examples hold true of every community and culture?* People from different cultures and communities act and react in a variety of ways. This is a good time to explore any differences your students may name. If none arise, this could be a potential area for investigation.

At some point during the lesson, either as a lesson launch or during an end-of-lesson share, bring students together to discuss how being able to identify our own emotions and the emotions of others helps us be better friends, more empathetic classmates, and more effective communicators. This could take place as a whole-class or small-group discussion or a more personal written or digital reflection and share. If students need more support in this skill, consider drawing on your shared experiences with stories and characters, reaching back into books you've shared to offer specific moments to explore together.

OUTCOMES AND WHAT TO LOOK FOR

Students should be able to identify, name, and demonstrate facial expressions or body language that conveys emotion. Can students

▶ list common emotions and act out or show what they might look like?

▶ discuss subtleties and specifics of language used to show emotions?

▶ identify and explain emotions present in media?

▶ explain why it's important for us to be able to identify emotions in ourselves and others?

▶ recognize how context, culture, and the range of human ability contributes to expression of emotion?

▶ notice and respect how different people react in different ways?

FOLLOW UP

Refer back to the co-constructed charts from this lesson any time it might be helpful to remind students to be aware of their own emotions or the emotions of others. This might be during a literacy or writing lesson, when discussing a character, or during a discussion of a sensitive issue. You might also offer students emotion check-ins, giving them a moment for a quick private reflection or time to jot in a notebook. These check-ins are for the students' own metacognition, not for sharing with others. We often use this strategy before, during, and after a conversation, dispute, or learning activity.

WRITE WITH US

⏻ **In this section's Try Its, what connections did you make to empathy in your own life?**

⏻ **What students did you think of as you read this section? What do you think brought them to mind?**

⏻ **When do you see empathy in your classroom? How can you provide more opportunities for your students to grow their empathy?**

⏻ **Share your ideas. #ReadTheWorldNow**

RESPONDING AND CONNECTING:
Communicate with Emojis

TRY THIS WHEN . . .

◼ you are helping students grow their digital communication skills

◼ students discover the emoji keyboard and are using winky faces (or poop emojis) in lieu of a clear explanation of their ideas.

Emojis are, perhaps, not beloved by all educators. We get it: a cartoon (of, say, an alien head) is not the same thing as a nuanced explanation, and the imprecision of emojis can lead to serious misunderstandings: Is that laughing face laughing *with* me or *at* me? Is that pouty face telling me that someone is annoyed at something unrelated to me, or is it meant to be an insult? However, emojis can also be hugely helpful in clarifying digital communication: they give us a way to compensate for the lack of intonation, emotion, and body language in typed communication. Emojis provide a way for students to show feeling. To help students become stronger online communicators, we can develop classroom guidelines and common expectations for emojis that enhance—rather than complicate—online communication.

WHAT TO DO

Gather students together and let them know that today you're going to do an inquiry into how using emojis might help or hurt their communication efforts. Ask students to look over the emoji options on their devices and brainstorm with a partner about which emojis might be useful for certain situations, such as writing or reacting to book reviews, crafting a response to a video, having a digital discussion, or doing a mood check-in. Create a chart (this might be a great one to try digitally) of common emojis that the class agrees will enhance and amplify communication; add any guidelines needed for your community. Now give students an opportunity to try the emojis out right away in a few quick digital notes to classmates.

After students have received some emoji comments, ask them to revisit what they thought and how they felt when they received them. You might ask students:

▶ *How did receiving an emoji feel? Do you think that's what the person who gave it to you intended?*

▶ *Did you get any emojis that you want to try using?*

▶ *Did you get any that made you feel confused, sad, or angry? Why? How can we address that?*

Helpful Language

Which of the emojis feel meaningful to the work we do at school?

Which emojis would you like to get in a comment or see in a discussion?

Let's agree right now what this emoji will mean if someone uses it in our class. Of course, we can't guarantee that people outside our classroom will have the same understanding.

We can show respect to each other with the emojis we choose. Think about what an emoji is saying before you include it, and ask yourself, "Is this really what I want to be saying to a friend or in school?"

How many emojis do you think are appropriate for a response? Why?

OUTCOMES AND WHAT TO LOOK FOR

This lesson gets the classroom community on the same page about how emojis can enhance their interactions, what the common meaning is of those emojis, and any other community guidelines that need to be established. Can students

▶ identify emojis that are helpful in furthering understanding of comments, reactions, and conversation?

▶ identify emojis that might demonstrate empathy, understanding, and perspective taking?

▶ identify emojis that are easily misinterpreted, enigmatic, negative, or unwanted as part of the community?

▶ establish and follow guidelines for emoji use?

FOLLOW UP

Over time the class may wish to add more emojis to the chart, take some off, or clarify use. Of course, you may have a student or two who forgets or misuses emojis. When this happens, remind students of the shared expectations that they created together and offer opportunities to demonstrate growth.

Room 302 Emoji Chart

If you want to say . . .	Then use . . .
I strongly agree with what you are saying. I agree with this. You've done a fantastic job.	😍 😊 🙂
This is funny! It made me laugh! • Always make sure the person intended to use humor; we don't want to laugh at anyone.	😄 😆

This example of a chart used by a fifth-grade class features emojis that the class agreed would be acceptable to use during their digital interactions.

RESPONDING AND CONNECTING:
Use Different Lenses

TRY THIS WHEN . . .

■ you're planning a unit, a lesson, or a series of lessons to support students in reading short informational texts, blogs, or videos

■ you're addressing current events that affect your students and classroom, or that relate to overarching topics of study.

Beyond the time we devote to them in class, current events make their way into our classrooms through resources our students access and through concerns that students bring to school. In these situations, it's often the case that only one element of the event surfaces, without context or multiple viewpoints. We can show our students that any topic or issue is multifaceted: we can work with them to build our understanding in a holistic way, intentionally seeking out perspectives other than our own. This work helps students see how additional perspectives can offer us a more thorough understanding, a compassionate course of action, or an educated stance that anchors discussion and debate. Additional perspectives may even change our thinking. In short, getting the full picture makes us better members of the wider community.

WHAT TO DO

Kristin likes to launch this lesson by passing around a few kaleidoscopes and asking students to look through them, describing how the image changes. She encourages students to connect their changing views with reading, noting that what we think or pay attention to can change based on the intention behind the reading. Another option is to show students a quick video of 3-D sculptures that change as the viewer adjusts their point of view (for example, try an online search for videos using the term, "sculpture changes at different angles"). This provides an engaging and concrete way to demonstrate how our perception is affected by our own perspective. In art, our perspective is the spot where we're standing. In reading, our perspective is influenced by our background, experiences, biases, and beliefs.

Decide on two articles that students can read independently and that show different perspectives on the same topic. If you are struggling to locate full-text articles that feel appropriate for your students or that have the perspectives you are looking for, consider using smaller snippets—a few paragraphs—of a text intended for adults. We often select portions

Questions We May Ask to Consider a Text from Multiple Viewpoints

- Who's telling this information? Why?
- What information aren't they telling us?
- What values, cultures, or beliefs are represented in this story?
- Where am I in this story? How does my experience color my understanding?
- What's on the other side of the story?
- How might people around the world interpret this message?
- How does the author attract my attention? Do those techniques guide my thinking in any way?
- Do illustrations or photos provide additional information?
- Where can we go to find more information?

of opinion articles from different resources, using small selections of the text that feature descriptive language or quotes that reveal the author's perspective. Once you've introduced the concept of perspective, provide students with the first article—or excerpt—to read independently or with a partner, and ask them to describe the author's perspective, citing evidence from the text. Then, give students the second article or excerpt.

Use the questions below to prompt discussion among students.

▶ *What do you notice about the perspective of each article?*

▶ *How is the language different in the two articles?*

▶ *What information is shared or left out from each side?*

▶ *How does understanding the various sides of an issue help you be a more critical reader?*

▶ *Why do you think people need to understand sides of an issue that they may not agree with?*

These questions—particularly the last question—may not be fully answered in a single discussion. Consider this lesson to be the beginning of a larger conversation that will last throughout the year. Revisit these questions as you explore more topics of study and as you encounter situations in which not everyone agrees—in current events, in real life, and even in the pages of a book.

During these discussions we, as teachers, want to make sure that we take a back seat to the conversation. We want students to look at and talk to one another, not to feel as if they are in a question and answer session. To encourage this kind of discussion among students, you might try these strategies:

▶ Set students up in a circle, or facing one another, while you sit off to the side.

▶ Write or type questions and give them to students to read or share with the group. Give each student a silent nod when it's time for them to chime in with their question.

▶ If students turn toward you, turn the discussion back to the group and ask them: *Who would like to build on that thinking? Who will carry that idea on?* or *Who would like to respond?*

▶ Offer a talking object that students pass from one to another to signify who has the floor, leaving the teacher out of the equation.

▶ Jot notes to students rather than interjecting.

Above all, let silence sit. Let the students fill the silent moments with their own ideas, thoughts, and reactions.

To end the discussion, we might ask students to respond with a bit of micro-writing to a given prompt such as *What are you taking with you from this discussion?* This can be done on sticky notes, on chart paper, or with a digital tool. You might allow them to choose if their response will be shared or not.

OUTCOMES AND WHAT TO LOOK FOR

This lesson asks students to begin the work of being keen observers of perspective. Can students

▶ identify an author's perspective based on the information explicitly and implicitly stated?

▶ engage in critical analysis of a topic or issue to determine which perspectives may be missing from a source?

FOLLOW UP

Offering multiple perspectives isn't about offering many stories for the sake of curiosity—it's about good teaching practice and habits for life. When we make a habit of giving students multiple texts on a topic, we teach them to expect to closely read, analyze, evaluate, and synthesize on a deeply cognitive level (Cummins 2018). Each time students are reading an article online about a current event, consider: Does it represent multiple viewpoints? What other articles could be added to enrich their understanding of the situation? Then, ensure that student get to see those other perspectives.

Applying these same principles to our own reading can help us make this a habit in our classrooms. Consider which sources you use most often and compare them with sources that offer a differing viewpoint. How does the language shift? What information is shared or left out from each side? Where does the article connect with your emotions, and how does it do that?

RESPONDING AND CONNECTING:
Lay the Foundation for Discussions

TRY THIS WHEN . . .

▪ you're ready to have students reflect on and synthesize a learning experience

▪ you want to ensure that all students feel heard and safe in a discussion.

When a topic is close to home and close to the heart, it's not uncommon for teachers to shy away from discussing it in the classroom: in many schools, it has become an unspoken rule to avoid the ire of the community. However, we must also consider that, without open discussion, biases and misunderstandings can be left to fester. We create a positive school climate not by teaching lessons in equity, citizenship, and diversity in isolation, but by addressing these as a habit for living. If we do not address difficult conversations, we run the risk of signaling to students that challenging or emotionally-charged topics are not to be explored. As educators, many of us bring feelings of discomfort into our classrooms because when we were young an adult in our life signaled there were topics "not to be discussed." In a 2017 interview, Beverly Daniel Tatum affirmed that when children's questions are labeled as something that should not be talked about, children associate emotional responses to those topics that may include fear, shame, anger, sadness, and confusion (Anderson 2017). But, if not in our classrooms, where else will children find a safe space to ask and discuss big issues of the heart? Today we find ourselves in a world that needs to be heard, respected, and affirmed. And the only way to build empathy and grow understanding is to talk about it.

WHAT TO DO

Identify a point in your plans when you think students will benefit from a thoughtful discussion. It might be when you are reflecting on a particularly challenging day's learning, or perhaps after reading a rich text. When you reach this point, offer students a 3–2–1 format for focusing their ideas, thoughts, and feelings. You'll find a blank 3-2-1 page located in the book's online digital resources at Hein.pub/RTW-Resources. The structure can be tweaked any number of ways. We might ask students to

▶ write down three things they've learned from the text, two questions they have, and one thing they enjoyed (a version that the organization Facing History and Ourselves often uses)

The Water Walker

☐ The Mother Earth water walkers walked all around the Great Lakes. — Celia

☐ They carried a pail of water with them. — Zander

☐ Nokomis used 11 pairs of sneakers and 3 knees walking! — Diana & Maria

☐ Why did they think walking could help? — Alex, Carson & Rhett

☐ Are there still water walkers today? — Ben, Anna & Elise

☐ We felt challenged by the idea that someone would give up so much for something like water. It made us want to learn, think, and do more about this topic.

Third-grade students used the 3-2-1 structure to guide a conversation about their reactions to the book The Water Walker / Nibi Emosaawdang *by Joanne Robertson. The teacher prompted:* Write down three things you learned from the book, two questions you had, and one thing that was confusing or challenging to understand. *Students first jotted in their notebooks, then shared, discussed, and came to a consensus about what to include on their chart. The teacher noted student names where appropriate.*

This printable tool can be downloaded at Hein.pub/RTW-Resources.

Helpful Language

Consider your words as you write.

If you're not sure what to write, go back into the texts and see what might be there that you missed the first time around.

Let's take a minute and talk about how the ideas that were just shared build on one another.

What patterns are you seeing emerge here?

Does anyone have, or can anyone think of, a perspective that hasn't been shared already?

Has your thinking changed about this? How so?

▶ write down three things they learned, two questions they have, and one idea that challenged or changed them

▶ write down three things they are feeling, two things they want to comment on, and one burning question to discuss or research.

Notice how each of these variations

▶ asks for responses regarding the student's learning or the student's perspective—not "correct" answers

▶ includes at least one prompt related to the student's opinions or ideas

▶ values the student's questions as a starting point for discussion or learning more

▶ uses the 3–2–1 strategy as a funnel that concentrates initial impressions into a more refined question or idea.

For younger students, we can use this strategy in a whole-class discussion, in conversation, or by inviting students to draw and write their thinking.

For example, in one fourth-grade class the teacher read aloud *The Day You Begin* by Jacqueline Woodson. This story, about owning our identities with pride, brought up many different kinds of emotions and connections for students. After reading, the class used the 3–2–1 strategy with the following prompts:

Write down three thoughts or feelings you had while you were reading.

Write down two thoughts or feelings you think someone else might have had while reading.

Write down one thing you'd like to do after having read this book.

The teacher crafted these prompts to encourage students to think in a way that would increase the empathy and understanding of the classroom community and help them internalize the message in a way that would have a lasting impact. While she knew that she wouldn't accomplish this in one lesson, this read-aloud, accompanied by myriad read-alouds and learning conversations across the year, would have a lasting impact on her students.

As you decide which prompts to provide students for the most impact, consider how each type of prompt will lead them to think in different directions and how it will focus student understanding of the resource, discussion, or experience. In some cases, you may wish to offer students a choice or allow them to design their own reflections.

If you want students to . . .	Try . . .
identify the most important new learning of the day to promote retention	Jot down _____ pieces of new information, _____ facts, and ideas from the resource.
see the importance of questions and/or launch a mini-inquiry	Write down _____ questions you have about the text.
have practice in showing empathy	Write down _____ emotions you were feeling. or Write down _____ emotions that someone else in the story might be feeling. or Write down _____ emotions that someone else in the world might feel about this.
identify the words that speak most strongly to them	Write down _____ quotes, ideas, phrases, or words from the text that you want to take with you.
synthesize a single lesson or text with other learning moments to develop a wider understanding	List _____ personal connections. or List _____ connections to another text. or List _____ connections to the world.
focus on key words and understanding of concepts	Write _____ words that are new to you, that have been used in a new way, or that you'd like to discuss.

Options for 3–2–1 reflections. Indicate the number of responses you would like students to give three, two, or one where the line is located.

The 3–2–1 reflection serves as a preparatory exercise for a larger discussion in the class. You might choose to embark on this discussion as a whole group or in smaller groups depending on your students. The purpose is to offer a starting place that can take students to a more in-depth discussion about a text, resource, or topic. You might have students share one item they wrote down as a way to kick off the discussion or ask one student to share and then prompt with questions like *Who has something similar?* or *Who would like to offer a different idea?* As students speak, help them connect their ideas to one another, see patterns in their responses, fill in gaps in perspective, and notice when they've developed new ideas. Again, we carefully moderate our own role, taking care to listen more than we speak and to ask questions instead of tell.

If moving to a discussion seems overwhelming, you might instead try asking students to form an inside circle and an outside circle, partnering with the person across from them. Students share at your direction, then rotate to a new partner. You might ask students first to share their three items, then to rotate and share their two items with a new partner, and so on, ending with a final partner for reflection. This strategy can also be used as a warm-up for the discussion: when you gather the class, you can prompt students to talk about someone else's idea that challenged their own.

OUTCOMES AND WHAT TO LOOK FOR

The purpose of this reflection is to help students identify their own thinking and think through different lenses as they prepare for a discussion. Can students

▶ use the given prompts to dig deep and consider their own learning, emotions, and reactions?

▶ share their thinking and listen attentively to others?

▶ use the reflection as a way to prepare themselves to participate in a class discussion?

FOLLOW UP

Once students are familiar with this strategy, allow them to take ownership of the labels for 3–2–1. Have students contribute ideas as a class or design their own structure for responding and connecting. You may want to have students meet in partners or in small groups to discuss their responses. This can be done randomly or by collecting student responses and creating some intentional groupings to begin the next day's class. You may wish to reflect on student responses in order to determine the next steps for learning and adjust their sequence of lessons.

The 3–2–1 strategy is just as useful to adults as to children. In reflecting on a lesson, you might write three things that showed students were moving toward the learning target, two questions they probably still have, and one adjustment you need to make. Or perhaps a more individual focused response might be three students whom you need to circle back with, two students whose ideas you want to amplify, and one student whom you need to do a better job of connecting with.

Not every discussion will require or even benefit from this kind of structure—sometimes it's best to simply ask kids to turn and talk to a partner and honor the organic groupings that take place within our rooms. Consider the following as you plan discussion options in your classroom:

▶ Will students benefit from a great deal of teacher facilitation or less teacher facilitation?

▶ Can students be matched to small groups or partner randomly? Would an intentional pairing support or deepen a conversation?

▶ Does this topic have the potential to get heated? What supports before, during, and after discussion can be put in place to address this?

▶ Are there any specific students who will need additional supports to be successful?

▶ Does this discussion need to take place face-to-face or digitally?

▶ What structures are most likely to ensure a high level of engagement and energy for this discussion?

Join the Conversation:
Difficult Conversations

"There are difficult conversations that will occur in our classroom. If we don't make space for them, then where will kids learn how to have them?"

#ReadTheWorldNow

Hein.pub/RTW3.3

RESPONDING AND CONNECTING:
Write to Process Thinking and Emotions

TRY THIS WHEN . . .

■ you are delving into topics, issues, or resources that have the potential to elicit strong emotions from students

■ a classroom discussion is becoming one-sided or heated

■ you notice emotions bubbling to the surface that students need time to process.

Writing is one of our best tools to help students make sense of the world around them. We can use writing as a strategy for students to consider their own thoughts, give voice to things they might not otherwise say, process strong feelings, reflect, and even communicate with us.

WHAT TO DO

The chart on the next page shows several ways we might utilize writing as a way for students to process thinking depending on the nature of the conversation and subject matter.

You'll notice that these strategies rely primarily on students writing independently. While there are times when we want students to connect with an audience for their work, we also want to be mindful that often students need time to process their thinking in a more private manner. These private opportunities offer students time to identify their thoughts and emotions, explore them in a safe and nonjudgmental way, and process their thinking before sharing in a more public way like a discussion, blog post, or video.

Your response to students' writing depends on the situation—if students are writing to you, you may wish to follow up with them by either writing back to them or having a conversation. In other situations, it may help to debrief with a colleague, school social worker, or coach to analyze what worked well in a challenging situation and what steps you might take the next time around. As we reflect on this work, it's important for us to remember our role as educators. Students may feel or think things that we disagree with. It is our duty not to ensure all students think and believe as we do but to teach them to think for themselves. Our work is to help cultivate critical, thoughtful, and empathetic children in the hope that they will go on to embody these qualities in their adult life and, we hope, take steps to make the world a better place.

When . . .	We might try . . .	Examples
we need students to be aware of how their thinking shifts and changes as they get new information	using a three-column organizer that helps students privately identify beliefs and thinking before, during, and after reading or talking	▶ Column 1: *At first I thought . . .* ▶ Column 2: *Some new information I'm hearing is . . .* ▶ Column 3: *Now I think . . .*
we want to honor each student's process for thinking and feeling	giving students two to four minutes for private journaling using a thought prompt or sentence stem	▶ *This makes me think . . . because . . .* ▶ *This makes me feel . . . because . . .* ▶ *Something I wish my classmates could understand is . . .* ▶ *Something I'm confused about is . . .*
we want to check in on students' emotions	giving a paper or digital survey	▶ *How are you feeling right now?* ▶ *Is there anything you'd like to share with me about today's discussion?* ▶ *What can I, as your teacher, do in the future to help discussions like this go more smoothly?* ▶ *What do you wish your classmates could understand right now?*
we want to help students process or think through a difficult discussion	prompting students with a sentence stem	▶ *Something that is weighing on my heart from today's discussion is . . .* ▶ *I think a next step for the class with this topic is . . .* ▶ *In order to move forward I need . . .* ▶ *One thing that would have helped our discussion go more smoothly is . . .*

- This makes me think...because...
- This makes me feel...because...
- Something I wish my classmates could understand is...
- Something I'm confused about is...

This makes me think that the government of the starving people's countries should pay more attention to the hungry people. Something I'm confused about is why the government of those countries aren't doing a lot. Why don't they focus more on the people.

This makes me feel bad because In america, we take all this stuff for granted, and we can't even emagine 1/1000 of what these people are going through.

Eva

Fifth-grade students write to process their thinking, revealing their understandings and new directions for learning.

- This makes me think...because...
- This makes me feel...because...
- Something I wish my classmates could understand is...
- Something I'm confused about is...

Something I wish my classmates could understand is how kids all around the world have the same dreams as us. and are struggling to stay alive because of world hunger.

This makes me think that world hunger is still a big problem around the world.

This makes me feel because kids are around the world are struggling to stay alive just because of hunger.

These printable tools can be downloaded at Hein.pub/RTW-Resources.

OUTCOMES AND WHAT TO LOOK FOR

The message we are sending to students here is that their feelings matter and that writing is a way for us to process our thoughts and emotions, a safe space to work through tough topics. Can students

▶ stop and write about their thoughts, reactions, feelings, interpretations, or questions when faced with a tough topic, resource, or conversation?

▶ reflect on how things went during a class and how they might have gone better?

▶ reflect on how they will move forward, or what action they might wish to take?

FOLLOW UP

Navigating difficult topics in the classroom is complex work. These reflection moments help students process their thinking, and they help us, their teachers, understand how we can better support and coach them. When taken together over time, reflections can provide evidence of how our students are learning and growing. Rather than looking at these reflections as one-time events, look at the arc of students' reflections across the year. What growth do you see? In what areas do you see the need for more growth?

Helpful Language

Let's take a few minutes to reflect on what we're thinking.

I see a lot of you have strong feelings about this. Let's take a moment to write about our feelings.

Will you help me by sharing some of your thoughts about our discussion today? I've put a link to a quick survey on the board. As always, these answers will be kept private.

Let's draw about how we are feeling. Do a quick sketch in your notebook.

Student Privacy

Trust is an important part of the student-teacher relationship, and we let students know when work is to be shared or kept private. We take student desire for privacy very seriously and maintain that privacy to the greatest extent possible. That said, we also know that sometimes students use these moments to share deeply personal information that requires action on our part. Always use your professional judgment and talk with the support staff at your school in the event that a student divulges information that indicates they are in danger or wish to do harm to themselves or others.

TRY IT!

RESPONDING AND CONNECTING:
Foster Listening Discussions

Helpful Language

Let's think about some things we might say or do when we want the other person to know we are really listening to them.

What might we say when we want to acknowledge that someone else thinks differently than we do?

What else would you like to hear during a discussion?

TRY THIS WHEN . . .

- you are establishing a classroom community at the beginning of the year

- you notice that students have mastered basic discussion techniques and would benefit from instruction on how to further their skills

- you anticipate a discussion or situation that might come with strong emotions.

When we were new teachers, the accepted wisdom was that discussion skills could be easily addressed by teaching students to disagree using polite language. In truth, the language of discussion goes much deeper than merely stating your own opinions nicely. Discussions should have language that honors the thoughts, beliefs, and ideas of others and demonstrates that the speaker is taking a listening stance to truly understand and honor the other person's beliefs, even if they do not agree with them. Using listening language is essential in today's classroom as our students come from a wide variety of backgrounds and beliefs, even in communities that may, at first, appear homogeneous. By teaching students how to listen, we can then support them in responding to the ideas of others.

WHAT TO DO

Ask students to take a minute and either talk or write about how people might demonstrate a listening stance during discussions. Then, create a

This chart was created by a team of fifth- and sixth-grade teachers after synthesizing ideas that their classes came up with, in order to honor the thinking of the students while offering some new language for them to try out during discussions. Teachers decided to organize the phrases into different categories to help students find the language they were looking for to address different situations.

Acknowledge what the other person is saying or acknowledge the risk they are taking	Or ask for more information	Then, give your own thoughts, ideas, opinions, or questions	Acknowledge when someone else has challenged your ideas or changed your thinking
So what you're saying is . . . I think what you're saying is . . . That's an interesting viewpoint I hadn't considered before. Thank you for sharing your thinking. Thank you for taking a risk in sharing.	Can you tell me more about . . . ? I'm not sure I understand. Can you give me another example? What do you mean when you say . . . ?	I agree with you because . . . Another way we might look at this is . . . I had a different reaction to this, which was . . .	I hadn't thought about it that way. I'll have to think about that. I appreciate that you shared a different opinion from mine. This was a helpful conversation. Now that you've said that, I'm thinking. . .

chart with students that shows examples of language they might use when having a discussion or conversation. Honor the language of your students; listening language comes in many forms.

Beginning with ideas from students provides us an opportunity to model respect for them and show that we hear their thoughts and honor their ideas. Then, as we add to the chart, we can weave in language that builds upon student ideas. Phrases like the ones listed below introduce new framing and build a more robust language repertoire for future conversations.

▶ *When you said _____, that made me think of _____. Maybe we can add that too?*

▶ *I like the way you're thinking. Could we build on that idea and also say _____? May I write that on the chart?*

▶ *The other day I heard a friend say _____. What do you think about adding that to our chart as well?*

Additionally, you might work with students to consider how body language conveys a listening stance. Create a chart with students with drawn or photographed examples of body language that can help support strong and open discussions. As in the Build Our Empathy Vocabulary Try It (pp. 127–129), remind students that context, culture, and range of human ability may also contribute to body language and expression of emotion.

Once you have established expectations and supports, help students internalize and practice using this language in discussions. You might try these strategies.

▶ Model using this language yourself during lessons and discussions.

▶ Give students multiple opportunities to practice using the language by turning and talking with partners.

▶ Coach into conversations as students practice by prompting students with sentence stems as they talk.

▶ Set intentions for using language during conversations. Reflect on language use after.

▶ Give students reminders of these language tools, perhaps on charts or bookmarks.

Sharing Our Ideas

Thank you for sharing, [student's name]. I would like to add on . . .

I agree with [person's name] because . . .

I would like to respectfully disagree with the idea that . . . because . . .

I was interested in what [person's name] had to say, but I was wondering . . . [question about what the person said.]

Third-grade students tried on using new phrases to make their discussions more productive and show they were listening to each other. In this class, the teacher also chose to make discussion groups smaller to give students more opportunities to practice and participate, moving from groups of six or seven students to groups of three or four students.

Fourth-grade students worked together to choose a few key phrases that would help them show they were listening to each other, were considering what group members said, or had a different idea to offer.

OUTCOMES AND WHAT TO LOOK FOR

The outcome of this lesson should be a general consensus among classmates for how to proceed in classroom discussions and the addition of some tools to help students accomplish this. Can students

▶ consider a time when they were in a discussion that went well or didn't go well?

▶ identify key language?

▶ think of ways to honor other people's ideas and perspectives during a discussion?

▶ find language and body movements that show they are listening and thinking about what others have to say?

FOLLOW UP

Revisit these strategies for practice and keep language visible for students until they have internalized it in their spoken and written comments to one another. Take a coaching stance: offer opportunities to revisit a chart before commenting, give students opportunities to revise their comments, and prompt students to use the language as they carry on conversations or make comments by using visual tools (charts) or voice-overs (sentence frames that you prompt students to use during discussions). It is also helpful to model and encourage a revision mindset when it comes to language and the way we coach and respond to students. We might pause when talking and say, *Let me rephrase that using one of our sentence stems* or *Let me try again*. Showing students that they can review their words or have another go at it helps establish a classroom atmosphere in which growth and change for the better are valued. Even our interactions with colleagues can be models of close listening for our students.

WRITE WITH US

⏻ As you consider how you might help students respond and connect, how are you feeling right now? What thrills you? What scares you?

⏻ What more do you want to know, talk about, practice, or watch? Take some time to watch Dr. Brené Brown's *The Power of Empathy* (bit.ly/1CvgPCn). Journal a bit here about how Brown's work connects with the work in this chapter.

⏻ In the video, Brown says: "Rarely can a response make something better. What makes something better is connection" (2013). How does this quote connect to you, to your students, and to your teaching practice?

⏻ What will your first step be in bringing this work to your classroom?

⏻ Share your ideas. #ReadTheWorldNow

4 *Student Agency*
Rethinking Action for a Better World

As students begin to read the world and take a more empathetic stance on the stories of others, they also begin to identify problems they want to fix. Some of these students address local concerns, like the first-grade class that developed public service announcements to raise awareness about train safety—a critical issue in a town with three railroad lines. Other students realize that the problems they would like to fix affect people in faraway places, such as the fifth graders who passionately researched issues of child labor in chocolate production and started a campaign to encourage others to buy certified fair trade and labor-free products. Or the group of kindergartners who raised funds to donate mosquito nets to protect children in areas plagued by malaria. At times, students find themselves deeply embroiled in issues of equity, race, and adult power struggles, as the students of the National Teachers Academy did when Chicago's mayor decided to close their successful South Side elementary school. With the help of teachers Mia Leonard and Autumn Laidler, students researched, wrote letters, and spoke at press conferences. They raised difficult questions about why their city would want to close a school that had been central to their community—a community largely made up of people of color—to replace it with a selective enrollment high school. In the end, they were able to keep their school, largely due to the efforts of these students and teachers and their community.

If we look around, we see a generation of young people poised and ready to make an impact on the world, whether it be by doing a kind act on the playground, performing a public service in the community, raising awareness about an issue, collecting donations for those in need, making a personal pledge to change a behavior, contacting members of government, or protesting for a cause they believe in.

As Kristin's first-grade student said in the quotation on the right, kids *can* change the world, at any age, and it's our job to support them to do so. In each of the situations described here, students were empowered to take action on an issue that mattered to them. It is this sense of agency and energy that propels students to see themselves as someone who can make

You'll see that kids can help change the world!

—Moey Dworkin-Cantor, first grader
(quoted in *Inquiry Circles in Elementary Classrooms*, Daniels and Harvey 2009)

151

a difference. We believe that students can take action in ways that change the world, both big and small. As teachers, we have the power to make the space for this work, building opportunities for students to take the reins and follow their questions about the world to a place that sparks an action for change. In this chapter, we'll discuss how to do it.

What Does It Mean to "Take Action"?

There are many times in our curriculum when we ask kids to share what they have learned from reading, research, or long-term inquiry work. These "going public moments" are important opportunities to let students stretch their creative legs, apply writing and speaking skills, share their learning, and assess how they have grown. However, taking action goes a step further and aims for real impact on an issue. In the work ahead, we define taking action as working toward a specific change that affects others. This means students' work must be created with a purpose, audience, and intended impact in mind.

To work toward their specific change, students who are taking action might

▸ talk with other students and community members

▸ post a well-researched comment

▸ record and share a quick video teaching the important parts of what they've learned

▸ engage in and/or advocate for conscious consumerism related to their issue

▸ write a letter or email to a government official or person in power

▸ write a letter to the editor and send it to the local paper

▸ write a blog post

▸ start a social media campaign

▸ design and distribute posters or pamphlets to raise awareness

▸ create a piece of artwork

▸ build a photo essay

▸ craft and deliver a presentation

▸ write and perform a play or spoken word poem

▸ make a Common Craft–style video

▸ engage in a volunteer opportunity

▸ organize a symposium or workshop

▸ start a fund-raising or donation campaign and educate potential donors

▶ create and publish video public service announcements

▶ film a documentary.

The examples here are part of the process of taking action, but not the whole process. The piece that we create, the action we take, is one step in a larger process—from initial spark to reflection on impact—for guiding students into informed, thoughtful, and effective actions.

Action Supported by Understanding and Empathy

In many elementary schools there are already structures in place or ways that students are engaging in action-oriented events. We can reframe these events in a way that adds to the experience and potential impact students can have. For example, many schools have a yearly food drive to benefit a local pantry. This experience could just be boxes outside classrooms without students really understanding the *why* of the drive, or it could be a meaningful opportunity for students to understand and act with empathy. At one school in Chicago—in anticipation of a yearly student council–sponsored food drive—teachers began to pull resources that would help students develop an understanding of the multifaceted issue of hunger and the services food pantries provided. They also looked for materials to address student miscon-

Sixth-grade students in Ben Kovacs' class write as they consider their impact on the school's food drive.

Seventh- and eighth-grade students advocated for lower class size and library funding as they marched with Chicago teachers during a labor strike.

A Word About Our Role

This work of taking action can begin to feel like it's stepping into sensitive territory. As adults, we have developed ideas about how things should be: our backgrounds, political leanings, and ideas about the world have been developed over years of experiences. As teachers, we help students explore issues in a way that is both respectful of who they are and their families' values while providing the resources, structures, and platforms for students to develop their own ideas about the world around us.

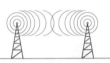

Join the Conversation:
Action-Oriented Learning

"How did I make an impact, and how can I be of useful help in the world?"

#ReadTheWorldNow

Hein.pub/RTW4.1

ceptions and stereotypes related to hunger. They reached out to the student council members and the representatives of the food pantry and asked them to speak to their classes about the specific needs of the pantry and why those needs were important. Teachers supported students in reading, unpacking, and considering perspectives they hadn't heard before. As they learned from these resources, students developed an understanding that there was a great need year-round, not just before the holidays. As a result, the students began to discuss how they might continue their work in supporting the local pantry beyond the yearly drive.

Students began to realize that the strategy they'd used in past years to try to gather the most items to win a pizza party—donating many small items without considering how useful the items really were—was hurting the food drive effort. With this understanding came discussion about the personal cost associated with not winning the reward versus the benefit from making more thoughtful choices about what they would donate. Instead of glossing over this, teachers took the time to hear students out, gave them space to write about their feelings, and left room for discussion, disappointment, and the eventual understanding that the impact far outweighed the outcome of a contest. Ultimately, when all was said and done, students took time to reflect and consider what they had learned, what more they wanted to know, and how they might continue to take action in the future. In one sixth-grade classroom, students gathered in front of the total donation they would send to the pantry later that day to write and process their thinking. In another classroom, students planned a mini-inquiry based on questions that had come up during the process about hunger in other parts of the world. In yet another classroom, students composed a letter to the student council sharing what they had learned and encouraging council members to rethink the reward for collections. By supporting and encouraging students' understanding and empathy, the school's teachers had made the food drive more meaningful for students and more effective in meeting the needs of the local pantry.

Laying the Groundwork for Taking Action

The types of issues and topics that drive students are not limited to any one subject area; however, they are all connected by one common thread: people. It is hearing the stories of others that inspires students—and adults—to action. Inspiration lives in everyday moments. As the teacher in the room, we help students harvest those moments and plant seeds for action.

While we cannot control whether our students feel called to take action, we *can* create an environment that supports their curiosity, their interests, and their sense of agency—all of which are ingredients in becoming invested in an issue and taking action. You might try these approaches:

▶ **Tune in to what's in your kids' news.** As our fellow educators James Beane (1997), Smokey Daniels (2015), and Sara Ahmed (2015, 2018) remind us, when we are clued in to what students are thinking, talking, and worrying about, we can be responsive to potential opportunities to help them do something about it. Let kids' news and interests influence your decisions about texts and topics of study as well.

▶ **Model your own curiosity, passion, and action.** Be on the lookout for opportunities to share what you wonder and what moves you.

▶ **Model compassion.** Let your actions show your students that, in your classroom, the norm is that people care and do whatever they can to help.

▶ **Give students time to wonder and to dwell in ideas.** Be mindful of when students may need more time to read, talk, and explore ideas that come up.

▶ **Establish structures that support discourse.** Refer back to Chapter 3 to ensure that kids are prepared to discuss and listen to ideas.

▶ **Explore new genres and media.** Provide support for the skills, strategies, and dispositions needed to unpack new genres and media.

▶ **Flood students with resources.** Choose resources carefully, grouping them around central themes or big ideas.

▶ **Embrace overarching concepts and questions.** Focus on ideas, such as "the struggle for power," rather than marching across a publisher's scope and sequence or through a linear timeline of history.

▶ **Connect work across the curriculum.** Establish an understanding of inquiry that ranges across content areas.

▶ **Normalize taking action.** Discuss situations in which people have taken action, and make taking action a theme in the texts you share with your class. (See page 184 for a list of picture books that feature people taking action.)

As our mentor Stephanie Harvey says, we're not necessarily making every kid an activist, but we're leaving room for that to happen.

Setting Students on a Path to Action

While students sometimes decide on their own that they want to take action, it's more often the case that if we want them to understand the process of taking action, we'll need to help them. We can show them how action is a real possibility, from considering issues they care about with an eye toward making a difference to mapping out and implementing a plan. We may also see natural places for action within our curriculum if there is a topic that sparks interest for our students.

When we—not our students—are choosing a path toward action, we are mindful of ensuring that our own ideas, interests, and passions don't overshadow those of our students. This means making space for conversation, letting kids dwell on ideas, and listening carefully for what resonates with

Questions That Guide Our Action

1. **Why is this important?** Establishing the importance of our action gives purpose and drive to the work that students are doing. This positions students to have a solid base in purpose, not compliance.

2. **What's the best way to take action?** In many ways, this becomes a genre study of the ways adults and, increasingly, kids get things done. Students consider various options and weigh the impact of each option to develop a plan to guide their action. The result is much more purposeful than "everyone makes a movie."

3. **Who needs to hear my message?** When students consider who their audience is, they are really asking, "Who has the power to make this better?" This question is closely tied to the one above as students explore the most effective way to create change.

4. **What will this cost me?** When students consider what an action will cost them, they are developing an understanding of the cost-benefit ratio of taking action. If they want to promote energy conservation, they must conserve energy and that might mean they will have less time to do something they enjoy, like playing video games.

5. **How am I changed?** Perhaps the most important step is to help students reflect on how this experience will change them. How will they adjust their behavior? What lessons will they take with them? How will they make different choices moving forward?

them. Students may not come up with a plethora of ideas when they first do this work, and that's OK. It's up to us to provide time for them to take action, starting with a few simpler opportunities, then spiraling in scale and depth across the year and grade levels, to drive the learning. Some iterations may be more effective and challenging than others, but each iteration, no matter how big or small, will build students' fluency in thinking as they grow their skills.

Action-Oriented Teaching

The Try Its in this chapter are a scaffold for guiding students while they take action, either on an issue that they have spontaneously chosen or on an issue that you've given them guidance to identify. At the heart of this chapter's work of action-oriented teaching are the five questions that guide our action (listed on the left). When we anchor opportunities for students to take action in these questions, we offer them an opportunity to engage on a deeper and more personal level. We might use these questions to guide a conversation with a student or student group, or we might plan lessons associated with each one, as we've done in the Try Its in this chapter. The questions can be used together to help students consider their action in a holistic way or individually to direct students to think about particular components of the process.

WRITE WITH US

⏻ What about the idea of students taking action sparks excitement for you? What sparks concerns?

⏻ What are some ways you've taken action in your own life?

⏻ What effect did your actions have on you and on your issue?

⏻ How might you share these experiences with your students?

⏻ How might this work align with the required skills or content (or both!) in your curriculum?

⏻ What do you notice about the Questions That Guide Our Action? What do you wonder?

⏻ **Share your ideas. #ReadTheWorldNow**

About This Chapter

This chapter builds on students' understanding and empathy—the goals of the previous two chapters—to help them take meaningful action.

INSPIRING STUDENTS TO ACTION

Here, we transition students from learning from and about other voices and perspectives to considering how they would choose to take action in their own lives.

TRY IT

PLANNING FOR IMPACT

To maximize the action's impact, we challenge students to consider two important factors: who might help them achieve their goal and whether the project is manageable in terms of personal cost.

TRY IT

ACTING WITH PURPOSE AND HEART

This section lays out possibilities for action based on the goals students identified in the previous section.

TRY IT

INSPIRING STUDENTS TO ACTION:
Identify What We Care About

TRY THIS WHEN . . .

- you and your students are looking for a topic that they might take action on

- you want to establish a mindset for thinking about interests, passions, and issues

- you notice students are encountering resources, issues, or events that might be important to think and act on

- students are reading or viewing a resource set that might inspire them to develop a stance and take action.

It can be challenging for our students to sit down and say, "I want to do something about [insert issue here]" at a moment's notice. Sometimes inspiration strikes like lightning and other times students plan and care for many idea seeds at a time. We can support students by offering creative ways for them to gather thinking, ideas, concerns, or cares.

WHAT TO DO

We've found that students have the most success in generating and curating ideas when given large paper and markers. However, if students are adept at digital drawing or prefer to work on a device, make that option available as well. Here are some ways to help students identify the things they care about in the world:

▶ Put up a graffiti wall in your classroom where students can write or draw when an idea strikes them. This works well if you are looking to gather issues over time for a later period, such as a genius hour rotation or passion projects. The class can update the wall as they encounter new resources that spark their interests.

▶ Ask students to make a collage of things they care about using hand-drawn pictures or images collected from magazines and the internet. Students often start with concrete topics (soccer) before moving into more issue-based thinking (equity between male and female soccer teams).

▶ Prompt students to develop an "I Care About" map in a notebook, on a poster, or on a device. Offer time to talk, share, reflect, and adjust. Ask the classmates to notice trends—consider collaborating with a teacher in a different school, community, or country to compare as well. This can offer students affirmation through similarities and a push in thinking.

No matter which option you choose, begin by modeling for students how you stop, reflect, and jot to gather your own thinking. For example, show students how you begin by first mapping out general topics that you care about using pictures and words. You might then revisit each one to add further thinking, ask questions, and identify areas that you want to know more about. Some students may already be aware of the potential for taking action within a topic, whereas others may not yet be aware of any potential issues. Either way, students will benefit from time to read about their topics of interest or do research to further inform their maps.

For our youngest students, we often create a class map, asking each child to create a small drawing with a caption. Then we discuss trends that we notice across the class in order to identify areas of interest, helping students make connections to things they care about and possible actions they might take. Some of our students are not familiar with having conversations about topics beyond their own experiences. Their initial approximations might include a list of likes, objects they enjoy, or places that are important to them. We can scaffold them into thinking about what more they might want to learn about these topics, what questions they have, and how they can connect their own experiences and world to something greater.

If you find that students need more support in any of the suggested methods, the following questions and prompts are helpful in quick conferences as students work:

▶ Encourage students to revisit the texts and resources we've studied as a class. Ask: *What is still bothering you? What are you still thinking about? What do you wish could be different?*

▶ Prompt students to consider their own life and identity. Ask: *What communities are you a part of? What personal challenges or interests do you have? What is unique to you or your family?*

▶ For students who are already thinking about the world beyond their own lives, ask: *What problems do you see in the world that you'd like to solve? What more do you want to know about those problems? What do you wish everyone could know?*

▶ Have students do a quick silent gallery walk around the room to see if the work other students are doing sparks ideas.

▶ Group students into partners or groups of three to talk and collaborate as they work, or have them create a poster that represents each of their thinking.

Once students have developed some ideas, gather them back together to share their thinking and model how to zoom in on areas of interest using

Helpful Language

What issues are you thinking about right now?

I see you've written down some things that are important to you. What questions do you have about these? What do you wonder?

Who would you like to help in the world?

What have you read or watched lately that is weighing on you?

How might we make a difference? What more can you say about that?

What do you already know? What do you want to know more about?

your own map. You might star a few possibilities that feel relevant, timely, and accessible or choose something because it feels connected to something else your class has learned recently. As you evaluate your map for potential places to learn more, model asking yourself some guiding questions: *Is this an issue that feels pressing? Do I already have an idea of a problem that might be solved here? Is there a problem to solve here? What aspects do I need to learn more about?* Modeling how to evaluate whether there's really enough content to dig into can be especially helpful when students' first ideas include things they like—such as video games or a favorite toy. We might say something like this:

> ***I notice*** *I wrote "cats" on my map. **I wrote that because** I like cats a lot. I miss my cat from when I was growing up; he was a good friend. **A question I have is,** What problems or issues are there about cats? I'm going to try and learn a little more. Maybe there are some things I can do to help cats, but I'm not sure this will get me through several days of reading and research. Before I start reading about this, I'm going to go back and look for something else I might dig into as well.*

Then, ask students to do the same: star possible areas of interest, talk with classmates, and explore ideas. As students do this work, circulate, talking with them to help them articulate their ideas and gathering some information about what directions kids are considering. You will want to look for possible groupings to leverage the power of the small groups and to assist students in the learning journey to come. We also find that allowing students to share this work can help them crowdsource ideas. To share, students might gather in partnerships or small groups, or they might hang their work up for a gallery walk.

Revisit protocols and guidelines for respectful and kind sharing behaviors, due to the personal nature of this work. Remind students of what it looks like to be a supportive listener, referring them back to any previously created charts and encouraging them to move forward with the same level of empathy and kindness they wish to receive.

OUTCOMES AND WHAT TO LOOK FOR

In this lesson, we want students to be able to find ways to express what is on their minds and hearts. Can students

▶ identify people, issues, topics, organization, or places that they feel connected to and want to help?

A teacher models creating a map using digital sketchnoting. She shares her map by projecting it for the whole class to view and then talks through each image, jotting more ideas and questions on sticky notes and placing them around the map. She will revisit this map as she considers where she wants to dig deeper, learn more, and take action.

Fifth-grade students take time to reflect on issues that matter to them.

FOLLOW UP

These maps are the starting point for students to take action. Additionally, they can be one of the many ways that you collect authentic data about your students in order to build connections and customize the curriculum to students' interests and passions. You may want to prompt students to leave blank space in their maps so they can add to them as the year goes on.

Students will have a wide range of responses on their maps, from simple everyday concerns and likes to global issues. This speaks to their background knowledge, shared learning, experiences, and biases. Prompt students to share and listen to one another to develop a wider vision for what issues may be out there, and to evaluate carefully which issues involve problems that affect people and where they might make an impact on those problems.

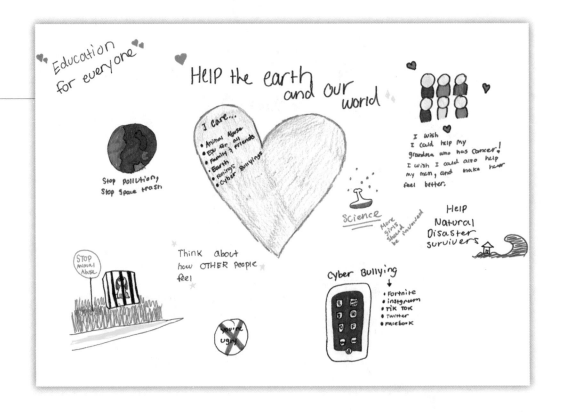

INSPIRING STUDENTS TO ACTION:
Build Students' Understanding with a Multimedia Tech Set

TRY THIS WHEN . . .

■ you and your students have identified a topic (or topics) to learn more about

■ you're gathering resources to support students in developing their understanding about why and how to take action on an issue

■ you want students to spend the majority of their time understanding and identifying the issues and critically consuming content rather than searching for information online.

Whether students are identifying topics to dig into or an opportunity to take action presents itself, a multimedia tech set offers students resources to build context and make informed decisions. By providing a few options at the click of a button, we invite kids to seek more and go beyond their initial questions and understandings. Multimedia tech sets can be helpful in a wide range of other classroom situations as well: to supplement print resources, to ensure students are experiencing resources at an accessible reading level, to gather resources for less traditional topics, and to preview a unit's content.

WHAT TO DO

The process for building a multimedia tech set starts with a spark. When you're using this lesson as part of taking action, the spark might be the topic you and your students identified in the previous Try It. If this is the case, you will be looking for sources that help students grow their understanding of the topic and learn about potential current issues that relate to the topic. Once you've curated the multimedia tech set, you'll be working to help students deepen their understanding of the "spark" topic you identified in the previous Try It, sharing the new tech set with students and using structures to help students interact with the tech set.

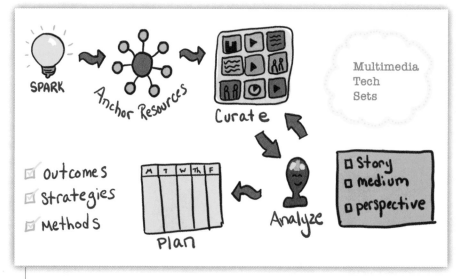

Multimedia Tech Set

Let Yourself Geek Out

Geek out: "to become excited or enthusiastic about a favored subject or activity" (*Merriam-Webster*, n.d.b).

We push ourselves to geek out by developing our own intellectual curiosity, asking ourselves:

- What do I think I already know? What do I think about this?

- What don't I know about this? Whom might I ask?

- Are there different ways of looking at this? What do other people think?

- How does this connect to other topics or issues?

- How might this affect other people? Places? Issues?

- What is the history of this? What has already happened and why?

- Which people have a stake in this issue?

- Is there an inequity here? Who has the power? Does that need to change?

- Is there a problem that could be solved? What solutions have people already tried?

- What impact does this have on my own life? The lives of people I know and care about?

Find Resources

Start with reputable websites and databases. As of this book's publication, we consider these our anchor resources—the tools that we turn to again and again:

Websites
Newsela
Time for Kids
Scholastic Kids
Wonderopolis
The Kid Should See This
National Geographic Kids
BrainPOP

Podcasts
Wow in the World
Brains On!
But Why
Short and Curly
The Past and the Curious
Tumble Science Podcast for Kids

YouTube Channels
The Brain Scoop
Crash Course Kids
SciShow Kids
Minute Physics
Mike Likes Science

School Research Databases
Encyclopedia Britannica Kids
Safari Montage
PebbleGo

Next, broaden your search to other sources, using your own judgment to weigh sources. Letting yourself get curious is fun *and* it will give you a sense of the process your students might go through as they dive into inquiry-related learning. As a result, you'll be able to share and coach authentically when they are working. As educator John Spencer (2018) says, research should be fun. It should feel like geeking out. Be sure to connect with your school and local librarians during this phase as well as any other experts in the school or our Personal Learning Network (PLN) community who might have insight into the topic.

Our purpose in building and sharing multimedia tech sets is to offer students diverse reading opportunities in both the stories they tell and the media presented. As you compile your tech set, ask yourself:

▶ Have you represented, to the best of your ability, resources at a wide variety of age-appropriate levels?

▶ Have you included a range of media, such as informational articles, e-books, videos, images, primary source documents, first-person accounts, news articles, opinion columns, blog posts, essays, infographics, and podcasts?

- Have you analyzed the resources to consider the impact they will have on a student's overall understanding of the topic or issue?

- Have you vetted resources to ensure they are not perpetuating stereotypes or single stories?

Analyze the Multimedia Tech Set as a Whole

You've found some incredible information! But does what you've found tell the whole story? Look over what you've curated so far and ask yourself:

- What stories does this tech set tell?

- Which stories aren't represented yet?

- Have I done my due diligence in presenting varying perspectives?

- Does this tech set have a wide range of media?

- Will every student find an entry point in these resources?

If your analysis shows you places where your tech set needs to be stronger, re-research to find the additional sources it needs. Look back at "Reconsider the Texts You Share with Students" in Chapter 3 for additional support in considering the texts in your tech set.

Make the Multimedia Tech Set Shareable

Now, decide how you'll give students access to the tech set you've created. The chart on the next page outlines options for sharing. Keep these questions in mind as you decide how to share the tech set:

- How will the students access the tech set in school? At home?

- What lessons from Chapters 2 and 3 will students need to apply in order to interact with the resources? Do they need a refresher in any of those lessons?

- Will every student find an entry point into these resources?

Watch, Talk, Think

Something I learned is . . .

A question I have is . . .

This makes me think of . . .

I wonder how . . .

I'm surprised that . . .

A QR sheet like the one shown here, created with a word processing program, gave third-grade students a quick and simple way to access resources. The teacher printed QR codes linking to individual articles, videos, or podcasts and placed them at stations around the room.

Medium	What It's Good For
Digital Bulletin Board (e.g., Padlet)	▶ Digital bulletin boards allow you to gather many resources in one place and present them in a visual way. They offer the ability to organize material and can act as a free-form collection place. ▶ They make it easy to collaborate with other teachers, students, and librarians. ▶ They can be revised and refined for future use.
School Learning Management System (LMS) (e.g., Edmodo, Google Classroom, Schoology, Seesaw)	▶ Your LMS may already have a way to organize and share links with students through folders, assignments, or a class feed. ▶ Younger students may find this format familiar and easy to navigate if you are already using it for other purposes, making accessing and responding to resources simple and streamlined.
Class Website	▶ If you already have a website and students use it on a regular basis, adding resources is a quick and natural choice. ▶ Websites provide longevity and the ability to organize sources by type, in order of challenge level, or by question or subtopic. ▶ A class website can also be helpful if you'd like to embed short instructional videos in which you teach students how to interact with the resources or discuss what they might consider as they dig into each resource.
QR Codes	▶ QR codes work well in stations around the classroom where students interact with different types of resources (video, image, infographic, data, map, article) or with resources that present different perspectives or ideas. QR codes might take students directly to the resource, to a short blurb about how to interact with the resource, to a compelling question, or to a lens to read through. ▶ In a classroom with limited devices, teachers might preload media onto the device and leave it at the station. Some stations could feature print resources and others could use QR codes to access digital resources. This maximizes the impact of a few devices and gives all students an opportunity to apply their digital literacy skills. ▶ QR codes are also easy to print and send home so students can access the resources from anywhere.
Google Slides	▶ Google Slides offers a unique way to share resources. Teachers might include an image, QR code, or link, or directly embed videos right into a slide. Google Slides also gives students the option to leave comments and thinking using the comment feature. ▶ Google slides have a clean and simple layout that can be organized as a workflow for students. They are easily editable, allowing you to update and customize tech sets for students.

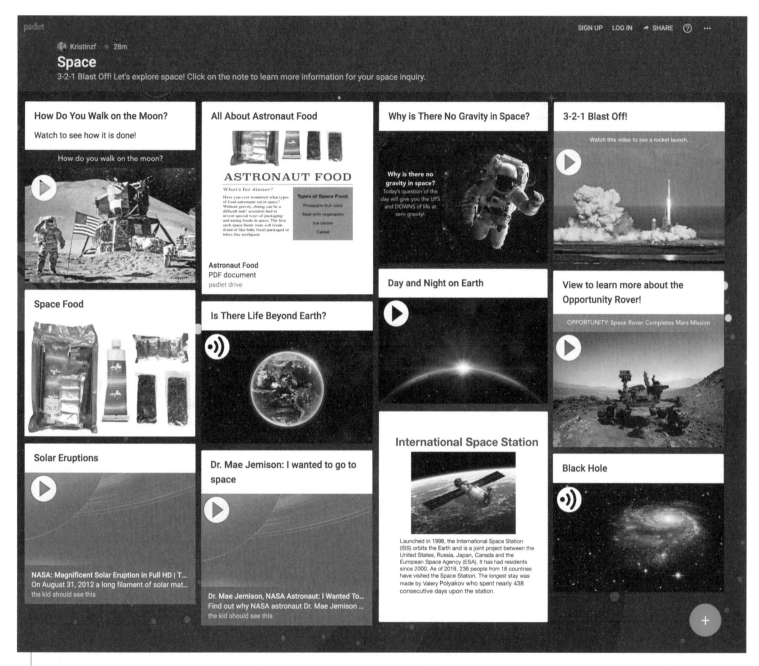

This multimedia tech set is shared using Padlet, a type of digital bulletin board. Information is organized in a visual layout with articles, videos, images, and podcasts that are curated by the teacher. As students embark on their space inquiry, they use this site as a launchpad for all their research.

Get Students Interacting with the Multimedia Tech Set

Now that you have a tech set and a method for sharing it, it's time to decide how to structure how students will interact with it. We've gathered five of our favorite methods in this Try It. As you look through them, ask yourself:

▶ Which option will help students meet objectives or learning targets?

▶ What strategies will students need to know (or refresh) for each option?

▶ Which option seems to be the best fit for my students' current needs and preferences?

Whole-Class Introduction Followed by Independent Use of the Texts

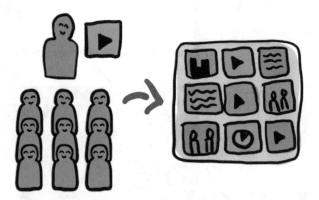

Introduce the set through a whole-class image or video study. Gather students together at your whole-group meeting place so they can see the detail in the images you are about to show. Then model the skills you expect students to use. Provide active practice of the strategy; guide them to look closely at the images, ask questions, and make inferences to make sense of what they are seeing. Engage them in turn and talks and a debrief before releasing them to continue the work on their own or in partners. Allow students to explore the resources in the set at their own pace and in an order that they choose. In this model, the teacher may meet with small groups and confer with students to support skills.

Gradual Release of Responsibility

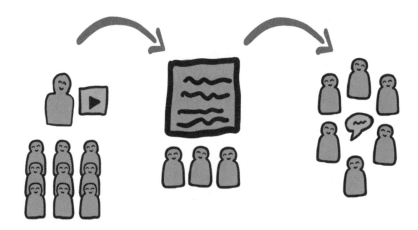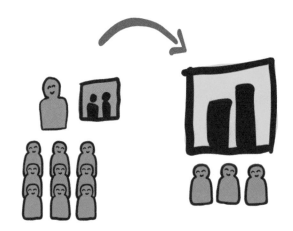

Follow a linear path of minilessons, using a gradual release of responsibility each day: model, guide, practice. This works best when your students are less experienced interacting with certain media or the topic is especially challenging. For example, we might do a whole-class image study and then have students try another image study with a partner or in a small group. During the next lesson, we might model how to interact with a text and then ask students to continue on their own.

Students Following a Path at Their Own Pace

Allow students to navigate through the resources at their own pace, starting with the most accessible resources first and slowly building to more complex ones. When using this option, organize the resources to show the order in which they should be used. On Padlet, we might create columns that indicate the order. On a website, we might separate resources into sections or separate pages.

Stations

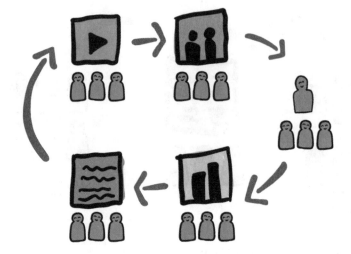

Have students move through a station rotation model. Record a quick two-to three-minute video lesson for each station to get students started on more independent work. This frees you to observe, confer with, or meet with groups during the rotations. If you're working with other teachers, divide and conquer! Each teacher can be in charge of recording the lesson for the station.

Workshop

A workshop approach offers the instruction and support that students need while preserving time for them to practice independently. Like the gradual release of responsibility option, this option begins with modeling and guided practice. However, it provides more time for student practice and also includes time to share a particular resource, method, tool, or new idea (in a quick face-to-face share, a digital format, or a quick whole-class share) and to get feedback from peers.

OUTCOMES AND WHAT TO LOOK FOR

We want students to engage with a wide variety of resources and consider how those resources work together to tell a rich story. Can students

- ▶ access information in a variety of formats: video, article, website?
- ▶ apply reading and thinking strategies to comprehend various resources?
- ▶ document new learning and questions in drawing and writing?
- ▶ connect resources to one another, finding common threads of information and big ideas?
- ▶ develop an increasingly complex understanding by synthesizing multiple resources?
- ▶ analyze sources with different perspectives?

FOLLOW UP

You may find that you can use some multimedia tech sets year after year, updating them each year to reflect the most current information, resources, and needs of your students. For resource sets that don't have a curricular connection every year—such as a set created to address a specific current event, student question, or inquiry project—you might create a bulletin board or place in your classroom library for students to scan a code and access the resource set during independent reading.

Join the Conversation:
Tech Sets

"One of the secrets to really making great multimedia tech sets is to allow yourself to sort of go down the rabbit hole."

#ReadTheWorldNow

Hein.pub/RTW4.2

TRY IT!

INSPIRING STUDENTS TO ACTION:
Ask Questions to Understand an Issue

TRY THIS WHEN . . .

■ students have identified a topic or issue they'd like to take action on but have yet to understand the scope of the issue

■ students have dug into research and are unsure of the best way to take action or how they can help.

Children instinctively ask questions when they encounter cognitive dissonance as youngsters. As Warren Berger points out, questioning is essential now and in the future as "complexity increases and change accelerates" (2014, 2). Yet our education system tends to discourage this practice, intentionally or unintentionally. By valuing students' questions, we can encourage them to drive their own learning, to gain understanding, and, most importantly, to care. In this Try It, we'll focus on equipping our students with skills and strategies for generating a range of diverse questions as they focus on an issue related to their topic. Students will rely on the introductory tech set that you curated in the previous Try It to inform their questions. Then, in the next Try It, they'll have opportunities to dig deeper to try to address these questions in the tech set or in any new resources you bring into the classroom.

WHAT TO DO

Share your own topic with students on the projector and model asking whatever questions come to mind. It can be helpful for students to see that asking questions can be challenging but we can work through those challenges. Try to talk through your thoughts as you work, to show students what this work looks like inside your head. It's OK to pause and think silently when necessary—students need to know that we sometimes need to give something some thought. Give students paper and pencil or a digital way to jot any of their own ideas down so as not to interrupt the flow.

As you model, try using one of the following questioning lenses to better understand the issue you're studying:

Understanding: What questions do we need to answer to help ourselves fully understand what's happening right now and why?

Context: What questions would it be helpful to answer in order to know the history behind this topic? Context questions help us to understand the overarching question, *How did things get this way?*

Join the Conversation:
Asking Questions

"If you have a question about something, and are given the time and space to pursue that, then you care about it because you own it."

#ReadTheWorldNow

Hein.pub/RTW4.3

Perspectives: What questions might people in different roles ask?

Solutions: Which questions might help me get to possible solutions or actions?

For example, if we were focusing on the topic of recycling at school, we might use the *perspectives* lens, considering the questions that a teacher, a student, a custodian, and a principal might ask.

Once you've modeled how the process might go, give students time to jot down their own questions independently. Then, have them share and view each other's questions in groups, actively looking for new ideas and feedback.

We often find that a quick gallery walk helps students who feel stuck find new ideas. You might also use one or more of the following prompts to help students generate more questions.

▸ *What do we need to know about here? Can we glance over our resources to get the gist and then come up with some more questions?*

▸ *What might other people know that we don't know?*

▸ *What questions might someone ask if they didn't agree that this is a problem?*

▸ *What questions would each person who is involved with this topic have?*

▸ *What solutions have already been tried? What happened? Which solutions haven't been tried?*

You might stretch this process over a series of a few short sessions, giving students ample time to read, view, talk, and write and ensuring they have opportunities to discuss and be inspired by others' questions. If students are working on separate topics, you might even gather a list of questions that could be applicable to other students' topics on a class chart. For example, in one third-grade class a student asked, "Why hasn't anyone fixed this problem yet?" The teacher wrote this question on the board and asked students to consider if this question would apply to their topic. If it did, he prompted them to write it down and then ask any follow-up questions they came up with.

OUTCOMES AND WHAT TO LOOK FOR

We want students to go beyond the initial first few questions they might have about a topic. Can students

▸ use lenses to generate many questions about a resource?

▸ collaborate in groups to generate, discuss, analyze, and refine questions?

▸ identify questions that will lead to further inquiry and action?

Helpful Language

What do we wonder about here?

What questions do you need to answer in order to really understand this topic?

What is one question another group had that you want to add to your list?

Do you have any other questions that will prompt you to think about why this learning is important?

What new questions do you have after exploring the resources?

Can you bully by embarrassing someone?

Can you bully by accident?

What should we do if we see this?

Can you be cyberbullied by your friends?

Why is cyberbullying worse sometimes?

How do teachers fee about cyber bullying?

How does it affect the person getting bullied?

When can this happen?

Are there apps that are worse for cyberbullying?

A small group of fourth graders generated questions to guide their learning. Students then used these questions to guide additional reading and research.

▶ take on different roles to anticipate what support or challenges they may encounter in taking action (for example, the cost of a proposed idea, or opposing viewpoints)?

▶ consider how they might address counterpoints or potential barriers to a solution they are proposing?

FOLLOW UP

As students begin to answer questions, they will inevitably have more. Encourage this type of thinking: it leads students to questioning that will take them to a deeper understanding of the topic, and it reinforces their own curiosity, which is an essential skill for lifelong learning. As students move into research or inquiry work in the next Try It, make time during the process for them to stop and reflect on how they are addressing their questions and to note any new ones that have arisen. Prompt students to keep thinking in this way through the language you use during conferring and small-group work, using phrases like *What more do we wonder about this? What else are you curious about?* and *What new questions do you have?*

TRY THIS WHEN . . .

- students have many questions about a topic and need the time and space to explore them

- you've identified something worth exploring and taking action on that is not already included in your curriculum.

Now that students have gathered their questions, we launch into the investigative phase. This might be a short burst—a few days of intense reading and research—or it could stretch into a longer period of time if you choose to weave it into the required curriculum and standards.

WHAT TO DO

At this point, you may find that your students are in different places: some students may have a strong sense of the problem they want to address, and their purpose for further investigation is to answer their follow-up questions and identify potential solutions. Other students may be in a more exploratory place, still building their background knowledge in an effort to develop their understanding of potential issues or problems associated with the topic.

To begin, consider what resources students will use to try to answer their questions. Often, we find that revisiting the tech set can yield enough information. However, this could also be an opportunity to add new texts, such as print resources in your classroom or recommendations from your school librarian. This can also be an invitation to work on students' internet research skills. When considering whether you should curate resources or allow students to use kid-safe search engines, ask yourself:

▶ **How much time do we have, and how do I want students to spend that time?** Tie this time to skills that you would like to develop or reinforce. If those skills are internet search skills, then it's worth coaching students through that process, devoting minilessons to how to access school databases or how to do a keyword search. School librarians can be instrumental in this process. If the skills you're looking to work on are more about working with resources, like those discussed in the Try Its in Chapter 2, then it may be better to do some legwork ahead of time to beef up the multimedia text sets and gather additional print resources.

▶ **What do I find when I search?** Are you able to find kid-friendly resources quickly and efficiently, or are you pulling up college-level dissertations on the first page of results? If you check your go-to resources, can you find pertinent information? What do you have available in the classroom or library? If students will be relatively successful quickly so they can get to the business of learning, then we can let them practice doing that work. If not, it's best to curate.

▶ **How complex is the topic?** We may also need to do some legwork to ensure that what our students find is appropriate. Some topics can turn up disturbing images or content. As teachers, we have to ask, What's appropriate for this age level? How much is too much? We often support students in investigating above and beyond the canned topics that curriculum publishers think schools want to teach. However, we also trust our instincts about what is and is not appropriate for the children we teach. We may even go as far as connecting with parents to explain why students aren't searching the internet on a particular topic without guidance.

▶ **Now that the students have some specific questions, would it be helpful to involve an expert?** Hearing from someone in the field—even if it's just a quick interview chat via Skype, FaceTime, or Google Hangouts—can deepen students' understanding, spur new thinking, and even make kids aware of future career possibilities. We often survey our parent community at the beginning of the year to see who might have a skill set that could benefit our students in a situation like this. Teacher-supervised student blogs, a class Twitter account, or a class Instagram account are great places to seek more information from friends and specialists. It's easy to do just a little bit of research and find a museum, researcher, or organization that can provide more information.

A third-grade student uses his classroom Twitter account to tweet questions to experts in the field.

Gather students together and let them know that they will have an opportunity to explore and address their questions. For our youngest students, we might start this process as a class, using a read-aloud and shared or interactive writing to gather, sort, and synthesize information. We would then teach them to research by reading pictures, captions, maps, and other features. With all students, we use the workshop model, spending short bursts of time modeling skills and strategies and then providing long chunks of time for students to investigate independently or with small-group think partners.

As students delve into their resources, we step into the role of co-learner and coach. We might

▶ pull a small group to support their reading of a particular resource or to apply a strategy

▶ teach a minilesson on how to keep our questions at the front of our mind as we read and research

▶ model how to synthesize multiple sources or thinking

▶ prompt students to revisit their questions and add new ones

▶ help students create a plan to organize their small group to do efficient and peaceful work

▶ converse with students in order to deepen their understanding, encourage them to process what they're reading, and help them begin to develop a vision for what's next

▶ teach a lesson on collaboration skills to promote effective group work.

This process, inquiry, can be messy. It follows students' learning, not a rigid structure. With this in mind, it's difficult to plan down to the minute in advance. On the pages that follow, to give you an idea of what this looks like, we offer a few ideas of how this work might unfold over five days in the primary grades and the intermediate grades.

In Katie Plamondon's kindergarten classroom, students reference an anchor chart that reminds them of the many ways they can research a question. When researching, kids fluidly move between text, tech, and a thinksheet to gain new knowledge.

A Sample Five-Day Investigation for Primary Students

Day 1	Day 2	Days 3 and 4	Day 5
The teacher sets the tone for the day by telling students that today they are going to start learning about some answers to their questions. He keeps the shared question chart in an easy-to-access-and-view place near him. He then models with a read-aloud of an informational text, focusing on using text features to gather information. Students practice in pairs by documenting new learning and questions in drawing, writing, and turn and talks as he continues to read. Students then go to their tables to continue the process with a digital version of the same text. This text is accessible to all students through a "read to me" function. The teacher coaches pairs as they read and talk, prompting them with thinking stems like *This image shows me . . .* and *That's making me think . . .*	The teacher gives a quick procedure minilesson reminding students of how good researchers interact with their resources—reading all the parts of the resources, stopping to talk and think, and gathering new learning. He then releases students back to their tables to begin their investigation. There they find baskets filled with source sets: images, books, printed articles, QR codes, and artifacts for students to use for research. Working in teams, kids gather around a large piece of chart paper to document new learning using pictures and words (for young learners, the size of the chart paper allows everyone to write and work at the same time and gives space for a range of fine motor skills). The teacher meets with small table groups to support their reading and thinking process. As he does, he's taking note of any new vocabulary to add to the content word wall on a picture card.	The teacher begins with a minilesson responding to needs he's seen over the last few days. He might focus on a strategy for nonfiction reading or support students in thinking about what they are reading by modeling some new prompts. He might also choose to teach a procedural lesson to address work habits or collaboration. Or he might focus on meeting with small groups: supporting students who need it, teaching students what researchers do when they feel like they're done, and prompting students to do deeper thinking as they work. He might also teach explicit lessons on how to access additional resources as students exhaust the materials in their class.	On the last day of the cycle, the teacher gathers the students together with all their notes and new knowledge. They talk in partners and as a class. He asks them, *What have you learned? What problems did you find? What solutions did you find?* As students talk, he starts an interactive writing piece on chart paper. He begins to demonstrate for students how to summarize and synthesize their learning, then releases students to do so on their own. At the end of the session, the students have a clear idea of what the problem is and what solution they would like to take action on. They then create a work plan for the next step of the inquiry.

A Sample Five-Day Investigation for Intermediate Students

Day 1	Days 2, 3, and 4	Day 5
The teacher gathers students together to launch the investigation phase. She models looking over her questions and prompts them to do the same. She might take this first day to teach students how to choose which sources to start with based on what they want to learn about. She shows how she skims and scans digital resources or checks the table of contents, headings, and pictures in a book to decide if it would be a good starting point. She is sure to note that she wants to start with the easiest resources first. She's mindful to not keep students at the meeting place too long, because they are eager to dig into their own topics. As they go off to work, she reminds them to revisit the tech sets and the bins of books that she's put out for them. She might start with a small group of her students who need the most support to help them choose which resources to start with.	The teacher plans minilessons in response to what students need. She might teach a digital literacy lesson, modeling with a video, infographic, or website; demonstrate using a digital book and how she transfers her print skills to the digital text; apply new digital reading strategies; teach a procedural or collaboration lesson; synthesize information from multiple sources; conduct database or internet searches; or revisit informational reading and note-taking skills. She watches as students work, looking at what skills they are applying, what skills they are ready to develop, and which skills she might introduce. She is careful to keep her lessons short and to the point so that students have time to read, talk, think, and jot their new ideas and learning. As students work, she is prompting them to consider what problems they are finding and what potential solutions other people have tried. Some students may encounter solutions presented in their resources, while others may need to devise innovative solutions of their own.	On the last day of the investigation, students take time to reflect on and synthesize their new learning. They tease out what the problems are and what the solutions to those problems might be. They might take time to analyze those solutions through the lens of their own action, brainstorming ideas for how they could get involved.

One final thing to keep in mind: even with intense research, it's possible that students will not find answers to every single one of their questions—some questions are unanswerable or are too complex to fully answer. The goal of this work is not to check off every question as answered; it is to ensure that students are deepening their understanding.

Materials you will need

Wednesday	Thursday	Friday	Monday
PuT iN PLaN's	reD BOOks	Cimboor	Shar With CLAS

← Will   Vivian Will   Vivian

Resources: iF YOu LIVeD WiTh The Sioux InDians
the LEGEND OF the BLUEBONNet

In this work plan, designed for first grade, students use a template to share the workload, identify individual subtopics, and plan for research process and product across several days. As early as first grade, we build awareness and understanding of proper citation by asking students to name two resources they used. At this age it doesn't have to be done in APA format, but we expect students to name books, websites, or specialists they have learned from.

One tool that we use to help support our learners in becoming independent is a work plan. This work plan, designed for a class of fourth and fifth graders, includes boxes to prompt them to establish a focus and consider where they will begin searching for information before they get started. Model filling out your own plan and using it when conferring with students and small groups.

You can find printable work plans at Hein.pub/RTW-Resources.

OUTCOMES AND WHAT TO LOOK FOR

The heart of this Try It is to give students time to investigate their questions to develop a better understanding of the issue at hand. Can students

▶ use their questions to drive their investigation?

▶ access resources and apply strategies to read, view, listen, and think?

▶ use search skills to find reliable and useful resources, where appropriate?

▶ identify and use topics and subtopics to organize small-group work, strategize, and gather and connect new learning?

FOLLOW UP

In the next Try It, students will use what they've learned to start planning an action they will take on the issue they've researched.

STUDENT WORK PLAN

1. What do we want to find out?

2. What are some subtopics or follow-up questions?

4. What keywords or phrases can we use when searching?

3. What resources can we start with? Who will look at each resource?

Who needs to know what we've found out? Who is our audience? What do we know about them?

How can we connect with our audience?

Taking Action Plan: Be detailed; say who will do what and when.

Materials:

Questions for the teacher:

WRITE WITH US

⏻ Where are you seeing excitement from your students in this work?

This work can sometimes look "messy," as it means that kids are likely conferring with each other, asking questions, trying things out, and getting things wrong. Take a moment to reflect:

⏻ Where are you seeing messiness?

⏻ How might you support your students through this messiness without taking the reins?

⏻ Share your ideas. #ReadTheWorldNow

PLANNING FOR IMPACT:
Make a Plan to Take Action

TRY THIS WHEN . . .

▪ students are ready to move from doing the gathering and synthesizing work of inquiry to going public and connecting with an audience or taking direct action themselves

▪ you notice students are ready to consider how to position what they've learned, or create something with an intended audience in mind.

The purpose of this Try It is twofold. First, students will analyze the ways in which they might have an impact on the issue they've immersed themselves in. Second, if appropriate, they'll consider what their possible audiences are and what the ask would be for each of those audiences.

This transition from learning about an issue to seeing one's role in relation to the issue is crucial to developing student agency. When we ask students to consider whom they want to connect with, to share their work with, and to inspire to action, we teach them that their words have power. This position carries students beyond an assignment, an inquiry, or a classroom and into the work they will be engaged in as members of society.

WHAT TO DO

Begin by modeling with your inquiry, using think-alouds to help students understand the process. For example, inspired by several social media posts about straws, third-grade teacher Tiana Ortega investigated more and decided that she wanted to take action. Then, she modeled thinking through what the possible audiences and actions might be. We often begin this work by thinking through our own model inquiries with students and demonstrating how we consider whom to share our learning with. We might begin by gathering students on the carpet and sharing the synthesis work we've done on our topic by projecting our notebook using a document camera or sharing a digital document or graphic. We model thinking about what we've learned, what feels important, and what ideas we have for doing something about the issue. We evaluate any solutions that we've read about, brainstorm new solutions if appropriate, and narrow in on what we'd like to do to take action. Here's what this sounded like in that third-grade class:

Class, as you know I've been really immersed in learning about how harmful straws are for animals in our environment. I've learned so much about

single-use plastic straws: why they are a problem and different ways companies and people are addressing the problem. I've also read some opinion articles from people with limited mobility who rely on straws in order to drink. Here's what I've learned:

▶ **The problem is** that after we use them, straws are harmful for animals in our environment.

▶ **It would help if** people didn't use straws—or, at least, didn't use as many.

So I'm feeling like I'm ready to take some steps to make a difference when it comes to this topic. Today I'd like your help in considering some possible actions that I might take and what my audience might be for those actions. Here are my initial thoughts:

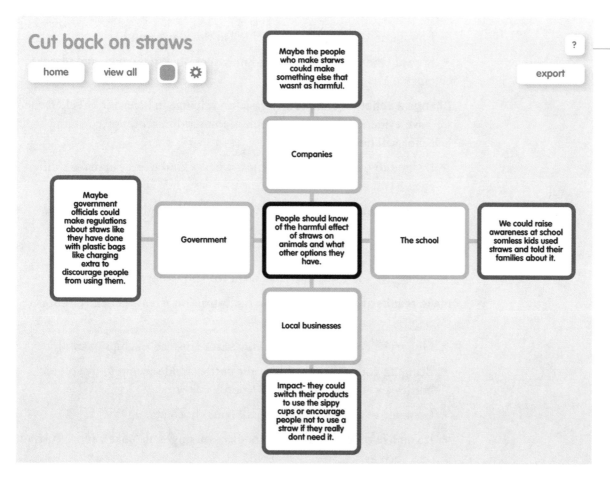

Cut back on straws

home | view all | ⬛ | ⚙

Maybe the people who make staws coukd make something else that wasnt as harmful.

Companies

Maybe government officials could make regulations about staws like they have done with plastic bags like charging extra to discourage people from using them.

Government

People should know of the harmful effect of straws on animals and what other options they have.

The school

We could raise awareness at school somless kids used straws and told their families about it.

Local businesses

Impact- they could switch their products to use the sippy cups or encourage people not to use a straw if they really dont need it.

export | ?

Students helped co-create this chart by coming up and typing their ideas directly into it. After the class co-created this graphic, it remained projected in the room so that students could use it as a mentor as they worked with their own small groups to try making their own maps of audiences and asks.

▶ *I can help by* not using straws.

▶ *I can have even more of an impact by* convincing other people not to use straws.

On the map that the third-grade teacher built with her students, notice how she began by naming groups of people who might have an effect on the issue and then considered what those groups might do. From here, work with students to consider who else might help and how. Use the following list as necessary to spark ideas:

Ways We Ask Other People to Help Us Take Action

Call people to action. We use a call to action when we want people to support us in our own direct action.

▶ Join us Saturday to pick up trash in the park.

▶ Please donate to help us . . .

▶ Join me at a peace rally after school at the playground.

▶ Spread kindness! Add your kind messages on a sticky note and place outside Mr. K's door.

Change a behavior or belief. We ask for a change in behavior or belief when we have evidence that many people thinking differently or changing their behavior will help.

▶ Be kind to others: you never know when a kind word can make a difference.

▶ Recycling matters! Make sure you get it in the right can every time.

▶ Everyone can do something about bullying. Be an upstander, not a bystander!

▶ Show that you care. Everyone wants to know they matter.

Make a substitution. We ask for a substitution when that substitution results in the change we want to make.

▶ Hungry? Try one of these yummy snacks instead of chips or candy!

▶ Bringing your own reusable water bottle could save up to five plastic bottles a week from going in a landfill.

▶ Look for a "fair trade" label on all your chocolate.

▶ If you like one of these classic books, you might also like a more current one, such as . . .

▶ Save fossil fuels and bike to school. Your exercise will result in fewer carbon emissions.

Spread the word. Sometimes we ask people to spread the word, because the best way we can take action is to educate as many people as possible.

▶ Always look both ways at a train crossing.

▶ Know the signs of choking! Here are three things you need to know . . .

▶ Bicycle helmets save lives.

Change a policy or law. When we contact people in power, we often advocate for a change in rules, policy, or law to help our cause. We can also encourage others to reach out for the same purpose.

▶ Contact the city council to install speed bumps on a residential street where kids play.

▶ Ask a business to find more environmentally friendly packaging.

▶ Call a congress person to address summer safety for students.

Students then move to working with their groups to engage in a similar process, beginning with completing the following sentence stems:

▶ *The problem is . . .*

▶ *It would help if . . .*

▶ *I can help by . . .*

▶ *I can have even more of an impact by . . .*

Then, students can brainstorm possible audiences and asks that support their goal. They might begin by naming potential audiences or asks, but the work isn't complete until they've identified at least one clear ask for each audience or at least one clear audience for each ask.

To foster student agency and to aim for a real impact on an issue, we want students to consider their audience as someone other than us, their teachers. While teachers can be great feedback engines, students need to connect with organizations, people, or other students in order to see their work making an impact. As students are working, confer with them. Can they identify who target audiences may be for their message by applying their current knowledge about society and government? If not, a quick minilesson about your community's governing structure or about individuals' jobs within a corporation might be of help.

> **Helpful Language**
>
> *Who might have the power to change this? To make a decision about this?*
>
> *Who can help us solve this problem?*
>
> *Whose job is it to control or manage this?*

Think and ask ourselves . . .

Who else is affected by this?

Who might care about this?

Who can change this?

This is our potential audience.

Students in a fifth-grade classroom considered these three questions as they worked in small groups to discuss potential audiences for their work.

OUTCOMES AND WHAT TO LOOK FOR

This Try It requires students to shift from taking in and synthesizing information to seeing themselves as active agents in the world. Can students

▶ identify a problem?

▶ identify a way to bring attention to the situation?

▶ identify ways in which they, personally, might help?

▶ identify ways in which they might inspire others to help?

▶ understand how different audiences might have different capabilities for help?

▶ identify ways in which different audiences might help?

FOLLOW UP

In the next Try It, the students will continue this work by considering how viable their plans are.

PLANNING FOR IMPACT:
Consider Cost and Impact

TRY THIS WHEN . . .

■ students have drafted initial action plans and are ready to move forward with considering the costs of what they are asking and the potential impact of their plan.

Here we teach students to understand the term *cost* as it relates to time, personal sacrifice, or another variable and to weigh the cost against the potential impact of the action. A brilliantly planned action with a sizeable planned impact will not have any effect if its cost is so high that it's not possible to execute. Our goal is to maximize impact while keeping the cost of the action doable and sustainable. In this Try It we also discuss with students the importance of not asking others to do what we wouldn't do ourselves: it is one thing to hang up a poster asking someone else to do something; it's quite another to actually do it yourself.

WHAT TO DO

Open up a conversation about cost and impact with your students. For older students, it might sounds something like this:

> *We've been deeply immersed in learning about _____ and I can tell you are ready to take action. Yesterday you finished your planning page to identify several possible actions that you might want to take. I know it's tempting to pick just one! But before we do, we need to think about the cost of each action.*
>
> *You know the word* cost *can mean how much money you'll need to spend to buy something, and sometimes our actions have a monetary cost. But many times, cost can be other things too: our time, a personal sacrifice, doing something that is less convenient, or asking people to do things they might not want to do. Today I want to share one way that we can use to analyze the cost of our different actions. This helps us make informed and reasoned decisions.*

For younger students, we keep our language direct and to the point:

> *Friends, we have quite a few ideas on our class chart. Let's talk about each idea and write down what we will have to do for each one. Let's think about each one in a special way. Do you ever do this when you go to the store? You think carefully about which choice to make. Hmmm . . . Do I want this . . . or this? Why? Our first idea was to write some announcements for the school. Turn and talk about how many kids we will reach if we do that. Will we reach more or fewer*

A first-grade class surveyed school staff to help evaluate possible actions they would like to take. They then followed up by surveying fellow students and interviewing the school principal to determine if they could get funding or would need to raise funds.

kids if we make posters instead? What do we think will get our message to more people? Let's think about each of our ideas in that way. We call that impact.

We then model for students—with our own issue—how to use one of the following options for assessing cost.

Conduct a survey. When we suggest to students that they conduct a survey, we are acknowledging that we, as learners, sometimes need to reach out to a test audience to see what their thoughts are. Digital tools like Google Forms or online survey sites can help students reach out to audiences beyond the school community. Surveys might present a potential audience with a variety of options to see how they would react. Students might ask: *Would you be more willing to pay a charge for a plastic bag at the store or bring your own bags? How likely are you to remember your own bags? How much of an inconvenience is it to bring your own bags?*

For younger students, posting a piece of chart paper with their question in a place where their audience is likely to see it—outside the school office or where caregivers arrive for drop-off and pickup—and asking people to respond in writing is an easy way to capture feedback.

Support: Give students an example or write an example survey for your own topic. Provide students with sentence frames and language to help them work their questions in a way that will get them useful information. You might include language like:

Would you be more willing to _____ or _____?

How easy would it be for you to _____?

What is a reason you might not want to _____?

What would convince you to _____?

What might help you remember to _____?

Build a chart. Compare the various solutions to a problem by using a chart to explore different costs associated with each one. In this option we might also consider the potential to have a widespread impact. In the following example, from a fifth-grade classroom, the teacher walked students through a variety of actions, costs, and impacts.

Possible Actions to Take	Start a cyberbullying education campaign by creating posters to hang around school and writing morning announcements.	Use our class social media account to send out facts about cyberbullying and urge people to do something.	Stand up to cyberbullies. Tell an adult.	Teach parents about cyberbullying and what they can do.
Possible Costs and Impacts	Time: we will need time to research and create the posters and announcements. Could have an effect on our school.	A little bit of time; might have a farther reach but might not affect our school.	Could become a target. Could really help someone out that is in trouble. It would mean a lot to them.	Organize a way to get to parents, time, and maybe time outside of school. We think this would help a lot because parents should watch what kids are doing.

Another option is to use a chart like the one below (adapted from Zemelman 2016, 80) that asks students to examine several scenarios for taking action. Unlike the example above, it also includes another component to consider: *How much fun is this going to be?* This is actually a very practical question: the more students see the work as fun or engaging, the more likely they are to maintain the energy needed for longer or bigger projects. At the same time, if we notice students choosing only options that they deem fun instead of gravitating toward those that have a higher potential for impact, we might help them come to a compromise by weaving in elements of both.

Possible Actions	**How strongly do I feel about taking this action?**	**How difficult will this be to do? What is the cost?**	**What impact will this action have?**	**How much fun will this be to do?**
Option 1				
Option 2				
Option 3				

Support: Students might need some prompting to evaluate several different options in order to make informed decisions. With younger students, we might look at only a few options, but older students can dig a bit deeper and revisit their resources to find more. Just as there are multiple perspectives in any issue, there are often widely varied opinions on what a solution might be. Encourage students to consider all the options before latching on to any one way to take action.

Working with the tools in this Try It can help you and your students identify any safety issues or insurmountable costs that might prevent you from putting a specific option to work.

By the end of this Try It, we will want students to select the best option or options for moving forward. To do so, we ask them to look at their charts and discuss which options seem the most actionable, which options will have a strong impact, and which options have an approachable cost for the time allocated to the work. If students are struggling, ask them to meet with another group to share their ideas and get some objective feedback. Even our youngest students can engage in peer to peer feedback using language like *I think the best idea is . . . because . . .*

Small groups will likely want to choose one or two options if they complement each other. If the class is moving forward in work together, students might form groups at this point to take different actions related to the class topic. Further options for small-group work arise as students decide how to best implement their action. For example, the class may decide that a public service campaign on allergy awareness has the strongest impact. However, students might go about their campaign in different ways, crafting announcements, making pamphlets, designing infographics, or giving a teaching presentation to other classrooms via video chat.

A fifth-grade class explores the cost and impact of various forms of action.

OUTCOMES AND WHAT TO LOOK FOR

This Try It encourages students to take a reflective stance. Can students

▶ fully consider several options before narrowing in on one?

▶ consider what the cost of what they are asking might be for themselves or an intended audience?

▶ project the impact of various actions and use that estimation of impact to help them make an informed choice?

FOLLOW UP

The next three Try Its offer options for putting students' plans to work. Use one, two, or all of them as necessary:

▶ Try **"Take Action by Creating"** (pp. 195–200) if your students are looking for ways to influence others to support their action or to make a change.

▶ Try **"Take Action by Teaching Others"** (pp. 201–204) if your students want to deepen others' knowledge about their topic, especially if they have an opportunity to do this by teaching face-to-face.

▶ Try **"Take Action Directly"** (pp. 205–208) if your students are planning to take action directly through volunteering, collections, donations, or other direct options.

WRITE WITH US

⏻ **What audiences might be especially receptive to hearing from your students?**

⏻ **Where are your students likely to find *fun* in this work?**

⏻ **Based on the Follow Up notes on the previous page, which Try Its will you use in the next section? Why?**

⏻ **Share your ideas. #ReadTheWorldNow**

ACTING WITH PURPOSE AND HEART:
Take Action by Creating

TRY THIS WHEN . . .

■ students are looking for ways to influence others to support their action or make a change.

In our daily lives, we're surrounded by what we call mentor tech—real-world exemplars of high-quality multimedia—that aims to get us to take action: to buy something, to accept a viewpoint, to vote or donate in support of a candidate or a cause. The advertisements, blogs, and infographics that we see each day can be mentor tech for our students in their efforts to get others involved with their planned action.

WHAT TO DO

First, consider what genre you'd like to work with. See the table on the next page for genre suggestions. You might make this decision on your own, or you might show students a few examples and discuss which to use.

Next, we apply the genre study method Katie Wood Ray writes about in *Study Driven* (2006) to our real-world mentor tech. This approach gives students a taste of the genre and helps them identify what is effective. The first step is building a resource set that features grade-appropriate, real-world examples of the genre. The mentor tech examples you find don't need to be related to the issues your students are addressing. They just need to be well produced, interesting, accessible, and appropriate for your students. They should represent a wide range within the genre to help students see what is possible. For an example, see the mentor tech set we've created on public service announcements at tinyurl.com/ReadtheWorldPSAs.

Once you've collected mentor examples, you can begin work with students. View a few examples as a whole class to help students craft a vision of what's possible. Give students time to discuss what they notice in partners or small groups and to note those findings on a class chart. What do different examples from the same genre seem to have in common? What elements or techniques did they find effective or memorable? Next, offer students a place to access additional mentor examples. You might post them on your classroom website or LMS, create QR codes for students to scan, preload videos on devices for station rotations, or gather them all in a central place using Padlet or Google Slides. You might print out still images or graphics and give students the opportunity to interact with them up close, annotating

Helpful Language

What do you notice that you'd like to try?

How do you feel? How well did the text we looked at tune into your emotions?

What did you learn about the topic? How did the authors present things they wanted you to learn?

What do you think your audience would connect with?

What did you see that you want to try?

What story are the authors telling?

What do you see me doing here?

How might we organize this? What's most important?

What does my audience need to know before I ask something of them?

What graphics or images would help bring some energy to my writing?

What tone should I take? What visuals do I need?

Video Advertisements or Public Service Announcements	Public service announcements are videos that typically address a social issue and are designed to raise awareness in order to influence behavior and attitudes. **Tech Tip:** As of this book's publication, some apps we like for creating PSAs are iMovie, Clips, Powtoon, and WeVideo. To create video advertisements or PSAs, students can use apps and websites that will enable them to combine images, text, voice-overs, and music. Look for something that meets the needs of your students' age level and offers the ability for exporting to share with an audience. Students can also use these tools to do digital storytelling, a powerful medium for sharing personal stories as a means to take action.
Blogs and Vlogs	Blogs and vlogs offer students a place to write or talk in great detail about a topic. Blogs are typically long-form writing, including graphics and images. Blogging enables students to break their information into a series of blog posts, each tackling a subtopic of a broader issue at hand, or to write a longer post subdivided into sections. This format works best when students have a great deal of information they want to share with an audience or you want to integrate taking action with developing writing skills. Vlogs offer a more personal touch, relying on students to share information verbally; they are typically casual in tone, making the listener feel as if they are being directly spoken to. Vlogs are extremely useful for capturing the ideas of developing writers or for practicing speaking skills. **Tech Tip:** We often start our youngest students blogging through a classroom LMS system like Seesaw, which offers them the ability to record video and type or post handwritten work. With older students, we prefer dedicated blogging platforms like Kidblog or Blogger.
Infographics	Infographics blend icons, images, text, and design to share information visually. Work with your students to study mentor tech examples and note the features that convey information. Identify layout and design, the balance of text and visuals to tell a story, and representations of data as means to connect with the audience. Also, pay careful attention to structure; these micro-lessons will help students transfer what they know about text structure when they are ready to create an infographic. **Tech Tip:** Students can use any app or program that allows them to add and manipulate text, images, and graphics. Digital tools like Canva or Piktochart offer templates and guidance for infographics. You can also use a simple presentation tool like Google Slides or Keynote to create graphic representations. Younger students might choose to create simpler graphics using paper, markers, and scissors and then share these digitally via an app like Flipgrid so they can add their own narration and explanation.
Something Else!	Let students take the lead in identifying other ways that they might reach their audience. What ways are they seeing people communicate in the world? What can they create? We have seen students write digital books to be distributed to classmates, create flyers, write articles for existing outlets, or engage in photography and graphic design. Students might create interactive murals, adding components like captions, labels, and flaps; they might further enhance the interactive teaching moment by using QR codes that lead to voice recordings or augmented reality that gives the viewer a pop-up of a student offering deeper explanation. Although we like to avoid "boredom by slide presentation," we can support students in creating interactive slide presentations that ask the audience to follow links, watch videos, and discuss resources presented that have been created using many of the design features we studied with infographics. Whatever you choose, be sure to create your own project alongside students to model and scaffold their efforts. And, of course, more traditional outlets, such as letters to the editor or city officials, can also be effective.

them directly or using sticky notes. Ask students to continue this work in partners or groups of three, viewing, talking, analyzing, noticing, critiquing, and gathering their thinking. We typically use lessons like this over the course of several days to help students immerse themselves in the genre and build a list of exemplar qualities. Whether you do this work over a few days or in one session, make sure to bring students back together to revisit the chart you started together. This chart can serve as guidance for creation, feedback, minilessons, and later assessments.

Students will continue to come back to the charts you create together as they develop their own pieces. We recommend that you use the charts to drive quick minilessons that will help raise the quality of student work.

What we noticed about Infographics

- They use lots of pictures related to the topic.
- They have a title and a little introduction.
- They show information with graphs and charts.
- There is only some writing. We see subtitles, captions, labels and short paragraphs.
- They list sources at the bottom.
- Some are made by companies.
- They have maps.
- They have diagrams.
- They have icons.

Fifth-grade students shared their ideas for a class chart after exploring many examples of infographics from books and websites. The teacher later used this chart to develop an assessment checklist for students to use as they created their infographics.

Fourth-grade students in Eric Webb's class analyze documentary films as a genre study in order to create movies to inform about a cause.

Avoiding Ads

When sharing videos with students, we can use several strategies to minimize the ads, suggested video links, and extraneous content that often appear on online video sites. We might embed videos in a Google Slides presentation—like we did with the collection of mentor PSAs mentioned in the text—so that the video isn't surrounded by distractions. There are also sites like Quietube, TubeChop, and SafeShare.tv that will pull the video into its own window and offer some editing possibilities. Additionally, many LMS systems offer YouTube embedding that will remove distractions, and a site like PlayPosit allows you to add interactive pieces to guide student viewing. Check with your district technology team to determine the best option for your students.

Examining PSAs

① How does it begin?
- What do you see?
- What do you feel?
- How does it hook you?

② How does it tell a story?
- Emotion?
- facts?

③ What is the "ask" and how do you know? Is it effective? Why?

④ What craft moves stand out? Use of color, music, symbols, acting, camera angles...

⑤ What essential information did they include?

Which of these elements work for YOUR TOPIC?

Fourth-grade teacher Michele Giovanelli provided questions to guide students as they examined their mentor tech public service announcements. Students used these questions to guide their discussions as they worked in partners to view many examples of PSAs.

Based on the fifth-grade chart about infographics on page 197, those mini-lessons might include

▸ Is a particular image conveying the intended message?

▸ How can we use images more than sentences?

▸ How can we make clear diagrams?

Here, look out for the urge to overplan. Challenge your instinct to have students storyboard every frame and plan every word before they begin. Digital tools today offer so many creative possibilities that students need flexibility as they work to adopt, adapt to, and be inspired by the medium. Use planning and scaffolding tools with a light touch. Model for students how you might stray from an original plan in a way that is meaningful. Rely on just-in-time minilessons rather than a comprehensive plan from the outset. If you work alongside students and spy on yourself as a creator, you will find your next lesson right at your fingertips. Devote the bulk of class time to students working, experimenting, revising, and refining their work while you confer, support, and offer in-the-moment feedback. Keep the students focused on the clarifying questions *What will help your audience understand?* and *What will inspire them to action?*

As students near the end of their process, bring them back together to offer constructive critiques to one another and—when possible—gather some initial feedback from an intended audience using their original checklist. Let students make any last-minute edits that result from this feedback. When the pieces are complete, it's time to share them with the audience students have chosen. Whether the plan is to post students' work online, hang it in the hallways, or distribute it in some other way, decide how you will support students so the intended audience will see it. Students might

▸ write notes to their families and friends asking them to check out their work

▸ use a class social media account to announce or distribute the work

▸ use existing in-school communication systems, such as daily announcements, family newsletters, or the school website, to promote the work.

Students use a short form to plan documentary films.

A third-grade student shows off her business card, which she uses to promote her blog.

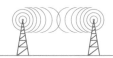

Give US feeDBack
When we get feedback we
see how our learning
impacts others. Please share
your new learning or questions.
Jot YOUR Thoghts
hear ↓

OUTCOMES AND WHAT TO LOOK FOR

The goal of this Try It is to help students internalize a process that they can transfer to any medium they wish to use to go public. Can students

▶ use mentor tech to notice and note the key elements of the genre?

▶ use a key elements checklist or chart (like the What We Noticed About Infographics chart on page 197) to create and reflect, taking into consideration their topic, intended audience, and voice?

▶ make adjustments and refinements as they work?

FOLLOW UP

Use the final Try It in this book, "Reflect on Our Actions," to help students consider the effect of this work.

Join the Conversation:
Genre Studies

"How can we create a public service announcement if we've never studied public service announcements? In order to write in a genre, you have to immerse yourself in the genre."

#ReadTheWorldNow

Hein.pub/RTW4.4

ACTING WITH PURPOSE AND HEART:
Take Action by Teaching Others

TRY THIS WHEN . . .

- students want to deepen others' knowledge about their topic, especially if they have an opportunity to do this by teaching face-to-face

- students have identified their classmates or other school-age children as their target audience

- students have an opportunity to present in public to their chosen audience.

Sometimes the most effective way to take action is to share what we have learned with others. Raising awareness can also be the first step in generating energy and excitement for more action-based work. Students might raise awareness within their own classroom or the school, in students beyond the school (using digital tools), and in the wider community. At times this teaching might be informal: students might stand up, tell what they've learned, and explain what we can do about it. We can also support students in a more formal approach, drawing on all we know about good teaching and sharing those practices with students so that they can put them to use.

WHAT TO DO

This work gives our students a sneak peek into our world as teachers. We make transparent the ways in which we design lessons for them; how we consider what they will read, view, listen to, or do during that time; and how we plan this work so that they can achieve the intended outcomes. This work calls on students to engage the learner, perhaps by providing hands-on work or experiential learning. Begin by taking a moment to reflect on the following:

▶ **What teaching strategies do you commonly use with your students that will feel familiar to them?** For example, these strategies might include read-alouds, discussions, turn and talks, explicit instruction, small-group practice, blended learning, image study, and exploring resources. Try brainstorming a list with students: What do *they* notice about the strategies you use? Which do *they* find the most helpful? Use this list as a starting point for your minilessons.

▶ **What strategies and skills have students developed during informational writing units?** For example, if students have been working

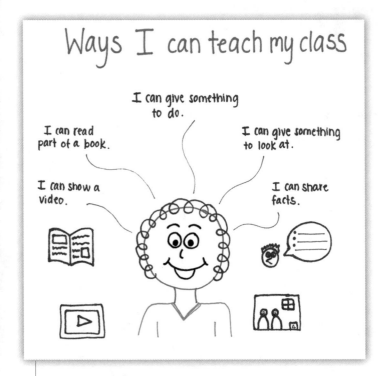

A first-grade teacher begins the process of helping students choose which information and resources they will use to teach their classmates about a topic of importance.

on how-to books, might that genre lend itself to taking action? Could students write a how-to book to be distributed to local businesses? Pull out any old charts or materials you've used during informational text units to help students consider options as they get to work.

▶ **What skills or strategies would you like to develop in your students?** When our students have a rich repertoire of strategies, we allow them choice; when we are looking to develop certain skills, we might focus on specific media that can help them tell a story. We might also guide kids to media that they need repeated practice with in order to build proficiency. As with reading volume, you have to blog a lot to become a good blogger and make movies a lot to become a high-quality director. We build skill where kids need it, just as we do across the curriculum.

If you've built a student-centered classroom, you've modeled teaching moves countless times across the year. By this time, students know how to turn and talk and how to have a discussion. Making a quick information chart of the ways you can teach, using examples from your own classroom practice, gets students' thinking on the right track. Provide varying levels of scaffolding to help students select a method if you are providing choice. Some students may be able to choose fairly independently while others may need more guidance.

If the entire class is using the same format, you might plan a quick lesson to share more details on how you plan. If students are using different formats, this work can be done in small groups. That might sound something like this:

I want to share a few tips with you about how I make a quick teaching video. I try not to overwhelm my students by putting in too many things. I also try to have a visual for each important piece of information that I'm sharing. I'm going to suggest that you talk with your group to identify the three or four most important pieces of information your audience will need and what visuals you might use in your video. I'll check back with you a little later to see how it's going.

Once students have planned their teaching or created the tool that will teach others, give them an opportunity to do a trial run of their teaching method with another small group, with you, or by using a video tool like See-saw or Flipgrid to collect initial feedback.

To check the impact of their lessons, students might choose to design a method for feedback such as a quick exit ticket on a sticky note or a digital platform. Or you can establish a common format for all students to use. We scaffold students in their responses with language stems in order to prompt deep thinking and respectful evaluation.

▶ *Something I learned is . . .*

▶ *I never knew that . . .*

▶ *Something that surprised me is . . .*

▶ *One thing I'm wondering is . . .*

▶ *I have a question about . . .*

▶ *Something effective you did is . . .*

▶ *I really liked how you . . .*

▶ *Next time you might try . . .*

▶ *It would be helpful to me if you could . . .*

▶ *The most interesting thing to me was . . .*

▶ *The thing you did that was most helpful was . . .*

▶ *Have you thought about showing . . . ?*

A student in Alison Cardoso's third-grade class prepares his materials for teaching his classmates what he's learned about issues with cacao harvesting.

Many times this teaching takes place face-to-face within our schools, with another class or invited community members as an audience. We can also teach beyond the walls of our classroom by capturing student projects and ideas on video or audio. Videos or podcasts posted to a classroom or school website or kid-safe channel allow easy ways for students to influence a larger audience. Using a tool like Flipgrid, students can post their videos to share and receive feedback. The Flipgrid community offers opportunities to connect with other classrooms across town or around the world.

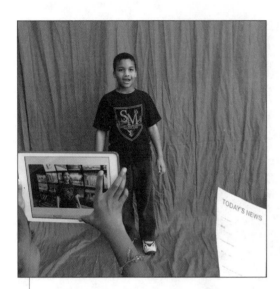

Students use a green screen to craft their own news show to educate others.

OUTCOMES AND WHAT TO LOOK FOR

This Try It turns the tables and asks students to be the teacher. Can students

▸ apply what they've learned about teaching strategies in order to educate their audience about their topic?

▸ determine what information to include?

▸ choose the best resources or activities for their audience?

FOLLOW UP

Use the final Try It in this book, "Reflect on Our Actions" on page 209, to help students consider the effect of this work.

ACTING WITH PURPOSE AND HEART:
Take Action Directly

TRY THIS WHEN . . .

■ students have identified that the best way to take action is to get involved some way.

Direct action—donation drives, volunteer opportunities, service projects, systemic or design innovations, or a myriad of other options—offers students hands-on opportunities to dig in and make an impact themselves. It might be something that occurs in the school or an action that reaches into the community. It can be small scale or have a widespread impact. Action takes many forms, from service-oriented projects to innovations in design to solve problems in the world. Some forms of action will feel accessible within the scope of the curriculum while others will require a bit more planning. Something to consider with action is that not every kid needs to take direct action, every time. It's one option in a toolbox of ways to respond.

WHAT TO DO

When considering what kind of direct action to take with students, two main questions drive our work:

▶ How will this action have a legitimate positive impact on the issue at hand?

▶ How will this action be meaningful to students and reinforce their sense of agency?

Whether you choose the kind of action the class will take on your own or you involve students in the decision, keep those two questions in mind as you choose and plan the action.

Next, we've listed some common methods for students to take action. We hope that this list will be a help as you brainstorm potential actions, but don't let it limit your thinking. As experts on the issues you've researched, you and your students may have even better ideas for action.

Volunteer or engage in community service. Students often find that issues they thought were geographically far away actually exist right in their own community or school. Service opportunities can be school based, such as organizing a way to help with recycling at school, or community based. Many times, schools are already engaged in these types of activities, so we suggest leveraging understanding, empathy,

Fifth-grade students from Grove Elementary School pack high-nutrient meals to benefit undernourished children at the non-profit organization Feed My Starving Children.

Helpful Language

How can we be most helpful here? What information do we have to back that up?

Are we capable of doing the things that this action would require of us?

How will we measure our impact?

Students at Sifton Elementary School raise awareness for kindness by alerting everyone who pulls into their parking lot that their action is to choose kindness.

and students' questions to guide action and help students develop a real understanding of their impact.

Power it up: Connect with organizers and specialists in the field or through an organization you are working with. Arrange for students to be able to interview that person before or during the opportunity as part of their research. Guide them in developing questions that help students examine different lenses.

Take care: Stay away from volunteer or service opportunities that are more about congratulating volunteers than about affecting the issue, causes without verified backing, and events that overstep the voices of those they are attempting to support. Taking action is never about the opportunity to get out of the classroom for enjoyment or as a reward. (Although we hope students find joy in the work!) It's about changing the hearts, minds, and actions of the children we teach.

Organize a day of action. A day of action is when a school community decides to alter their behavior for an entire day in order to directly observe the impact that they had for that day. For example, in one kindergarten classroom, students planned a day of kindness. They asked each student in the school to do three kind things for someone else during the day. They then calculated their impact, with the help of their fifth-grade buddies, by totaling the number of kind acts that had taken place as a result. At another school, third graders organized a recycling awareness event.

Power it up: Challenge students to consider how they can encourage authentic participation and ensure that students who were not a part of the initial research will understand the issues in a meaningful way. What materials can they share with teachers or present to classes?

Take care: Don't let change fall by the wayside after a single day of action. Encourage students to develop a plan for how the day will kick off long-term changes in behavior. In one fourth-grade classroom, students encouraged the school to participate in Earth Hour (www.earthhour.org/). Afterward, they created a guide to saving energy, which was then shown on the school's video morning announcements each day to encourage continued energy-saving practices.

Collect donations. Donation drives—for coats, clothing, food, or other essentials—can offer much-needed assistance. Students can gather by class or as a school and then participate in delivering if the option is available. Donation drives can occur year-round, seasonally, or to address a specific crisis.

> **Power it up:** Plan the drive with a local organization that can use and distribute what is collected. The organization can also let your team know what is most needed.

> **Take care:** Local donations may, in fact, be going to families or students in your very own school or classroom. Proceed with care and compassion. Avoid labeling donation boxes with the names of specific schools. Instead, focus on organizations as the recipients.

Raise funds. Raising funds is a good option when students encounter nonprofit organizations they would like to support, particularly if the organizations are working in places where students would like to help but don't have access to. Often, organizations can use monetary donations more effectively than physical goods.

> **Power it up:** Fund-raising can go awry quickly. It's inequitable for students whose families cannot or choose not to participate, and it can be taken out of the students' hands by well-meaning parents. Instead, try to help students find ways to raise the money themselves like the fourth graders at Grove Elementary School who held a gently used item sale during lunchtime.

> **Take care:** Be aware of district policies about what you can and can't do regarding fund-raising. Be mindful of the ties that organizations have, fully researching them before supporting them.

Use design thinking for change. There is one last option that we wish to explore. The current push for science, technology, engineering, and mathematics (STEM) education in our schools offers opportunities for students to use design thinking and innovation. STEM programs aren't just about coding: a well-rounded STEM curriculum also supports students in developing inventions and innovations and exploring

As students explore coding and robotics and engage in multiple experiences with design thinking, encourage them to consider: Now that you've made this, how might you use it?

A third-grade student invented a "close reading" finger light using a watch battery, a Light-Emitting Diode (LED), pipe cleaners, and electrical tape. This light helped him highlight text and track his reading. He thought others could benefit from it as well, so he produced additional lights in an after-school STEM club and distributed them to students throughout the school.

What is design thinking?

John Spencer and A.J. Juliani define design thinking as a "way of solving problems that encourages positive risk-taking and creativity" (2016, 52). The Stanford school identifies five stages of the design thinking model: empathize, define, ideate, prototype, and test. Experts agree that the model is cyclical, and students may move between stages fluidly as they revise, rethink, and re-design multiple times. For more information, visit Stanford d.school's K12 Lab website: stanford.io/2pOr2fC.

their potential impacts and applications. What if our students were inspired to take action by designing solutions to problems and issues in the world? Isn't that what leading experts in the field do? We've been following stories of student inventors closely over the last few years, and we are starting to see our own students rise to this challenge, like the third graders who designed finger flashlights for at-home reading, the sixth graders who designed a hydroponic gardening program at their school after working with a local community farm, or the fourth graders who helped research and design an accessible playground to meet a community need. In each of these cases, teachers and students anchored their work in empathy for those whom they sought to design for.

OUTCOMES AND WHAT TO LOOK FOR

Can students

▶ use their information and research to determine how or where they might make an impact with direct action?

▶ take action in a meaningful, thoughtful, and sensitive way?

FOLLOW UP

Use the final Try It in this book, "Reflect on Our Actions," to help students consider the effect of this work.

Stacy Hansen and her fourth-grade students in Waukee Community School District partnered with Enabling the Future (http://enablingthefuture .org/) to build a prosthetic arm for a child as a way to take action.

ACTING WITH PURPOSE AND HEART:
Reflect on Our Actions

TRY THIS WHEN . . .

■ you are wrapping up any action-oriented experience.

The essential last step in our action-oriented process is to make space and time for reflection on the work we've done. While this reflection may or may not have an effect on the issue at the center of the work, it is vital for students in naming and considering their own agency. We ask students to stop and consider the impact they've made, the effect the work has had on them, and how they might go further.

WHAT TO DO

We often find that the best reflection comes in the private spaces in our notebooks, at least at first. Ask students to join you in your common meeting area with notebooks and pens or pencils. Play soft music, turn down the lights, display any work the students have created, and ask them to draw or write about their experience with taking action. You might offer some free space at first and then trickle out some sentence stems or merely post a list of prompts on the board for students to access. For our youngest students, consider asking them to record video reflections. We remind students not to rush through the prompts: this is heart work and it takes time. We encourage them to choose one and stick with it, writing longer than is comfortable before moving on to another.

Helpful Language

Take a few minutes and look at the work we've accomplished together. Now, free-write in your notebook.

Give me a thumbs-up when you know which thought prompt you want to start with. Try to write as long as you can just from that prompt.

Look back over your notebook. What other thoughts do you have?

Will you jot one big reflection on this sticky for our class chart? Choose something you feel can be public.

Let's Reflect!
- At first I thought...but now I think...
- This work felt important because...
- The things I'm keeping with me are...
- I still want to...
- I plan to continue...
- Some ways my thinking has changed are...
- Something I'd do differently in the future is...

I think...
I feel...
I hope...
I wonder...

Sentences stems like the ones featured in these charts (the first for a fifth-grade classroom, the second for a first-grade classroom) offer students support in reflecting on their experience taking action.

At the end of our time, we might ask students to choose one idea to share more publicly on a sticky note. Of course, we go back and read and respond to their journals later, mining for data to use in our next cycle of learning, but a class share on a sticky gives all students a quick snapshot of how they've learned, changed, and (we hope) grown over the course of their work. Students can share their sticky with the whole group verbally, post it at their seat and then have a gallery walk to read what others have learned, or snap a photo of the sticky and share it visually on a digital bulletin board.

Taking action made me feel powerful, like I could do something. There are people who will get a meal because of what I did.
—Paul, fifth grader

This felt important because people need to know about how coral is endangered and what they can do about it.
—Dara, fifth grader

I want to tell more and more people about what I learned. I want to tell everyone!
—Isah, first grader

This makes me happy because I helped make food for hungry kids.
—Isadora, fifth grader

I still want to find a way to help people save food. Why does so much go in the garbage?
—Mikayla, fourth grader

I feel good to know something I did will be good for people.
—Booker, first grader

OUTCOMES AND WHAT TO LOOK FOR

This Try It requires students to step outside the frenetic pace of the school day and consider the impact of their work on themselves and the world around them. Can students

▶ stop, think, and write about their experience and the impact it's had on them?

▶ use scaffolds like sentence stems to go deeper with their thinking and reflection?

▶ acknowledge their impact and make a plan for the continued work they might want to do?

FOLLOW UP

Read through the writing that students completed in this Try It to assess the degree of impact the work has had. These words from our students offer meaningful data—often more meaningful than numerical scores. As you read, or as you debrief students about this work in conversation, pay close attention to the specific resources that made an impact and which strategies students felt were most effective for them. Keep your findings in mind when planning your next unit or school year.

WRITE WITH US

⏻ Think back to when you began this work with your students. Now, consider the work they're doing at this point in the process. What differences do you see in their sense of agency?

⏻ What feels hard about this work? What are the easy steps you can take to overcome that?

⏻ What feels exciting about this work? What can you do to keep that excitement at the forefront for you and your students? Jot down three things that piqued your interest as you read this section.

⏻ Now, go find a colleague (or a group of colleagues) and talk through those three things with them. What, from that conversation, reinforced your original thinking? What took your thinking in a new direction?

⏻ Share your ideas. #ReadTheWorldNow

Go #ReadTheWorldNow

Maybe you've already tried some of the lessons from this book, or perhaps you're considering where to start. More than once we've had a fellow educator raise their hand at the end of a workshop or conference presentation to ask a simple question, one that might also be on your mind right now. *Where do I start?* We ask that you take a minute and consider, *What makes sense for you and your students?* We don't advocate for trying to do everything at once or even everything in one year. We start where it makes sense for our students, our school, and our community. Choose one thing, just one, and give it a try. Oftentimes we see educators overprepare in order to get started. We suggest instead that you jump right in; even after just one lesson, you'll have infinitely more information about your students' learning than before you started. Open your classroom to colleagues; collaborate with your students. Be brave, take risks! We are teaching in exciting times and we firmly believe it is the best time to be a student and the best time to be a teacher! We are the pioneers, the wayfarers in the ocean navigating by the stars—listening to our guts and hearts, traveling paths that are familiar and yet unknown.

We have one last invitation to you. The Questions That Guide Our Action in Chapter 4 can also be applied to our own teaching lives. We've included a getting-started version of this for you to use as a planning tool on the next page. Revisit it frequently and update as your practice evolves. Think about what matters, write it down, rip out the page, and stick it to your bulletin board. Come back to it regularly and use it to help guide your next steps. You'll find a blank version located in the book's online digital resources at Hein.pub/RTW-Resources. Download a printable version of the plan and start over when you need to. It all starts with just one step. We believe in you. You've got this. Go read the world.

Those who authentically commit themselves to the people must re-examine themselves constantly.

—Paulo Freire, *Pedagogy of the Oppressed,* 1970 (60)

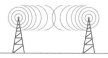

Join the Conversation:
Closing Recording
"Let's read the world together."

#ReadTheWorldNow

Hein.pub/RTWE.1

GETTING STARTED

⏻ Why is this work important?

Now that you've read this book, we invite you to decide why this is important to you. What will keep you going when it gets challenging? What will you hold on to as your "so what?" for this work?

⏻ What's the best way to take action?

Or in this case, what's the best way to get started? Where will you begin? What's a just-right fit for your class? Your situation?

⏻ Who needs to hear my message?

Who will you enlist to do this work with you? Who needs to know that you're ready to take this journey with and for your students?

⏻ How am I changed?

What do you know now that you didn't know before? What do you think now that you didn't think before? What will you do differently moving forward?

⏻ What will this cost me?

Everything costs something: time, a shift in mindset, the stress of taking a risk. What will this action cost you? How will you overcome costs that feel like a stretch?

This Action Plan can be downloaded at Hein.pub/RTW-Resources.

Frequently Asked Questions

We often get questions from teachers about the impact of digital tools in the classroom. These range from management questions to larger inquiries about curriculum and instruction. We have shared some of our thinking and conversations about these commonly asked questions below. We hope you'll join in this dialogue with us online. #ReadTheWorldNow

 Can technology really support social-emotional learning?

Hein.pub/RTWFAQ1

 What's the next big thing in educational technology?

Hein.pub/RTWFAQ2

 How do I assess when teaching with technology?

Hein.pub/RTWFAQ3

 Are primary kids too young for learning with technology?

Hein.pub/RTWFAQ4

 How do you manage using devices in the classroom?

Hein.pub/RTWFAQ5

Does this work meet standards?

Hein.pub/RTWFAQ6

 What if my supervisor doesn't think this work is necessary?

Hein.pub/RTWFAQ7

 How can I find time to fit this work in?

Hein.pub/RTWFAQ8

 How can professional development help in this work?

Hein.pub/RTWFAQ9

 Where can we find resources to do this work?

Hein.pub/RTWFAQ10

References
and the Shoulders We Stand On

Adichie, Chimamanda Ngozi. 2009. "The Danger of a Single Story." Address presented at TEDGlobal, Oxford, July. www.ted.com/talks/chimamanda_adichie_the_danger_of_a_single_story?language=en.

Ahmed, Sara K. 2018. *Being the Change: Lessons and Strategies to Teach Social Comprehension*. Portsmouth, NH: Heinemann.

Allington, Richard L. 2002. *Big Brother and the National Reading Curriculum: How Ideology Trumped Evidence*. Portsmouth, NH: Heinemann.

———. 2003. "The Three Principles of Reading." Keynote address presented at the CCIRA Conference. Denver, Colorado.

———. 2012. *What Really Matters for Struggling Readers: Designing Research-Based Programs*. 3rd ed. Boston: Pearson.

Allington, Richard L., and Rachael E. Gabriel. 2012. "Every Child, Every Day." *Educational Leadership* 69, no. 6 (March): 10–15.

Anderson, Melinda D. 2017. "Do Conversations About Race Belong in the Classroom?" Interview with Beverly Daniel Tatum. *Atlantic*, September 5. www.theatlantic.com/education/archive/2017/09/beverly-daniel-tatum-classroom-conversations-race/538758/.

Apkon, Stephen. 2013. *The Age of the Image: Redefining Literacy in a World of Screens*. New York: Farrar, Straus, and Giroux.

Atkins, Laura, Stan Yogi, and Yutaka Houlette. 2017. *Fred Korematsu Speaks Up*. Berkeley, CA: Heyday.

Ayers, William, Gloria Ladson-Billings, Gregory Michie, and Pedro A. Noguera, eds. 2008. *City Kids, City Schools: More Reports from the Front Row*. New York: New Press.

Baldwin, James. 1985. *The Price of the Ticket: Collected Nonfiction, 1948–1985*. New York: St. Marin's/Marek.

Baldwin, James, and Raoul Peck. 2017. *I Am Not Your Negro*. New York: Vintage.

Barrett, Peter, Yufan Zhang, Fay Davies, and Lucinda Barrett. 2015. *Clever Classrooms: Summary Report of the HEAD Project (Holistic Evidence and Design)*. Report. February. www.salford.ac.uk/cleverclassrooms/1503-Salford-Uni-Report-DIGITAL.pdf.

Bass, William L., II, and Franki Sibberson. 2015. *Digital Reading: What's Essential in Grades 3–8*. Urbana, IL: National Council of Teachers of English.

Beane, James A. 1997. *Curriculum Integration: Designing the Core of Democratic Education*. New York: Teachers College Press.

Beers, Kylene, and Robert E. Probst. 2017. *Disrupting Thinking: Why* How *We Read Matters*. New York: Scholastic.

———. 2013. *Notice and Note: Strategies for Close Reading*. Portsmouth, NH: Heinemann.

Berger, Warren. 2014. *A More Beautiful Question: The Power of Inquiry to Spark Breakthrough Ideas*. New York: Bloomsbury.

Bishop, Rudine Sims. 1990. "Mirrors, Windows, and Sliding Glass Doors." *Perspectives: Choosing and Using Books for the Classroom* 6, no. 3 (Summer).

Bomer, Randy, and Katherine Bomer. 2001. *For a Better World: Reading and Writing for Social Action*. Portsmouth, NH: Heinemann.

Borba, Michele. 2016. *UnSelfie: Why Empathetic Kids Succeed in Our All-About-Me World*. New York: Touchstone.

Boyd, Danah. n.d. Danah Boyd. Accessed April 1, 2019. www.danah.org/.

Brown, Brené. 2013. *The Power of Empathy*. RSA Shorts. Vimeo. https://vimeo.com/81492863.

CASEL. n.d. Accessed April 1, 2019. https://casel.org/.

Castek, Jill, Julie Coiro, Laurie A. Henry, Donald J. Leu, and Douglas K. Hartman. 2015. "Research on Instruction and Assessment in the New Literacies of Online Research and Comprehension." In *Comprehension Instruction: Research-Based Best Practices*, 3rd ed., edited by Sheri R. Parris and Kathy Headley, 324–44. New York: Guilford.

Center for Media Literacy. n.d. "Five Key Questions Form Foundation for Media Inquiry." Accessed April 1, 2019. www.medialit.org/reading-room/five-key-questions-form-foundation-media-inquiry.

Chang, Jeff. 2016. *We Gon' Be Alright: Notes on Race and Resegregation*. New York: Picador.

Ciampa, K. 2014 "Learning in a Mobile Age: An Investigation of Student Motivation." *Journal of Computer Assisted Learning* 30, no. 1: 82–96. doi:10.1111/jcal.12036.

¡Colorín Colorado! n.d. "Books for Kids." Accessed April 2, 2019. www.colorincolorado.org/books-authors/books-kids.

Common Sense Media. 2015. "The Common Sense Census: Media Use by Tweens and Teens." Common Sense Media. November 3. https://www.commonsensemedia.org/research/the-common-sense-census-media-use-by-tweens-and-teens (21).

The Conscious Kid (blog). n.d. Accessed April 1, 2019. www.theconsciouskid.org/blog.

Cook, Gareth. 2013. *The Best American Infographics, 2013*. Boston: Mariner Books.

Cook, Tim. 2017. Commencement address at MIT, Cambridge, MA, June 9.

Cooper, Bridget. 2010. "In Search of Profound Empathy in Learning Relationships: Understanding the Mathematics of Moral Learning Environments." *Journal of Moral Education*, February 12, 79–99.

Cummins, Sunday. 2018. *Nurturing Informed Thinking: Reading, Talking, and Writing Across Content-Area Sources*. Portsmouth, NH: Heinemann.

Daniels, Harvey "Smokey." 2017. *The Curious Classroom: 10 Structures for Teaching with Student-Directed Inquiry*. Portsmouth, NH: Heinemann.

Daniels, Harvey "Smokey," and Sara K. Ahmed. 2015. *Upstanders: How to Engage Middle School Hearts and Minds with Inquiry*. Portsmouth, NH: Heinemann.

Daniels, Harvey "Smokey," and Stephanie Harvey. 2009. *Inquiry Circles in Elementary Classrooms*. DVD. Portsmouth, NH: Heinemann.

Danticat, Edwidge, and Leslie Staub. 2015. *Mama's Nightingale: A Story of Immigration and Separation*. New York: Dial Books.

Darling-Hammond, Linda, Brigid Barron, P. David Pearson, Alan H. Schoenfeld, Elizabeth K. Stage, Timothy D. Zimmerman, Gina N. Cervetti, and Jennifer L. Tilson. 2008. *Powerful Learning: What We Know About Teaching for Understanding*. San Francisco: Jossey-Bass.

Draper, Sharon M. 2010. *Out of My Mind*. New York: Atheneum.

Emdin, Christopher. 2017. *For White Folks Who Teach in the Hood . . . and the Rest of Y'all Too: Reality Pedagogy and Urban Education*. Boston: Beacon.

Engle, Margarita, and Rafael López. 2015. *Drum Dream Girl: How One Girl's Courage Changed Music*. Boston: Houghton Mifflin Harcourt.

Everett, Chad. 2017. "There Is No Diverse Book." *Imaginelit* (blog), November 21. www.imaginelit.com/news/2017/11/21/there-is-no-diverse-book.

———. n.d. *Imaginelit* (blog). Accessed April 1, 2019. www.imaginelit.com/.

Fergus, Edward, Pedro Noguera, and Margary Martin. 2014. *Schooling for Resilience: Improving the Life Trajectory of Black and Latino Boys*. Cambridge, MA: Harvard Education Press.

Fountas, Irene C., and Gay Su Pinnell. 2017. *The Fountas & Pinnell Literacy Continuum: A Tool for Assessment, Planning, and Teaching*. Portsmouth, NH: Heinemann.

Freire, Paulo. 1970. *Pedagogy of the Oppressed*. Translated by Myra B. Ramos. New York: Seabury Press.

———. 2017. *Pedagogy of the Heart*. London: Bloomsbury.

Freire, Paulo, and Donaldo P. Macedo. 1987. *Literacy: Reading the Word and the World*. London: Routledge & Kegan Paul.

Frey, Jacob, dir. 2014. *The Present*. Vimeo. https://vimeo.com/channels/staffpicks/152985022.

Furedi, Frank. 2015. *Power of Reading: From Socrates to Twitter*. London: Bloomsbury Continuum.

Glover, Matt, and Ellin Oliver Keene, eds. 2015. *The Teacher You Want to Be: Essays About Children, Learning, and Teaching*. Portsmouth, NH: Heinemann.

Goulston, Mark, and John Ullmen. 2013. "How to Really Understand Someone Else's Point of View." *Harvard Business Review*, April 22. https://hbr.org/2013/04/how-to-really-understand-someo?referral=03758&cm_vc=rr_item_page.top_right.

Hare, Rebecca Louise, and Robert Dillon. 2016. *The Space: A Guide for Educators*. Irvine, CA: EdTechTeam Press.

Harvey, Stephanie. 1998. *Nonfiction Matters: Reading, Writing, and Research in Grades 3–8*. York, ME: Stenhouse.

Harvey, Stephanie, and Harvey "Smokey" Daniels. 2015. *Comprehension and Collaboration: Inquiry Circles for Curiosity, Engagement, and Understanding*. Rev. ed. Portsmouth, NH: Heinemann.

Harvey, Stephanie, and Anne Goudvis. 2005. *The Comprehension Toolkit: Grades 3–6*. Portsmouth, NH: Firsthand/Heinemann.

———. 2007. *Strategies That Work: Teaching Comprehension for Understanding and Engagement*. 2nd ed. York, ME: Stenhouse.

———. 2016. *The Primary Comprehension Toolkit*. Portsmouth, NH: Heinemann.

———. 2017. *Strategies That Work: Teaching Comprehension for Understanding, Engagement, and Building Knowledge*. 3rd ed. Portland, ME: Stenhouse.

Harvey, Stephanie, Anne Goudvis, Katie Muhtaris, and Kristin Ziemke. 2013. *Connecting Comprehension and Technology: Adapt and Extend Toolkit Practices*. Portsmouth, NH: Firsthand.

Harwayne, Shelley. 1999. *Going Public: Priorities & Practice at the Manhattan New School*. Portsmouth, NH: Heinemann.

Hayhurst, Mike, dir. 2017. *The Pits*. The Bizzaro Company and Evening Squire Productions. Vimeo. https://vimeo.com/264791358.

Heard, Georgia, and Jennifer McDonough. 2009. *A Place for Wonder: Reading and Writing Nonfiction in the Primary Grades*. Portland, ME: Stenhouse.

Herman, Amy E. 2016. *Visual Intelligence: Sharpen Your Perception, Change Your Life*. Boston: Houghton Mifflin Harcourt.

Herold, Benjamin. 2014. "Growth of Online Reading Fuels New Achievement Gap, Researchers Say." *Digital Education* (blog), *Education Week*, September 30. http://blogs.edweek.org/edweek/DigitalEducation/2014/09/online_reading_achievement_gap_leu.html.

Hertz, Christine, and Kristine Mraz. 2018. *Kids 1st from Day 1: A Teacher's Guide to Today's Classroom*. Portsmouth, NH: Heinemann.

Hicks, Troy. 2013. *Crafting Digital Writing: Composing Texts Across Media and Genres*. Portsmouth, NH: Heinemann.

———. 2015. "More Updates from AILA: Notes Visual Literacy and the Digital Workplace." *Digital Writing, Digital Teaching: Integrating New Literacies into the Teaching of Writing* (blog), September 12. https://hickstro.org/2015/09/12/more-updates-from-aila-notes-visual-literacy-and-the-digital-workplace/.

Hobbs, Renee, and David Cooper Moore. 2013. *Discovering Media Literacy: Teaching Digital Media and Popular Culture in Elementary School*. Thousand Oaks, CA: Corwin.

Hoyt, Linda. 2002. *Make It Real: Strategies for Success with Informational Texts*. Portsmouth, NH: Heinemann.

Imafidon, Anne-Marie. 2018. Panel discussion at Chicago Council on Global Affairs Global Cities Conference, Chicago, IL, June 7.

ISTE. n.d. "ISTE Standards." Accessed April 16, 2019. www.iste.org/standards.

Jenkins, Henry. 2006. *Fans, Bloggers, and Gamers: Exploring Participatory Culture*. New York: New York University Press.

Jenkins, Steve. 2016. *Animals by the Numbers*. Boston, MA: Houghton Mifflin Harcourt Books for Young Readers.

Johansen, Dana, and Sonja Cherry-Paul. 2016. *Flip Your Writing Workshop: A Blended Learning Approach*. Portsmouth, NH: Heinemann.

Johnston, Peter H. 2004. *Choice Words: How Our Language Affects Children's Learning*. Portland, ME: Stenhouse.

———. 2012. *Opening Minds: Using Language to Change Lives*. Portland, ME: Stenhouse.

Kamkwamba, William, Bryan Mealer, and Elizabeth Zunon. 2014. *The Boy Who Harnessed the Wind: Creating Currents of Electricity and Hope*. New York: William Morrow.

Keefer, Tony. n.d. *Classroom Communities* (blog). Accessed April 1, 2019. https://classroomcommunities.com/author/tonykeefer/.

Keene, Ellin Oliver. 2008. *To Understand: New Horizons in Reading Comprehension*. Portsmouth, NH: Heinemann.

Kittle, Penny. 2013. *Book Love: Developing Depth, Stamina, and Passion in Adolescent Readers*. Portsmouth, NH: Heinemann.

Kleon, Austin. 2012. *Steal Like an Artist: 10 Things Nobody Told You About Being Creative*. New York: Workman.

Krashen, Stephen D. 1993. *The Power of Reading: Insights from Research*. Englewood, CO: Libraries Unlimited.

Krashen, Stephen D., Sy-Ying Lee, and Christy Lao. 2018. *Comprehensible and Compelling: The Causes and Effects of Free Voluntary Reading*. Santa Barbara, CA: Libraries Unlimited.

LaGarde, Jennifer, and Darren Hudgins. 2018. *Fact vs. Fiction: Teaching Critical Thinking Skills in the Age of Fake News*. Portland, OR: International Society for Technology in Education.

Lai, Thanhha. 2011. *Inside Out and Back Again*. New York: HarperCollins.

Lasseter, John, dir. 1986. *Luxo Jr [Pencil Test]*. Pixar. YouTube. www.youtube.com/watch?v=9L7wSAMPFH8&feature=youtu.be.

Lee & Low Books. 2019. "About Us." www.leeandlow.com/about-us.

———. 2017. "Classroom Library Questionnaire." www.leeandlow.com/uploads/loaded_document/408/Classroom-Library-Questionnaire_FINAL.pdf.

Lehmann, Chris, and Zac Chase. 2015. *Building School 2.0: How to Create the Schools We Need*. San Francisco: Jossey-Bass.

Leu, Donald J., Elena Forzani, Cheryl Burlingame, Jonna M. Kulikowich, Nell Sedransk, Julie Coiro, and Clint Kennedy. 2013. "The New Literacies of Online Research and Comprehension: Assessing and Preparing Students for the 21st Century with Common Core State Standards." In *Quality Reading Instruction in the Age of Common Core Standards*, edited by Susan B. Neuman and Linda B. Gambrell, 219–36. Newark, DE: International Reading Association.

Leyshon, Cressida. 2012. "This Week in Fiction: Mohsin Hamid." *New Yorker*, September 16.

Lifshitz, Jessica. n.d. *Crawling out of the Classroom* (blog). Accessed April 1, 2019. https://crawlingoutoftheclassroom.wordpress.com/.

Ludwig, Trudy, and Patrice Barton. 2013. *The Invisible Boy*. New York: Knopf.

MacMillan, Kathy, Manuela Bernardi, and Kathrin Honesta. 2019. *She Spoke: 14 Women Who Raised Their Voices and Changed the World*. Sanger, CA: Familius.

Mahoney, Joseph L., Joseph A. Durlak, and Roger P. Weissberg. 2018. "An Update on Social and Emotional Learning Outcome Research." *Phi Delta Kappan*, November 26. www.kappanonline.org/social-emotional-learning-outcome-research-mahoney-durlak-weissberg/.

Mangen, Anne. 2016. "The Digitization of Literary Texts." *Orbis Litterarum* 71, no. 3: 240–62.

Mangen, Anne, and Don Kuiken. 2014. "Lost in an iPad." *Scientific Study of Literature* 4, no. 2: 150–77. doi:10.1075/ssol.4.2.02man.

Martineau, Susan. 2016. *Infographics for Kids*. Paw Prints.

Martínez Lara, Daniel, and Rafa Cano Méndez, dirs. 2015. *Alike*. YouTube. www.youtube.com/watch?v=PDHIyrfMl_U.

McLuhan, Marshall. 1994. *Understanding Media: The Extensions of Man*. Cambridge, MA: MIT Press.

McQuivey, James. 2013. *Digital Disruption: Unleashing the Next Wave of Innovation*. Cambridge, MA: Forrester Research.

Meixler, Eli. 2017. "Barack Obama Warns Against the Divisive Nature of Social Media in Interview with Prince Harry." *Time*, December 27. http://time.com/5080099/barack-obama-prince-harry-bbc-interview/.

Merriam-Webster. n.d.a. s.v. "diversity." Accessed April 1, 2019. www.merriam-webster.com/dictionary/diversity.

———. n.d.b. s.v. "geek out." Accessed May 15, 2019. www.merriam-webster.com/dictionary/geek%20out.

Merrill, Stephen. 2018. "Flexible Classrooms: Research Is Scarce, but Promising." Edutopia, June 14. www.edutopia.org/article/flexible-classrooms-research-scarce-promising.

Michie, Gregory. 2009. *Holler If You Hear Me: The Education of a Teacher and His Students*. 2nd ed. New York: Teachers College Press.

Miller, Debbie. 2013. *Reading with Meaning: Teaching Comprehension in the Primary Grades*. 2nd ed. Portland, ME: Stenhouse.

———. 2018. *What's the Best That Could Happen? New Possibilities for Teachers & Readers*. Portsmouth, NH: Heinemann.

Miller, Donalyn. 2012. "Bless It All." *The Book Whisperer* (blog), February 12. https://bookwhisperer.com/2014/02/12/bless-it-all/.

Miller, Donalyn, and Jeff Anderson. 2011. *The Book Whisperer: Awakening the Inner Reader in Every Child*. New York: Scholastic.

Miller, Donalyn, and Susan Kelley. 2014. *Reading in the Wild: The Book Whisperer's Keys to Cultivating Lifelong Reading Habits*. San Francisco: Jossey-Bass.

Miller, Donalyn, and Colby Sharp. 2018. *Game Changer! Book Access for All Kids*. New York: Scholastic.

Mills, Michael S. 2016. "Student Preference of a Customized, Open-Access Multi-touch Digital Textbook in a Graduate Education Course." *Contemporary Educational Technology* 7, no. 2: 123–37.

Minor, Cornelius. 2019. *We Got This. Equity, Access, and the Quest to Be Who Our Students Need Us to Be*. Portsmouth, NH: Heinemann.

Mirza, Sandrine, and Le Duo. 2018. *People of Peace: 40 Inspiring Icons*. Minneapolis: Wide Eyed Editions.

Mraz, Kristine, and Christine Hertz. 2015. *A Mindset for Learning: Teaching the Traits of Joyful, Independent Growth*. Portsmouth, NH: Heinemann.

Mraz, Kristine, Alison Porcelli, and Cheryl Tyler. 2016. *Purposeful Play: A Teacher's Guide to Igniting Deep and Joyful Learning Across the Day*. Portsmouth, NH: Heinemann.

Murdoch, Kath. 2015. *The Power of Inquiry*. Northcote, VIC, Australia: Seastar Education.

Napoli, Donna Jo, and Kadir Nelson. 2010. *Mama Miti: Wangari Maathai and the Trees of Kenya*. New York: Simon & Schuster Books for Young Readers.

National Geographic. 2016. *By the Numbers 2.0*. Washington, D.C.: National Geographic Partners, LLC.

———. 2017. *By the Numbers 3.14*. Washington, D.C.: National Geographic Kids Parthers, LLC.

The National Child Traumatic Stress Network. 2008. *Child Trauma Toolkit for Educators*. www.nctsn.org/resources/child-trauma-toolkit-educators.

National Council for the Social Studies. n.d. Accessed April 2, 2019. www.socialstudies.org/.

NCSS Board of Directors. 2016. "Global and International Education in Social Studies." National Council for the Social Studies. www.socialstudies.org/positions/global_and_international_education.

Neebe, Diana, and Jen Roberts. 2015. *Power Up: Making the Shift to 1:1 Teaching and Learning*. Portland, ME: Stenhouse.

Nerdy Book Club (blog). n.d. Accessed April 1, 2019. https://nerdybookclub.wordpress.com/.

Noguera, Pedro A., Jill C. Pierce, and Roey Ahram, eds. 2016. *Race, Equity, and Education: Sixty Years from Brown*. Cham, Switzerland: Springer.

O'Donnell Wicklund Pigozzi and Peterson, Architects Inc.; VS Furniture; and Bruce Mau Design. 2010. *The Third Teacher: 79 Ways You Can Use Design to Transform Teaching & Learning*. New York: Abrams.

Palacio, R. J. 2012. *Wonder*. New York: Knopf.

Parr, Todd. 2011. *The Feelings Book*. New York: Little Brown.

Patall, Erika A., Harris Cooper, and Jorgianne Civey Robinson. 2008. "The Effects of Choice on Intrinsic Motivation and Related Outcomes: A Meta-analysis of Research Findings." *Psychological Bulletin* 134, no. 2: 270–300. doi:10.1037/0033-2909.134.2.270.

Paul, Miranda, and Elizabeth Zunon. 2015. *One Plastic Bag: Isatou Ceesay and the Recycling Women of the Gambia*. Minneapolis: Millbrook.

Pearson, P. David, and Dale D. Johnson. 1978. *Teaching Reading Comprehension*. New York: Holt, Rinehart, and Winston.

Phillips, Katherine W. 2014. "How Diversity Makes Us Smarter." *Scientific American*, October 1. www.scientificamerican.com/article/how-diversity-makes-us-smarter/.

Piaget, Jean. 1974. *The Origins of Intelligence in Children*. Madison, CT: International Universities Press.

Pillai, Tisha Deb, dir. 2017. *If You Fall*. Vimeo. https://vimeo.com/214239522.

Pillars, Wendi. 2016. *Visual Note-Taking for Educators: A Teacher's Guide to Student Creativity*. New York: W. W. Norton.

Ray, Katie Wood. 2006. *Study Driven: A Framework for Planning Units of Study in the Writing Workshop*. Portsmouth, NH: Heinemann.

Reynolds, Peter H. 2019. *Say Something*. New York: Orchard Books.

Richardson, Will, and Bruce Dixon. 2017. *10 Principles for Schools of Modern Learning*. Modern Learners. Report. http://s3-us-west-2.amazonaws.com/modernlearners/Modern+Learners+10+Principles+for+Schools+of+Modern+Learning+whitepaper.pdf.

Rideout, Victoria. 2017. *The Common Sense Census: Media Use by Kids Age Zero to Eight*. Common Sense. Report. www.commonsensemedia.org/sites/default/files/uploads/research/0-8_executivesummary_release_final_1.pdf.

Right Question Institute. n.d. Accessed April 2, 2019. www.rightquestion.org/.

Ritchhart, Ron, Mark Church, and Karin Morrison. *Making Thinking Visible: How to Promote Engagement, Understanding, and Independence for All Learners*. San Francisco: Jossey-Bass, 2011.

Roam, Dan. 2013. *The Back of the Napkin: Solving Problems and Selling Ideas with Pictures; with Update on Drawing Tools for iPad, Android and Windows Surface*. Expanded ed. New York: Portfolio.

Roberts, Kate, and Maggie Beattie Roberts. 2016. *DIY Literacy: Teaching Tools for Differentiation, Rigor, and Independence*. Portsmouth, NH: Heinemann.

Robertson, Joanne. 2019. *The Water Walker / Nibi Emosaawdang*. Translated by Shirley Williams and Isadore Toulouse. Toronto: Second Story Press.

Rogers, Simon, and Nicholas Blechman. 2014. *Animal Kingdom: Information Graphics*. Somerville, MA: Big Picture Press.

Rosenthal, Amy Krouse, and Tom Lichtenheld. 2015. *I Wish You More*. New York: Scholastic.

Routman, Regie. 2003. *Reading Essentials: The Specifics You Need to Teach Reading Well*. Portsmouth, NH: Heinemann.

Sanders, Rob, and Jared Schorr. 2018. *Peaceful Fights for Equal Rights*. New York: Simon & Schuster Books for Young Readers.

Satell, Greg. 2018 "These Are the Skills That Your Kids Will Need for the Future (Hint: It's Not Coding)." *Inc.* (blog), Mansueto Ventures, October 13. www.inc.com/greg-satell/here-are-skills-that-your-kids-will-need-for-future-hint-its-not-coding.html.

Schmidt, J. Eric, and Jared Cohen. 2013. *The New Digital Age: Reshaping the Future of People, Nations and Business*. New York: Knopf.

Schrock, Kathy. 2018 "Infographics as a Creative Assessment." Kathy Schrock's Guide to Everything. www.schrockguide.net/infographics-as-an-assessment.html.

Schugar, Jordan, and Heather Ruestschlin Schugar. 2018. "Deconstructing ETexts and EReading: The Effect of Text Structure and Purpose on Teacher Educators." *International Journal of Mobile and Blended Learning* 10 (March 2).

Schunk, Dale H., Paul R. Pintrich, and Judith L. Meece. 2008. *Motivation in Education: Theory, Research, and Applications*. Upper Saddle River, NJ: Merrill.

"Sculpture Changes Picture at Different Angles." 2016. DailyPicksandFlicks. YouTube, May 9. www.youtube.com/watch?v=PiYMol0VjWo.

Sensoy, Özlem, and Robin J. DiAngelo. 2017. *Is Everyone Really Equal? An Introduction to Key Concepts in Social Justice Education*. 2nd ed. New York: Teachers College Press.

Shellenbarger, Sue. 2016. "Most Students Don't Know When News Is Fake, Stanford Study Finds." *Wall Street Journal*, November 22. www.wsj.com/articles/most-students-dont-know-when-news-is-fake-stanford-study-finds-1479752576.

Smarty Pants. 2017. *2017 Clicks, Taps & Swipes*. Report. https://tinyurl.com/SmartyPantsResearch.

Spencer, John, and A.J. Juliani. 2016. *LAUNCH: Using Design Thinking to Boost Creativity and Bring Out the Maker in Every Student*. Dave Burgess Consulting.

Stagliano, Katie, Michelle H. Martin, and Karen Heid. 2015. *Katie's Cabbage*. Columbia, SC: University of South Carolina Press.

Stanford d.school. "K12 Lab." n.d. Accessed April 1, 2019. https://dschool.stanford.edu/programs/k12-lab-network.

Stanford History Education Group. 2016. *Evaluating Information: The Cornerstone of Civic Online Reasoning*. Report. November 22. https://stacks.stanford.edu/file/druid:fv751yt5934/SHEG%20Evaluating%20Information%20Online.pdf.

Steineke, Nancy. 2009. *Assessment Live! 10 Real-Time Ways for Kids to Show What They Know—and Meet the Standards*. Portsmouth, NH: Heinemann.

Tatum, Alfred W. 2005. *Teaching Reading to Black Adolescent Males: Closing the Achievement Gap*. Portland, ME: Stenhouse.

———. 2009. *Reading for Their Life: (Re)Building the Textual Lineages of African American Adolescent Males*. Portsmouth, NH: Heinemann.

Teaching Tolerance. n.d. Accessed April 1, 2019. www.tolerance.org/.

Thompson, Laurie Ann, and Sean Qualls. 2015. *Emmanuel's Dream: The True Story of Emmanuel Ofosu Yeboah*. New York: Schwartz & Wade Books.

Turner, Kristen Hawley, and Troy Hicks. 2017. *Argument in the Real World: Teaching Adolescents to Read and Write Digital Texts*. Portsmouth, NH: Heinemann.

Verde, Susan, and Peter H. Reynolds. 2018. *I Am Human: A Book of Empathy*. Abrams.

Vilson, José Luis. 2014. *This Is Not a Test: A New Narrative on Race, Class, and Education*. Chicago: Haymarket Books.

Wagner, Tony, and Robert A. Compton. 2015. *Creating Innovators: The Making of Young People Who Will Change the World*. New York: Scribner.

Whaley, Kayla. 2019. "#OwnVoices: Why We Need Diverse Authors in Children's Literature." Brightly, February 3. www.readbrightly.com/why-we-need-diverse-authors-in-kids-ya-lit/.

Witek, Jo, and Christine Roussey. 2014. *In My Heart: A Book of Feelings*. New York: Abrams Appleseed.

Wolf, Maryanne. 2007. *Proust and the Squid: The Story and Science of the Reading Brain*. New York: Harper.

———. 2018. *Reader, Come Home: The Reading Brain in a Digital World*. New York: HarperCollins.

Woodson, Jacqueline, and Rafael López. 2018. *The Day You Begin*. New York: Nancy Paulsen Books.

Zemelman, Steven. 2016. *From Inquiry to Action: Civic Engagement with Project-Based Learning in All Content Areas*. Portsmouth, NH: Heinemann.

Zemelman, Steven, Harvey "Smokey" Daniels, and Arthur Hyde. 2012. *Best Practice: Bringing Standards to Life in America's Classrooms*. 4th ed. Portsmouth, NH: Heinemann.

Zhou, Lily. 2018. "K12 Lab." Stanford d.school. Stanford d.school, February 5. https://dschool.stanford.edu/programs/k12-lab-network.

Ziemke, Kristin. 2016a. "Balancing Text and Tech: How It Isn't an Either/Or Scenario." *Literacy Today*, January/February, 32–33.

———. 2016b. "Beyond Text Literacy for a Digital Culture." *Literacy Today*, July/August, 24–25.

———. 2017. "We Are Made for Story." *ISTE Entrsekt*.

Zimmermann, Susan, and Chryse Hutchins. 2003. *7 Keys to Comprehension: How to Help Your Kids Read It and Get It!* New York: Three Rivers Press.

Ziv, Talee, and Mahzarin R. Banaji. 2012. "Representations of Social Groups in the Early Years of Life." In *The SAGE Handbook of Social Cognition*, edited by Susan T. Fiske and C. Neil Macrae, 372–89. Thousand Oaks, CA: Sage.